MW01409174

UNHIDDEN

Don Richardson

Second edition 2010

UNHIDDEN
by Don Richardson

Printed in the United States of America

ISBN 978-1-60791-345-3

CONTENTS

To my two beloved Carols

Author's Prologue

I call them *redemptive analogies*. As God has given us physical compasses that point to one place—magnetic north—he also ordains redemptive analogies, an incredible variety of them, as *cultural* compasses that point mankind to *one person*. That one and only one Person—the single most *magnetic* personality in the universe—is Jesus! Poignant longings he alone fulfills find symbolic expression in human cultures everywhere.

For my warring Sawi friends in the southern swamps of Papua, Christ became the ultimate *'peace child.'* For Papua's battle-prone Yali people and for the Hawaiians Titus Coan encountered in the early 1800s, Christ became the ideal *place or city of refuge*. In an earlier book, *Eternity in Their Hearts,* I present more than a score of other examples.

Each of the above analogies becomes an eye-opener for members of one human culture. Some concepts appeal to only a few thousand people. But none pertain specifically to scientists, scholars, academics, cosmologists—mankind's *intelligentsia*.

Inevitably, a daunting question rises. Has God also ordained an *ultimate* redemptive analogy—a premise so comprehensive, so definitive and even so scientifically confirmed that it may draw even skeptical academics to faith? Might the universe itself be one massive 'compass' fitted with an 'arrow' that—once found and loosed on its pivot—gives everyone who grasps it ample reason to step into God's loving embrace?

I believe the ultimate 'redemptive analogy' can be nothing less than a single set of propositions—a phalanx of laws perhaps—that binds what is true in every field of research into a comprehensive whole.

After decades of searching, I believe I have an idea how that ultimate 'redemptive analogy' can be formulated. I trace the beginning of my quest back to 1944. I was 9 years old. With my father's return from World War II, we lived for almost two years on my grandmother's farm at North Saint Eleanor's, Prince Edward Island, Canada.

Nanny owned two encyclopedias. One featured four fully illustrated volumes for youth in their teens. Walking home from Annie McCloud's one-room rural schoolhouse each day, I soon perused all four children's volumes and then turned to Nanny's 16-volume *adult* encyclopedia.

By the time we left Nanny's farm late in 1945, I was reasonably informed about the world. I could confidently affirm, for example, that Perth in far-away Australia was famous for its black swans. But physics and astronomy became my *special* interests. I begged star charts from a pilot at a nearby Air Force base. Flashlight in hand, while parents and siblings slept, I stole out to the farmyard at midnight to find stars not visible at nightfall. I even memorized their names.

Later, in Victoria, British Columbia, an eighth-grade substitute teacher in geometry class held up a plastic cube and pointed to one of its corners. "Please note," he advised, "that three sides of this cube come together at this corner. These three sides have something in common. Each side forms a 90-degree angle with each of its two neighbors."

He continued, "The fact that these three sides are able to stand at 90 degrees relative to each other proves that space itself—the space the cube occupies—has three dimensions. We call them *length, width and height.*" To pique our curiosity, he asked rhetorically, "For a *fourth* dimension to be added to the ones we call length, width and height, what do you surmise should also be true of *it*?"

His answer: "Ideally, a fourth dimension must share something as equally in common with length, width and height as length, width and height already share equally in common with each other. Adding a fourth 90-degree angle will not do because any fourth 90-degree angle is only a mirror image of an already-present 90-degree angle. *What else* can you name that shares genuine commonality with length, width and height? *Answer that question and you will have found the fourth dimension.*"

Like a Socrates teasing his students, the substitute left us to seek an answer on our own. His query was only a clever little aside for anyone interested—and I *was*! I wanted to ask him for his answer the next day, but our regular teacher returned. I never saw that substitute teacher again but eventually I discovered the answer for myself. *All three dimensions that meet at the corner of a cube are* ***aging*** *at the same rate; therefore,* ***time*** *is the fourth dimension, at least because time shares something as equally in common with length, width and height as length, width and height already share equally in common with each other.*

From then on, I read everything I could find about dimensions in theoretical physics and astronomy, with the latter subject leading me over into the realm of cosmology. I read a book by Albert Einstein.

Learning that Einstein was seeking a "unified field," I asked God to help him find it. I was sad when I learned that he died without finding it. I followed the rise and fall of Hoyle's and Bondi's "Steady State Cosmology" and its subsequent eclipse by "Big Bang Cosmology." I subscribed for years to *Scientific American* and *Sky and Telescope*, copies of which reached me two or three months late while I lived in Papua. I read and reread, noting especially cosmology's unresolved problems. Terms and phrases such as "quasars," "quarks," "strings," "membranes," "strangeness" and "microwave background radiation" joined my vocabulary.

My mind was open to be filled with a grander cosmology, but I did not expect to actually *find* one. I only wanted to be well-read enough to understand a unified field if and when someone else found it.

Then came the day when I began to uncover a series of 22 laws that by their very nature link everything with everything! I was staggered to think that this beautifully symmetrical legal package might actually be the unified field mankind has sought for so long and still seeks. Suddenly all my previous insights seemed like gentle breezes. This was a bracing wind from the Himalayas.

Over the years I have watched to see if emerging empirical discoveries refute the 22 laws in whole or in part. To my knowledge, they do not. It is my perception that all 22 laws become axioms to anyone who understands them. Or am I mistaken?

I believe that a unified field of truth not only exists but is also humanly knowable. It stands within reach of the human mind and must be sought until found. Accordingly I present herein what I believe has rightful claim to occupy that until-now empty conceptual throne.

More than that, I believe that the unified field presented here—if a critical mass of people agree it is logically confirmed and applicable to human life—has an incredible potential to motivate those who respond to love what is true and do only what is good.

So, reader, come join my quest for an ultimate redemptive analogy.

Don Richardson

Chapter One
The Harmony of Entities

> [Isaac] Newton . . . looked on the whole universe and all that is in it *as a riddle,* as a secret which could be read by applying pure thought to certain evidence, certain mystic clues which God has laid about the world to allow a sort of philosopher's treasure hunt . . . He believed that these clues were to be found partly in the evidence of the heavens and in the constitution of elements . . . but also partly in certain papers and traditions handed down . . . He regarded the universe as a cryptogram set by the Almighty.

From John Maynard Keynes, "Newton the Man," written for the Royal Society of London's tercentenary celebration of Newton's birth. Quoted by Rodney Stark in *For the Glory of God* (Princeton: Princeton University Press, 2003), p. 170.

Tackling Enigmas of the Cosmos

I agree with Isaac Newton. The universe does indeed resemble a cryptogram designed, at the very least, to lead mankind on a quest. After a "treasure hunt" lasting more than forty years, this author finds Newton's 'cosmic cryptogram' to be a 'chest' sealed with 22 'locks.' The 'keys' that open all 22 locks are 22 laws. All 22 laws are subtly hidden where one may least expect to find them—*in plain sight*! The goal is to find all 22 laws and fit them, lock by lock, *in the right consecutive order,* thereby discovering a startling solution to Newton's cosmic riddle.

It may surprise readers, as it does this author, to find that the first seven laws of the herein posited unified field of truth *necessarily predate the cosmos*! Sans those first seven laws, no cosmos!

These seven supremely ancient laws comprise what I call the *primary* unified field, which in turn is appended by a 15-law *secondary* field of truth associated with the origin of the cosmos, making the grander unified field complete with the above-mentioned 22 laws.

The seven laws of the *primary* unified field are sorted respectively into four *sets,* called 'harmonies.' The 15 laws of the *secondary* field likewise divide into a fifth, a sixth and a seventh 'harmony' respectively, making the grander unified field complete with *seven* harmonies. Foremost among the four primary harmonies is:

THE HARMONY OF *LAWS*

The second harmony rules *dimensions*—that basic kind of entity a substitute teacher caused me to ponder at an early age. It is called:

THE HARMONY OF *DIMENSIONS*

Dimensions are never found separately. Dimensions exist as inherent components of an entity known as a continuum; hence our third harmony governs the second-most-basic kind of entity, *continua.* It has two laws, one for each of two continua, hence:

THE HARMONY OF *CONTINUA*

The fourth harmony enfolds the last three of the primary unified field's seven laws. All three laws of this the fourth harmony pertain to entities designated by an entirely new noun—*Persension*—fully defined in the next chapter. Hence the final primary harmony is called:

THE HARMONY OF *PERSENSIONS*

Let me explain all four primary harmonies consecutively.

What the Harmony of Laws ordains

Clues pointing to the Harmony of Laws abound everywhere via what is surely the most taken-for-granted aspect of reality—the *serialization of everything*! Length 'comes with' width, height and time. *Quality* juxtaposes *quantity*. *Red*, a primary color, 'comes with' *yellow* and *blue*—making *three* primary colors. *Green,* a secondary color, 'comes with' *orange* and *indigo*, yielding *three* secondary colors. *White*, a fusion of primary and secondary colors, links with *black*, the absence of primary and secondary colors. *Matter* 'comes with' *energy*.

We are just beginning. *Solids* 'come with' *liquids* and *gases*. *Positive* charge co-exists with *negative* and *neutral* charges. *Flora* 'comes with' *fauna*, *male* with *female*, *hot* with *cold*, *sweet* with *sour* and other tastes, *rough* with *smooth* and other textures. *Sound* resonates in multiple pitches. *Music* flows in major and minor keys. *Gravity* co-exists with *magnetism* and other natural laws. *Stars* and *galaxies* and even *elements* in the periodic table come in a variety of categories.

Pressing on, one finds more than one kind of mathematics, multiple branches of physics, chemistry, engineering and philosophy. Myriad pairs of two and series of three or more components intermix on all levels of the cosmos. Eventually we pause to ask, "What are we *not* finding thus far?" The answer is—*conceptual aloneness!* Anything and everything one can name has at least one 'comes with.' A second question follows: do conceptually lone things just happen not to be found, or are they not to be found for the simplest and deepest of all possible reasons: *an extremely major universal law forbids conceptual aloneness?*

Could it be that every entity, to join the natural order of things, *must* have at least one 'comes with'?

In fact, an all-encompassing unified field by definition *demands* logical interconnectedness for everything that exists. If even one thing *by nature* exists in conceptual aloneness, a truly unified field of truth cannot be! If a unified field truly exists, *interconnectedness* becomes an inherent characteristic of all things. Thus the unified field itself must consist of an underlying series from which all lesser series—such as the samples given above—spring forth.

One may object that a unified field itself—by definition—lacks a 'comes with,' hence a unified field by nature violates any law that bans conceptual aloneness. This objection will be answered later.

Actually this author knows of one—just one—verifiably existing entity which scientific commentaries to date are content to leave starkly *unpaired* with anything else in the cosmos. How delightful! Finding one such entity enables me to test my premise by asking: Is that one lone entity alone *by nature* or has mankind simply failed to discover that it, too, really does have an overlooked 'comes with'?

If a universal law absolutely ordains serialization for all things—if indeed conceptual aloneness is universally forbidden—something else will be found that 'comes with' that anomalously lone entity! Conversely, if that one lone entity truly has no 'comes with,' we are free to conclude that conceptual aloneness is 'legal' after all.

When physicist Ernest Rutherford discovered the first subatomic particle, a proton, no one at first knew of anything that 'comes with' proton. Before long, further investigation uncovered the *neutron*—a fellow "nucleon"—and also the *electron*, two entities that combine with protons to form atoms. Proton's conceptual aloneness was temporary indeed! *Neutron* and *electron* emerged to rescue *proton* from apparent conceptual aloneness.

There is, however, another scientifically proven entity for which science has yet to name a 'comes with'—Albert Einstein's 'space-time continuum.' Does the space-time continuum truly lack a 'comes with'? Or has mankind simply failed to discover a hidden something that rescues Einstein's space-time continuum from conceptual aloneness just as neutron and electron rescued proton from the same state years ago?

Surely *symmetry* is also to be anticipated

'Symmetry' designates a balanced numerical or geometric design or structure that is also aesthetically pleasing to look at. Because *symmetry* characterizes so many other facets of reality—snowflakes, the periodic table of elements, etc.—surely something as major as an all-encompassing unified field will also somehow manifest symmetry.

Symmetry in a unified field requires components of the field to conform to a balanced design. The number of components that enables any segment of the field to fulfill that requirement is designated in the Harmony of Laws, below, as the *perfect number* of components for that segment. When each segment of the field contains its 'perfect number' of components, the field as a whole manifests symmetry.

The first law of truth, then, ordains both *interconnectedness* and *symmetry* for the primary and secondary unified fields. Hence:

THE HARMONY OF LAWS

> Every law in the primary and secondary unified fields 'comes with' a perfect number of co-laws.

The **'perfect number'** of laws in any one harmony is the number of laws that enables that harmony to fulfill the symmetry requirement of the unified field as a whole. Note that the Harmony of Laws, were it alone, would self-contradict by virtue of lacking a 'comes with.' Rather the above-expressed First Harmony is like a 'point' from which a coordinated set of other harmonies and their respective laws radiate with both unity and symmetry conserved.

In other words, as the unified field's first legal entity, Harmony One *obeys itself* by initiating a symmetrical 'series of series' in which each series serves as a 'comes with' for the Harmony of Laws. We will see that the Harmony of Laws joins with six other harmonies, making *seven* the 'perfect number' of harmonies for the grander unified field.

We will not know which symmetry design the unified field manifests until we discover subsequent harmonies and see how their laws arrange under Harmony One.

Pre-creation, Harmony One was a Harmony of *Laws* simply because laws were the only things there for it to harmonize. Post-creation, the grander unified field also conforms to Harmony One by guaranteeing that *every entity in creation* ultimately has a perfect number of co-entities *somewhere in space and time.* That is why, post-creation, the Harmony of Laws is appropriately co-named the Harmony of *Entities*.

Note that Harmony One negates *monism*—a philosophical theory which holds that everything derives from only *one* basic essence. The Harmony of Laws forbids ultimate singularity. How this relates to the being of God will be explained.

In physics, subatomic phenomena are basic to everything material. In philosophy, ideas are basic to all that is non-material. What follows in *Unhidden* does indeed find both subatomic phenomena and ideas resembling a 'carpet' under all the 'furniture' in the cosmos. But, looking under that carpet, we find that dimensions comprise the *floor*.

The unified field's next Harmony relates to the most basic kind of entity in all of existence—*Dimensions*!

Chapter Two
The Harmony of Dimensions

Mankind often recognizes part of a series only to leave it truncated, i.e., missing one or more components. For example, people used to describe the universe as having only three dimensions—*length, width* and *height*—those invisible things that make it possible for three 90-degree right angles to form the corner of a box. Albert Einstein was the first to discern what I learned as a teenager—that ***time*** is a fourth dimension integral to that key series. By adding *time* to length, width and height, Einstein brought a key unified field series to what this treatise finds to be its *perfect number—four*!

Unlike Einstein, most of us take dimensions for granted. We regard them as mere accessories to what is "really real," rather than as foundational to reality. To prepare readers for what follows, I suggest the following mental exercise. Look at any object—a chair, a table, a rock or a mountain. No matter what that object is, it has a certain length, a certain width and a certain height in space. Recognize also, like Einstein, that the object's continuance in time is integral to its presence in space.

Now ask yourself, "Which is more *real,* the object itself, or the space and time that provide a setting for it?" The object seems more real, but is it? Reflect that if space and time did not exist, the object could not be there. If space and time did not exist, neither could *we* be here to reason about space and time. Once we grasp that space and time are prerequisite to the existence of mere objects, events and even people, we are at last beginning to recognize dimensions as very, very *real*.

Since Albert Einstein, informed people no longer speak of three but of *four* physical dimensions: length, width, height *and time*.

Einstein's *next* insight took him a step closer to discovering the unified field he so earnestly sought. He discerned that length, width, height *and time* together constitute a four-dimensional ***continuum.*** What in the world is a continuum? Various dictionaries define a continuum as *something whose parts cannot be separated or separately discerned.*

If an entity consists of different parts, how can it be *impossible* to separate one part from the others or at least "separately discern" them? Elements in solution—salt in water, for example—are separable. Evaporate the water, salt remains. Even alloyed metals separate in a smelter, but a 'continuum' is a fusion of dimensions no 'smelter' can undo. Einstein and others call that fusion "the *space-time* continuum." In this present work, I replace Einstein's hyphenated *space-time* with the word 'extent,' renaming his discovery 'the *extent* continuum.' It is an invisible 'ocean' in which billions of galaxies swim like fish.

Has the extent continuum always existed, or did it have a beginning? Many cosmologists believe that the extent continuum—with a nascent cosmos embedded—originated by exploding from a miniscule point. Others posit an *oscillating* continuum, one that repeatedly explodes outward only to crunch inward (and has perhaps been doing so forever). As of this writing, neither group appears to credit Einstein's space-time (i.e., *extent*) continuum with any potential to exist *apart from the presence of matter, anti-matter and energy.* Theologians also, for other reasons, posit the extent continuum as co-created with the cosmos.

The incongruity of seeing the extent continuum as co-created with matter and energy

Apart from the extent continuum, the phenomena we call length, width, height and time reduce to absolute zero. Apart from the extent continuum, terms such as place, point, position, even *presence,* cannot even be described as meaningless let alone meaningful. With time reduced to zero, all things that require *duration*—existence, events, causation, motion, process, thought, will, etc.—are also utterly nil.

Cosmologists assume that every event has a cause, a trigger, a catalyst. Causation, however, requires a moment, however brief, and a point, no matter how small, in which to happen. This means that the four-dimensional extent continuum had to exist already to supply space and time for a cause to trigger its formation. Unless their inert space-time invented itself out of timeless spacelessness, surely it always existed.

If, however, the extent continuum existed *before* matter and energy, one may posit empty extent—the vacuum itself—as a 'raw material' from which matter and energy formed *without the above incongruity.* How, then, may particles of matter loaded with mass and charge and photons that fly at the speed of light be derived in, of and from inert extent?

To find an answer we must examine the nature of infinite space. Physicists used to see space as *homogeneous*, i.e., the vacuum is identical from place to place. An inch in New York equals an inch in Tokyo. Now, space is known to be *expanding with the cosmos*. So, if space can expand, may it also *contract?* Next question: just as areas of high pressure in our atmosphere balance areas of low pressure, does an expansion in one part of space *demand* an inversely equal contraction in space elsewhere?

Consider iron. Iron seems solid, yet space intervenes between iron atoms. But what of space itself? Do units of something else form *it*? If so, what separates units of *that*? More space! So the seemingly immaterial vacuum really is *infinitely solid!* Compared to space, iron is ephemeral. Space cannot be cleft for the simple reason that space would fill the cleft! So the answer is yes! Any expansion in infinitely solid space *requires a concurrent inversely equal contraction elsewhere in space.* Since space is thus altered cosmically, may it also be similarly altered *microcosmically*?

Posit the extent continuum existing originally in a state of perfect homogeneity. Lo!—point-moments are available for units of matter and energy to form microcosmically as inversely equal alterations in the homogeneity of pre-existing *extent!* It would be as if balls of ice and bubbles of steam pop up and are preserved in an already existing, otherwise uniformly temperate ocean. Everything is still just water; yet the balls of ice and bubbles of steam have their separate existence, too.

But—speak of altering space and our minds object, "Nothing is there to be altered!" In fact, though, space *is* there *and its density matters*! According to a principle of physics called *relativity*, if a pilot flies into a patch of sky where space is *contracted* relative to standard space, an observer in standard space will see his aircraft decelerate. But to the pilot—for whom contracted space is now standard—his speed remains constant. If he crosses a bit of sky where space is *expanded*, an observer in standard space sees his aircraft accelerate for the same reason.

Why then would matter formed via microcosmic alterations of space itself manifest mass, charge, spin and conservation laws? All such features trace logically to the *inverse equality* of the density changes that birth matter out of homogeneous extent in the first place. Conversely, positing matter as popping causelessly from non-existent points in absolute nothingness is futile. Imagine two theories vying to explain why matter manifests mass, charge, spin and comes replete with conservation laws. One theory explains the entire problem with a single plausible premise. The other offers an *implausible* postulate for matter but needs who knows how many added postulates to explain mass, charge, spin and conservation laws separately. Which theory would you choose?

As I will explain in Chapter 10, defining matter and energy as inversely equal density alterations in pre-existing extent is a *single* premise that *plausibly* explains mass, charge, spin and conservation laws as well. Surely this single premise is far more *intuitive* than positing matter and energy as popping out of nothing more than nothing with no *linked* explanation as to why something derived from nothing should manifest mass, charge and spin and be subject to conservation laws.

Why would scientists prefer any other explanation for the origin of matter and energy? Perhaps it is because they intuit the above premise as requiring an already-existing-prior-to-the-cosmos Shaper who ably arrays inversely equal density alterations in an ultra-versatile extent continuum and sustains them as a material cosmos over eons of time. Some scientists disregard *a priori* any line of reasoning that requires *Him.*

As all scientists aver, science applies to observable, measurable phenomena. The extent continuum itself becomes *manifest* to human measuring devices only when material things and energy events occur in it. Since prior to the cosmos, nothing material was there to be observed or measured, most scientists prefer not to credit the extent continuum with prior existence. Still, does not the *potential* for measuring and comparing preclude the *phenomenon* of measuring and comparing? A pre-existent extent continuum provides that potential, apart from which there could be no later phenomenon of measuring or comparing of anything material.

Why theologians see the extent continuum as a created thing

One might expect theologians to see pre-existing homogeneous extent as serving their cause by requiring an Alterer who uses it to form the cosmos. Alas, the potential for balls of ice and bubbles of steam to comprise inversely equal alterations of water while still remaining as water has been a hint overlooked by theologians as much as by scientists.

Centuries ago, it became an unfortunate theological convention to teach that God, to be truly "*transcendent,*" also had to be capable of existing "*before* time" and "*outside of* space," oxymoronically granting existence to time and space prior to their existence. Words like "before" and "outside of" have no meaning if space-time does not already exist!

Absence of time equals zero duration. If God existed "before" he created time, *how old* was God when he created time? With *zero* duration, God would have *zero* age—i.e., he would not exist. Likewise absence of space affords zero ability to experience *presence*, let alone *omni*presence. Does not God's attribute called omnipresence link I AM eternally with space-time? If God created space-time and only then became omnipresent, *he gained a new attribute*, negating another divine attribute, immutability.

When theologians first conceived of God creating *ex nihilo* (out of nothing), how did they define "nothing"? For them, "nothing" was simply a void, a vacuum. Little did they know that a vacuum really is versatile space-time. "Creating out of nothing" then translates to "creating out of space-time" (i.e., out of that which is immaterial) now. I contend that theologians who still favor *ex nihilo* creation over what I call *ex extenso* creation fail to see that 'nothing' long ago equates to 'space-time' now.

This aligns with Hebrews 11:3, which avers that *"what is seen was not made out of what was visible."* Does one describe *nothing* as "not visible"? Clearly God used an invisible yet already-existing *something* to create the cosmos. How "visible" is space-time? We see things and events occurring *in* it, but we cannot see *it!* What could the author of Hebrews say? Human language afforded him no way to say *space-time continuum* in his day, but he could have said "nothing" if that were his intent.

A question Einstein failed to ask regarding the extent continuum

Einstein, unaware that the Harmony of Entities forbids any one kind of dimension or any one kind of continuum to exist alone, failed to ask the next question: What other continuum consisting of which other kind of dimensions does the Harmony of Entities ordain as a co-entity for Einstein's extent (space-time) continuum?

Instead, Einstein unwittingly left his marvelous extent continuum languishing in *unlawful disassociatedness*! Neither he nor anyone else opted to ask, "Which other kind of dimensions in which other kind of continuum are the missing co-entities for this continuum with its four extent dimensions?" This present work attempts to bring Einstein's extent continuum 'in from the cold' by finding the missing 'co-entity' our First Law requires it to have. What could that co-entity be? Only one answer is credible: a *second continuum comprised of another kind of dimensions*.

Einstein sought a unified field expressed mathematically, i.e., via a set of formulas describing *how* the universe came to be without necessarily explaining *why* the universe exists. The unified field presented here seeks to offer much more than mathematics alone can express.

Just as the first harmony regulates *entities,* the second harmony governs the most basic kind of entity—*dimensions.* First, let me define the word 'dimension' as used in this work:

Dimension: a universal basis for comparisons of a kind

Wherever one travels in the cosmos, a potential exists to compare/contrast physical entity-events as longer vs. shorter, wider vs. narrower, higher vs. lower, or older vs. younger. Hence length, width, height and time qualify to be called dimensions. If the same can be said of any other kind of universal potential to compare/contrast, another dimension must exist that makes that comparison/contrast possible.

In fact, *two categories* of universal dimensions exist. Einstein's famous four—*length, width, height* and *time*—are joined by a second category with *three* until-now historically unrecognized dimensions comprising another continuum, introduced later. Complemented by a second continuum, Einstein's extent continuum conforms to the Harmony of Entities—and returns the favor! Each universal continuum rescues the other from violating the unified field's First Law.

Whereas the first harmony guarantees *more than one kind* of dimensions, the second harmony decrees what that multiplicity of dimensions must *do.* There is only one thing dimensions need to do.

THE HARMONY OF DIMENSIONS

> Like dimensions *inhere* as continua comprised of *sub*-continua.

The second harmony describes like dimensions as things that *inhere*, forming continua. Why not 'adhere'? 'Adhere' is a more common verb, but it fails the concept here. Things that 'adhere' can be separated. A Band-aid adheres but can be peeled away. Metals adhering as an alloy can be separated in a smelter. That kind of a union is mere *adherence.*

The union of four extent dimensions in the *extent* continuum is profoundly more than four things temporarily stuck together. The very definition of a continuum, as we saw, requires an un-dissolvable fusion of components. It is this kind of joining, a fusion beyond mere adhering, that this present treatise describes as *inhering.*

It follows that those other three dimensions in our yet-to-be-described second continuum must likewise manifest inherence. They, too, must be inseparable one from the others.

What happens when like dimensions *inhere*

Inherence requires the existence of each dimension in a continuum to become *integral* to the existence of its fellow dimensions. Were this not so, individual dimensions ultimately could somehow be separated or separately discerned; hence the composite would not be a continuum.

Melt and mix four metals—tin, copper, zinc and nickel. They *adhere* as a four-metal alloy. If these same four metals could *inhere* the way length, width, height and time inhere in the extent continuum, they would not form *one* alloy, but *four complete alloys in one!* In one alloy, *tin* would be found manifesting characteristics of copper, zinc and nickel. In a second alloy, *copper* manifests characteristics of tin, zinc and nickel. In the third and fourth alloys, *zinc* and *nickel* respectively remain basic while genuinely manifesting characteristics of all four component metals.

If tin, copper, zinc and nickel could merge that profoundly, they would indeed be a continuum. No smelter could melt them apart! Of course, that degree of merging is impossible with alloys of metal, *but that is exactly what happens when length, width, height and time 'alloy,' forming the universe-encompassing extent continuum*! Hence what we call the extent continuum really has *four sub-continua embedded within it!*

Science fiction authors frequently write about something they call "*sub-space*" (better called sub-extent or sub-space-*time*, because time is never excluded from space). Once again, as occasionally happens, fiction anticipates reality, *but this time only by one-fourth*. I contend that <u>four</u> *sub*-extent continua actually comprise the extent continuum! Living and moving simultaneously in all four sub-extent continua as one, we humans are quite oblivious to the separate existence of the extent continuum's four sub-extent continua. That is not the way things are, I posit below, for certain very odd sub-atomic particles physicists are currently studying.

The extent continuum's four sub-continua combine length, width, height and time in four different ways:

The extent continuum's four sub-continua

Sub-continuum A: *length* is base—width, height and time are added.

Sub-continuum B: *width* is base—length, height and time are added.

Sub-continuum C: *height* is base—length, width and time are added.

Sub-continuum D: *time* is base—length, width and height are added.

If a hypothetical space ship could exist exclusively in sub-continuum A, for example, it could accelerate forward or backward more rapidly in terms of *absolute length* than in other directions. A man living solely in sub-continuum A looks oddly elongated in one direction and as flat as the jack in a deck of cards in another. Anything existing solely in sub-continuum D might be able to move forward or backward in *time*.

Because we exist and move in all four sub-extent continua as one, we and our man-made vehicles—sans hindrances such as friction, gravity, magnetism or electrical charge—accelerate with common ease or difficulty in *all* spatial directions. As I reveal later, finding four sub-extent continua embedded in the extent continuum enables me to explain anomalies physicists are finding in sub-atomic particles known as *quarks*, anomalies currently known as *membranes*, *strings* and *extra dimensions*.

The four extent dimensions have three *friends!*

Everywhere the four extent dimensions enable us to make extent-based comparisons, three *value* dimensions are enabling us to make value-based comparisons as well! Just as we take extent for granted while moving in it, we also have failed for ages to acknowledge value dimensions as real despite the fact that we apply them continuously.

To help you grasp value dimensions as *real*, imagine a group of astronauts sitting in the dining hall of spacecraft X as they cruise between stars. One named Ed shouts "Aha!" Aided by his link to one value dimension, Ed has just *discerned* how to improve an instrument on the flight deck. Enabled by still another value dimension, Anita *enjoys* a savory dish from the kitchen. Crew chief Vince, tapping into a third value dimension, *resolves* to face a crisis he would rather avoid.

Suddenly spacecraft X enters a hypothetical sector of space where all three value coordinates are absent. In an instant, Ed, Anita and Vince become organic performing robots with zero self-aware *cognition*, zero capacity to *feel pleasure* and zero capacity to *will* on the basis of self-aware perception and delight. Until they re-enter space pervaded by the three value dimensions, Ed, Anita and Vince experience no more self-awareness, pleasure or ability to will than does their onboard computer.

Materialists demote the phenomenon we call *value* as lacking existence apart from our minds. "Value exists in the mind that invents it" is their mantra. It is also true, of course, that it is only our minds that enable us to sort out differences in the length, width, height, age and shape of objects and events. This present work premises that three value dimensions exist universally apart from our thought processes. We experience them only because they exist. Though we move objects about, we do not create the extent through which we move them. Nor can we invent the value grid that enables us, no matter where, to ponder or ignore, cherish or despise, choose or reject. I propose that these three value dimensions be identified as:

1) **Reason:** This value dimension enables comparisons as to what is logical/illogical, rational/irrational, wise/unwise, discerning/naïve, feasible/infeasible, organized/chaotic, practical/impractical, clever/inane, realistic/unrealistic, sorted/unsorted. Taken to infinity, reason becomes omniscience (an infinite capacity to *know*).

2) **Pleasure:** This second value dimension enables contrast as to joy/sadness, delight/disdain, pleasure/disgust, beautiful/ugly, lovable/unlovable, feeling/unfeeling, splendid/common, captivating/boring, rare/usual, etc. Taken to infinity, the second dimension constitutes omnisentience (an infinite capacity for *sensitivity*).

3) **Volition:** This third value dimension facilitates freewill, i.e., ability to apply options, including options *opposite* to what chemical stimuli and common sense advise. Volition enables comparisons as to what is constant/vacillating, enduring/transitory, strong/weak, steady/unsteady, able/unable, etc. Taken to infinity, volition constitutes omnipotence (a capacity for infinite *power*).

Other viable sets of terms for the three value dimensions could be *intellect, emotion* and *will* or *discernment, enjoyment* and *application.*

As we all agree, our ability to make extent-based comparisons attests that extent dimensions exist apart from our perception of them. Why not agree that the myriad value-based comparisons we constantly base our lives upon attest that value dimensions are just as real? Our self-aware parts float like bubbles in a value ocean just as our bodies occupy space and time in the extent continuum. The actual means whereby value dimensions enable cognition, pleasure and volition in sync with the chemistry of our brains and the brains of animals is presented later.

For far too long anti-value bias has detoured mankind away from the paradigm presented here. Even theists fail to credit value as tri-dimensional and as a continuum. Unlike materialists, theists credit value as existing apart from the human mind, i.e., in the mind of God, but still fall short by failing to posit value as evidencing *a framework of universal dimensions.* Accessing the unified field is impossible apart from a paradigm that begins by crediting value as a phenomenon linked to a genuinely universal dimensional basis. *This paradigm is the gate!*

Hence the universe has more than just *four* dimensions in just *one* continuum. It has *seven* dimensions in *two* continua. A fourth value coordinate cannot be found, for *three* is this series' *perfect number!* That is why the famous quote, *Cogito ergo sum*—"I think, therefore I am"—is too brief. Rather say, "I *think, feel* and *will*; therefore I am."

How we apply three value dimensions every day

Just as independently real length, width, height and time are basic in every possible way to our perceptions of size, shape, location and duration, three independently existing value coordinates enable us to compare persons, ideas, objects or events from a value perspective.

One may say, "John is *smarter* than Joe," rating John above Joe as to the *cognition* value dimension. One may add, "But Joe is *more fun* than John," rating Joe above John on the *pleasure* coordinate. A third comment could be, "But as for *persistence*, Bill is your man!"—rating Bill above both John and Joe in terms of the value dimension of *volition.*

Neither John nor Joe nor Bill is *devoid* of qualities related to a particular value dimension. All three men, indeed, manifest all three value dimensions, but not equally. Rather, one person may manifest a particular value dimension more notably than another.

An automobile may be rated as *functional* by reason, but its *beauty* and *durability* as per the second and third value dimensions also matter. Some lectures may be *instructive* rated by reason yet *boring* rated by pleasure and *non-motivating* rated by volition.

How sad that millions take their ability to make three-tiered value comparisons for granted. Yet every time we say or hear someone say, "My favorite is...," we encounter evidence that value dimensions exist. I urge everyone: do not disdain, do not trivialize, our ability to compare anything—even everything—in terms of this universal, tripartite value-defining grid. *It is mankind's most important and most wasted capacity!*

We saw that four extent dimensions—*inhering* as required by the second law—result in an extent continuum consisting of four embedded sub-continua. As explained earlier, this happens because any three *extent* dimensions are as inherent to the existence of the fourth as the fourth is inherent to the existence of the three. Just as truly, any two *value* dimensions are as inherent to the existence of the third as the third is inherent to the existence of the two! Thus, by that same second law, three infinite value dimensions—let's call them *omniscience*, *omnisentience* and *omnipotence*—by inhering together, constitute a Value Continuum consisting of *three infinite Sub-Continua!* I designate the Value Continuum's three Sub-Continua as follows:

1. **Value Sub-Continuum "A":** an *omniscience-based* sub-continuum with omnisentience and omnipotence eternally added.

2. **Value Sub-Continuum "B":** an *omnisentience-based* sub-continuum with omniscience and omnipotence eternally added.

3. **Value Sub-Continuum "C":** an *omnipotence-based* sub-continuum with omniscience and omnisentience eternally added.

When cognition, pleasure and volition do not just *merge*, but actually *inhere* as a continuum, the result is *a person*! When infinite cognition, infinite sensitivity and infinite volition inhere as a continuum, the result is an *omniscient, omnisentient, omnipotent* Person. Each is a Person via an eternal inhering of three infinite value dimensions. Accordingly, fusing the word *person* with *dimension* provides a new term—*Persension*—to designate the three Members of the Godhead. The Value Continuum's A, B and C Sub-Continua are thus named:

The Persension of Omniscience

The Persension of Omnisentience

The Persension of Omnipotence

Since Persensions do not recognize each other according to different physical features or sound of voice, how does each Persension distinguish himself from his fellow Persensions within the Value Continuum? Quite simply, each Persension knows which of the three infinite value dimensions *he* is the eternal source of!

At last "God" can now be defined as a mega-infinite tri-Persensioned Value Continuum eternally embodied in an infinite quadri-dimensional extent continuum. 'Mega-infinite' designates God as infinite in terms of *both* value and extent!

Any objection that a unified field itself, by definition, has no 'comes with' and hence violates the Harmony of Entities, its own first law, can now be answered as follows:

The unified field—the basis of all that can be *known*, *appreciated* and *acted upon*—is complemented by the tri-Persensioned Value Continuum as Knower, Appreciator and Applier of all that is true within the unified field. Thus the unified field has its own intrinsic, personal 'comes with.'

Were God to speak to us now, imagine him saying: "That you may know me in a more *definitive* way, I bid you recognize me at last as the triune Value Continuum, Creator of all." Might he even invite us now to call him by a new name, *Valcon*—for *Val*ue *Con*tinuum—in addition to his historically sacred names like Elohim, Adonai, Yahweh, Theos and God? I say this believing that "Value Continuum" is what timeless expressions like 'I am that I am' and 'God is a Spirit' have always represented. I caution, however, that knowing *of* God definitively does not equal knowing, enjoying and willing by way of personal encounter *with* him.

It follows that every philosophy or religion that denies God's tri-unity has been misinformed. Christians—despite their acknowledged inability to *define* the term 'Trinity' objectively—nevertheless have been correctly describing God as a Trinity for some 2,000 years. Indeed, the Value Continuum is a Trinity for precisely the same reasons that the extent continuum might be called a "quadity"!

How the three Persensions form an *echelon*:

The four extent dimensions—length, width, height and time—are *unranked.* Reverse the order of their four names. Jumble them. It makes no difference. There is no basis for defining *length*, for example, as a *ruling* extent dimension that is innately above width, height or time. The four sub-extent continua derived from the inhering of extent dimensions are likewise *unranked.* Not so with the three Persensions! The Value Continuum's Persension of Omniscience is known as "God the Father." The Value Continuum's mid-ranked Persension of Omnisentience is the Bible's "God the Son." Third in rank, the Persension of Omnipotence, is "God the Holy Spirit." The basis for ranking the three Persensions in this order will become apparent in chapter four.

These three are indeed three infinite Persons comprising one infinite Person. With equal validity they can say '*We are the Three who are One* and *I am the One who is Three.*' Though echeloned within the Value Continuum—the Godhead—all three Persensions participate equally in creating and ruling the cosmos.

How white light denotes Valcon as three-in-one

What we know as **white** is always a mixture of three primary colors. In the kind of light emitted by phosphors in computer and television screens, **red**, **blue** and **green** comprise white light. These are known to physicists as 'additive colors.' In the so-called 'subtractive colors' used by painters, **red**, **yellow** and **blue** or, in some cases, **magenta**, **yellow** and **cyan** serve as three primary colors that yield white. Consider any one primary color as symbolizing one of the three Persensions. White light itself then symbolizes the Value Continuum. How fittingly John the Apostle averred that "God is light" (I John 1:5).

Putting white light through a prism also reveals *secondary colors*, i.e., colors derived by blending two primary colors together. Secondary colors thus symbolize each Persension as harmoniously imparting what he himself most basically is to each of his two fellow Persensions.

God is *transcendent* as the Value Continuum!

Pantheists teach that God is part and parcel of the material universe as opposed to merely omnipresent in it. Biblical theology holds that God, though omnipresent in the cosmos, is nonetheless *transcendent* in that he existed before he created matter and even now and forever exists independently of matter. Unified field theology agrees that God is transcendent. God is the Value Continuum but matter is not made of value. Matter consists of altered extent, nothing more. Defining the extent continuum as eternally pre-existent does not make it equal to God. God inhabits the extent continuum. The extent continuum does not inhabit him. God as the Value Continuum utilizes the extent continuum to create. The extent continuum cannot utilize the Value Continuum for anything. The Value Continuum is omniscient, omnisentient and omnipotent. The extent continuum knows nothing, cares about nothing and can do nothing.

God is far more transcendent existing *in* the extent continuum than *without* it. That even he needs a place to be in no way diminishes him. Surely God prizes his immutability and eternal omnipresence more than 'transcendence' defined in ways that deny him both major attributes. Theology, as I believe the rest of this book demonstrates, finds poignant links to what is true in physical science if only theologians can adjust to pre-existing space-time as God's extremely versatile *hyper-body.*

Some readers of course will try to equate what I posit here with views of God advanced by Greek philosophers or thinkers from other religions. However, no such thinkers conceived of length, breadth, height and time as a pre-existing, functionally versatile continuum. Unified field premises differ!

With just 2 of 22 laws presented, we have barely begun to excavate a long-buried trove of hidden paradigms!

The beginning of a cosmic 'redemptive analogy'

As readers of my earlier works will recall, the analogy of a tribal father giving his only son as a 'peace child' enabled me to help warring people find peace with God and with each other by receiving Jesus as a Greater Father's Greater Peace Child given once for all mankind. Now I seek to link modern man's four-dimensional invisible extent continuum with the perception that three infinite value dimensions comprise an equally invisible Value Continuum, God over all!

Chapter Three
The Harmony of Continua

The dimensional inhering required by the Harmony of Dimensions, as we saw, results in two continua—an extent continuum and a Value Continuum. Recognize that the extent continuum, in and of itself, is infinite four-dimensional extent [space-time] with zero value. Know also that the Value Continuum, of himself, is infinite three-dimensional value with zero extent. *How then can the extent continuum have value and how can the Value Continuum have 'a place to be' in space-time?* The two laws of pre-creation's Harmony of Continua provide this answer.

THE LAW OF THE EXTENT CONTINUUM:

> The extent continuum yields its four sub-extent continua *infinitely* and *involuntarily* to the Value Continuum, rendering the Value Continuum eternally *omnipresent* in the entire extent continuum.

THE LAW OF THE VALUE CONTINUUM:

> The Value Continuum—altering finite parts of the extent continuum *finitely* and *voluntarily*—creates two categories of 'creatons': *extent density alterons* and *value loci.*

A 'creaton' is anything that had a beginning in time.

About the Law of the Extent Continuum

The extent continuum—by yielding its four four-dimensional sub-continua infinitely and involuntarily to the Value Continuum—eternally adds four extent dimensions to the innately three-dimensional Value Continuum. Thus Valcon is, in fact, a *seven-dimensional* Being! How fittingly John the Apostle, four times in the Apocalypse, describes God as "a *seven*-fold Spirit." (See Revelation 1:4, 3:1, 4:5 and 5:6 footnotes.)

In other words, length, width, height and time are *secondary* attributes of God relative to his three *primary* attributes—omniscience, omnisentience and omnipotence. Ergo Valcon possesses a fourth 'omni-' as well. He is *omnipresent* throughout the infinite vastness of the extent continuum. That is why, no matter where Ed, Anita and Vince venture in the cosmos, they will not suddenly be reduced to mere organic robots.

Our bodies are a visible synthesis of brain, muscle, bone and nerves; but Valcon's "body" is the infinite, invisible extent continuum. Again, if it helps, think of the extent continuum as Valcon's "hyper-body."

Can the order of the above two laws be reversed? Not so! Valcon's ability to create by altering finite parts of the extent continuum presupposes that he is omnipresent in it.

About the Law of the Value Continuum

This law grants Valcon an option to reciprocate by altering *finite parts* of the extent continuum *finitely* in two ways, i.e., by:

1. **Changing finite parts of the extent continuum into "value loci."**

2. **Creating sub-atomic particle-antiparticle pairs and energy by altering the initially homogeneous (the same everywhere) density of finite parts of the extent continuum in inversely equal ways.**

How Valcon creates 'value loci'

Each of us is a value locus, i.e., a bit of space-time infused with value and co-existing with a brain and body. Just as Harmony III's first law assures omnipresence for Valcon, its second law enables him to create "value loci" by endowing his three values finitely and voluntarily to bits of the extent continuum. Any part of the extent continuum thus infused becomes an 'extent base' for a value locus—a finite bit of extent with its own ability to reason, enjoy and will. This is what we commonly call a 'soul.'' Creating a value locus does not require the physical density of extent to be altered, nor does the motion of a value locus require its extent base to move with it. Just as a spot of light is at home on any surface, a value locus has an extent base anywhere it happens to be.

How close is the link between Valcon and a 'value locus'? As stated earlier, if somewhere there existed a sector of the extent continuum where Valcon was absent, a value locus could not exist there. Entering that zone would leave a value locus reduced to an extent base indistinguishable from surrounding unaltered space-time.

Like Valcon, a value locus is seven-dimensional, but finitely so. It is unlike Valcon in another way. In the Value Continuum, value is basic, extent is added. In a value locus, extent is basic, value is added. For this reason alone it is indeed accurate to describe value loci as created "in the likeness of God." Omniscient omnipresent Valcon knows all that exists in the extent continuum. A value locus, occupying one point-moment at a time, knows only what exists within limited parameters.

How a value locus interacts with the world

A value locus learns of things external to itself by being linked to a body capable of receiving incoming electromagnetic waves, sound waves, chemical reactions, etc. A value locus—possessing its own innate but finite capacity to reason, enjoy and will—learns to interpret incoming messages, thereby perceiving the world external to itself.

Still, the actual shapes, colors, sounds, temperatures, scents, tastes and textures that we as value loci see, hear, smell, taste and touch are those that Valcon himself *projects* into all value loci in a standardized way. Valcon is the artist. We, value loci, are living canvases experiencing what is painted on them. Valcon is like an infinite Internet that is always "on." We are like PCs that turn "off" to sleep and "on" when we wake.

The Apostle Paul, in his Mars Hill address, describes the extremely intimate nature of our sadly under-appreciated dependence on God, saying: "[God] himself gives all men life and breath and everything else. . . . In him we live and move and *have our being*" (Acts 17:25 and 28, emphasis added). The second law of Harmony Three among the Seven Harmonies offers to explain the basis of our eternal dependence.

Though the 'projections' we receive 'on loan' from Valcon supply each of us with our moment-by-moment experience, how each value locus assesses or ignores, enjoys or disdains and applies or wastes what it experiences is innate to each value locus itself.

Free as we are to think, love and will, it is still true that no finite being in the entire cosmos enjoys total privacy. As surely as Valcon artistically paints shapes, colors, sounds, scents, textures and tastes on the canvas of our inner persons, he is also fully aware of every thought, feeling and intent that every being ever has formulated or ever will formulate. He is both the perfect assessor of integrity and an infallible prosecutor for every failure or crime.

More than that, Valcon creates the stimuli reaching us via our nerves and brain plus the matching sights, sounds, temperatures, scents, tastes and textures we experience as a result. Dementia results when physical breakdown inhibits a human brain's accustomed way of processing external stimuli for its resident value locus. Even so, the resident value locus, though increasingly isolated from its environment and confused, still remains self-aware with feelings of pain or pleasure, initiative or boredom.

Why do we experience *touch*, for example, in our *fingertips,* when every stimulus is being processed *in our brains*? Thank Valcon for the marvel of *projected* sensation. That is how *close* he is to us, yet how often we even doubt his very existence—he, the one who sustains our personal self-awareness moment by moment!

Consider, though, the far greater bonus that awaits value loci who change the above one-way flow of impressions from Valcon into a two-way interaction with him! Finding favor with Valcon enables a value locus to *worship* him and even experience the peace and joy he reserves for those who love him. Valcon also receives a personal bonus by creating us. He experiences myriad aspects of his creation via our appreciation of its wonders!

A second way the Value Continuum creates is by *altering* the actual *'density'* of finite parts of the extent continuum in inversely equal ways, resulting in a kind of creaton called *extent density alterons*, i.e., matter, anti-matter and energy. I explain aspects of that form of creation in a later chapter.

If Valcon created billions of galactic systems and quasars without value loci, there would be no one here to enjoy them *with* him. Or—if he created value loci with no vast universe to enjoy, value loci would be less able to marvel at his creativity and power. One of Valcon's three Persensions—Omnisentience—inspires him to *love*, and love requires something to love and be loved by; hence Valcon ordains citizen value loci as *the* major component of his vast creation.

To proceed, we must now learn more about Persensions.

Chapter Four
The Harmony of Persensions

The Harmony of Persensions holds three laws specifying the primary function that each Persension fulfills within the echelon of the Value Continuum:

THE LAW OF THE PERSENSION OF OMNISCIENCE:

> The Persension of Omniscience *discerns value* in himself and in everything subordinate to himself.

THE LAW OF THE PERSENSION OF OMNISENTIENCE:

> The Persension of Omnisentience *sustains meaning* for everything that is subordinate to the Persension of Omniscience and is also delightful to himself.

THE LAW OF THE PERSENSION OF OMNIPOTENCE:

> The Persension of Omnipotence *creates* whatever is both subordinate to the Persension of Omniscience *and* delightful to the Persension of Omnisentience.

These three phrases—*discerns value, sustains meaning* and *creates*—define the primary role of each member of the Value Continuum, the eternal Godhead, in launching and sustaining creation. Observe, though, that the true cause of creation is *the second* Persension—the Persension of Omnisentience, known to millions as God the Son.

The Persension of Omnipotence—known as God the Holy Spirit—does not give existence to anything merely because the Persension of Omniscience discerns it as "subordinate to himself." Only when the Persension of Omnisentience—finding an approved entity to be delightful—sustains meaning for it, does the Persension of Omnipotence cause that particular entity to pop into existence. That is why Valcon's servant John the Apostle, in his gospel, quoted God the Son incarnate as saying, "The Son … can do only what he sees his Father doing" (5:19). That is also why he guided John to declare (1:1), "In the beginning was the Word [the *meaning*-sustaining second Persension], and the Word was *with* God [as one Persension in the Value Continuum], and the Word *was* God [because each Persension is Deity]." Then comes: "*Through him* all things were made; *without him* nothing was made that has been made" (1:3). Note how John repeats the same thought reworded for emphasis.

Many ancient texts credit creation primarily to the Second Person. The law of the Second Persension undergirds all such texts.

Behold the *symmetry* of the four pre-creation harmonies:

I. The Harmony of Entities:
1 law depicted by a point: •
II. The Harmony of Dimensions:
1 law = 1 line of unit length: ______
III. The Harmony of Continua:
2 laws = 2 lines of unit length: ______ ______
IV. The Harmony of Persensions:
3 laws = 3 lines of unit length: ______ ______ ______

Next we will find this same symmetry, by extension, embracing also the 15 laws of the three yet-to-be-presented *creation-governing* harmonies.

Chapter Five
The Harmony of Existence-Meaning Combinations

We saw that the Persension of Omnipotence, in accord with his own special law, gives **existence** only to things for which the Persension of Omnisentience sustains **meaning** according to *his* own special law. Thus, throughout creation, existence is ever combined with meaning, leading one to ask, *how many kinds of existence* are combined with *how many kinds of meaning* in how many ways?

Prior to creation, there was only one kind of **existence**—Valcon's—an existence that is interminable, hence *unconditional.* Creating finite entities under the Law of the Value Continuum, Valcon grants some finite entities an existence that is unconditional, hence eternal, like his own. Valcon grants other finite entities an existence that is *conditional*, hence temporary. Anything Valcon creates subject to a condition may exist only as long as that condition applies.

Prior to creation, there was only one kind of **meaning**—Valcon's. As God, Valcon is not beholden to any other being; hence the meaning he possesses is *independent!* Creating finite entities in accord with the Law of the Value Continuum, Valcon endows some finite entities with independent meaning while ordaining dependent meaning for others.

Finite entities endowed with independent meaning are free to "do their own thing" subject only to the limits of their various capacities. No matter what they do, no penalties incur. But wait! If anything is that free, how can it be deemed subordinate to Valcon, hence creatable?

Such things, while not *volitionally* subordinate to Valcon, remain *involuntarily* subordinate to him as, for example, when animals, merely by "doing their own thing," keep an ecosystem balanced. Conversely, finite entities for whom or for which Valcon ordains *dependent* meaning must either be *volitionally* subordinate to him or at least be *involuntarily* subordinate to the laws of the unified field.

These two kinds of existence and two categories of meaning thus appear in *four* combinations, yielding an echelon that links creation with pre-creation by defining how everything created must manifest subordination to Valcon, hence:

Four ways existence and meaning combine in the cosmos

I. THE *SOVEREIGN'S* LAW

> The Value Continuum—*sovereign* of all creation—reigns with unconditional existence and voluntarily independent meaning.

II. THE *CITIZEN'S* LAW

> For 'greater' value loci—*citizens*—Valcon ordains unconditional existence linked with voluntarily dependent meaning.

III. THE *DENIZEN'S* LAW

> For 'lesser' value loci—*denizens*—Valcon ordains conditional existence linked with involuntarily independent meaning.

IV. THE *EXTENT DENSITY ALTERON* LAW

> For all other created things, Valcon ordains conditional existence linked with involuntarily dependent meaning.

About Existence-Meaning Combination #1

The foremost existence-meaning combination belongs to Valcon alone. It affirms that Valcon exists unconditionally with the right to exercise *independent* meaning. Ergo Valcon exists forever as a *rightfully* self-glorifying Being. Still, Valcon's independent meaning allows him to *forego* his right to exercise independent meaning should he so choose for the benefit of any part of his creation.

About Existence-Meaning Combinations #2 & #3

Valcon, in accord with the second and third existence-meaning (EM) combinations above, creates value loci in two categories. He creates 'greater,' i.e., 'second law,' value loci as *citizens* and 'lesser,' i.e., 'third law,' value loci as *denizens.* Citizen value loci—often described as "made in the likeness of God"—are, like Valcon, seven-dimensional beings, albeit finite. Citizens automatically share *unconditional existence* with Valcon; that is why citizen value loci, once created, cannot be destroyed. Citizens exist forever with or without a cosmos-interactive apparatus (a body). However, the *meaning* Valcon links with a citizen's unconditional existence must be *dependent;* otherwise a citizen value locus intrudes upon an EM combination that belongs to Valcon alone.

How, then, do citizen value loci fulfill *dependent* meaning? First, citizens consent to honor Valcon as Sovereign. Second, citizens consent to the seven harmonies of truth (or any reasonable similitude of them) as all-governing universal law. "Man shall not live by bread alone but by every word God speaks" and all similar texts echo EM Combination II—a law granting unconditional existence to citizen value loci in combination with dependent meaning.

Third law value loci—fauna of every shape and size—exist conditionally but possess the right to manifest independent meaning subject only to their limited capacity and intelligence. In other words, the third EM combination grants *denizens* the right to do as they please and are able as long as the condition attached to their existence still applies. If a leopard terminates a gazelle's conditional existence by slaying it, or steals prey from a fellow-leopard, the leopard violates no cosmic law. If a lion harasses or kills a leopard, the lion violates no eternal law. If a *citizen* value locus, conversely, afflicts a fellow value locus, the perpetrator violates his God-given dependent meaning, a serious matter.

Denizens do not know of Valcon nor do they even know that he ordains conditions they fulfill. Valcon alone guarantees that denizens, acting on instinct, unwittingly fulfill ordained conditions. Contributing to the balance of an ecological system is the most common condition Valcon attaches to denizen-level existence.

Over time various denizens—simply by scattering seeds far afield—unwittingly facilitated the growth of plant life that would later become seams of coal or hidden seas of oil for human use. Fossil records do indeed show that Valcon terminates entire species of denizens—dinosaurs, for example—when the purpose they once served conflicts with later purposes, such as ours. The reasoning capacity Valcon grants to denizens is necessarily more limited than the capacity he grants to citizens. Granting higher reasoning capacity to entities with independent meaning would enable them to *wreck*, rather than *balance*, eco-systems.

About Existence-Meaning Combination #4

The fourth EM combination links conditional existence with dependent meaning for everything below the denizen level, i.e., matter, anti-matter and energy. When electrons yield to the attraction of protons or rocks fall to the ground, extent density alterons are fulfilling dependent meaning. Unlike us, protons *et al.*—having no ability to choose—fulfill their dependent meaning involuntarily.

How Valcon creates matter, anti-matter and energy by varying the density of finite parts of the extent continuum will be explained later. For now, I simply aver that EM combination #4 governs quarks, anti-quarks, other sub-atomic particles, photons and other phenomena such as protons, elements, compounds, flora, galaxies and quasars. All such things exist subject to God working his purposes through them. Thereafter, the Persension of Omnipotence need only relax and the physical universe—across billions of light years—reverts to homogeneous extent. What then *are* Valcon's long-term purposes for creation? That I will soon explain.

From this point on, I refer to the fourth EM combination by an acrostic: The **L**aw **O**f the **C**onditional **E**xistence and **D**ependent **M**eaning of **E**xtent **D**ensity **A**lterons, hence: **LOCEDMEDA** (pronounced **low-ked-may′-dəh)**.

How, then, do matter and energy manifest dependent meaning? The answer: by conforming to the five laws of Harmony VI, **The Harmony of Extent Density Alterons,** presented later in this treatise.

By this time readers who have progressed to this level are asking: Can we know for sure that a unified field of truth exists and that the five harmonies the author has presented thus far plus the two harmonies he has yet to explain are what define it? Is God really a hyper-infinite Value Continuum consisting of three Persensions echeloned as specified here? Is the conscious part of each person really a self-aware "value locus" linked to an "extent base"?

Does the extent continuum really serve not only as God's personal, eternal "hyper-body" but also as the 'raw material' he uses to create matter, antimatter and energy? Are conservation laws really linked to the inverse equality of extent density alterations engineered by Valcon?

Harmony VI is key to a scientifically affirmable "Yes!" If the predictions Harmony VI enables me to make about subatomic particles and the cosmos are proved correct, the consequent validation of Harmony VI validates its six fellow Harmonies as well. To validate one and spurn the rest would be like trying to separate a living organism from its DNA.

Even so, I delay presenting Harmony VI because some readers will find the physics and cosmology it covers so difficult that they may never get to Valcon's seventh harmony—which has greater significance for one's personal relationship with Valcon.

In what follows, please do not accuse me of arrogance when I opine that the Seven Harmonies really are *the* unified field. I acknowledge in advance that if Harmony VI, after a fair examination, is *proven* to be erroneous in its broad scope—as opposed to in a detail here or there—I will be obligated to take much of this treatise back to the drawing boards.

Chapter Six
The Seventh and Final Harmony

Just as the five laws of Harmony Six will show how extent density alterons fulfill their dependent meaning *involuntarily*, the six laws of the seventh and final Harmony show what we as citizen value loci must do to fulfill *our* dependent meaning *voluntarily*.

Extent density alterons conform automatically to the five features of a sphere—volume, surface area, circumference, radius and diameter/axis—in both the micro and (as we will see) macro levels of the cosmos. Harmony Seven's *six laws of ministration* correspondingly define how citizen value loci are to utilize extent density alterons in their service for Valcon as well as for their own mutual blessedness. Adding Harmony Seven—the seventh set of laws—to the prior six Harmonies also enables us at last to discern how evil could originate and how Valcon is in the process of counteracting it.

Our name for Harmony Seven includes "Locedmedan" (low-ked-may′-dun), an adjectival form of the acrostic used to abbreviate Harmony Five's fourth law, Locedmeda—the Law Of the Conditional Existence and Dependent Meaning of Extent Density Alterons. The six laws of Harmony Seven are echeloned. Each higher-numbered law *outranks* and thus may *overrule* its fellow laws of lower rank.

Under the Harmony of Persensions the Third Persension (commonly called *Holy Spirit*) "gives existence to everything that is both *subordinate* to the First Persension (*God the Father*) and *delightful* to the Second Persension" (*God the Son*). It follows that value loci, as unified field citizens, must understand what is required for them to demonstrate their special kind of subordination to Valcon. In a word, value loci must learn to bless each other and all three Persensions, their Sovereign, by fulfilling all six of Harmony Seven's laws according to each law's rank.

In order of *descending* rank, Harmony Seven's six laws are:

The Harmony of Locedmedan Ministration

VI. The Law of Recompense

V. The Law of Beauty

IV. The Law of Abundance

III. The Law of Adaptability

II. The Law of Predictability

I. The Law of Efficiency

Valcon exemplifies *Locedmedan ministration*

In fact, Valcon himself fulfills the following six laws profoundly by providing this amazing cosmos made of extent density alterons (EDAs) to be our habitat as citizens of the unified field. Accordingly Valcon invites citizens to follow his example by ministering to him and to each other in ways consistent with Harmony Seven's six laws. Even denizens, by Valcon's design, unwittingly fulfill all six laws despite their independent meaning. Extent density alterons likewise, under Valcon's control, fulfill all six laws by providing everything field citizens require.

Consider now—this time in order of *ascending* priority—the six laws of Locedmedan ministration.

The First Law of Locedmeda—EFFICIENCY

The minimal Locedmedan rule governing how alterons and field citizens are to function in the cosmos is *efficiency*. It follows, then, that efficiency is an ideal for all interactions involving Valcon, citizens, denizens and extent density alterons; but it ranks at the lowest level of Locedmedan expectation.

Note how efficiency links with the ideal we call "frugality." All cultures intuitively honor Efficiency by advocating frugality with proverbs such as "Waste not, want not," "Haste makes waste," "A penny saved is a penny earned," "A stitch in time saves nine," "A bird in the hand is worth two in the bush." Even the very *words* found in such proverbs are used frugally. Every unified field citizen seeks how to think, speak and act ever more efficiently.

The Second Law of Locedmeda—PREDICTABILITY

For Valcon, citizens, denizens and alterons to function *predictably* is even more important under the seventh harmony than that they be efficient. Apart from Locedmedan Efficiency and Predictability, all the probability laws known to science would fluctuate randomly. Instead, Predictability ordains probability laws across the cosmos to fulfill reasonable, commonplace, everyday creature expectations. Gravity *predictably* moves all matter *radially*. A magnetic field *predictably* selects ionized matter only to be moved toward or away from magnetic poles. Hydrogen and oxygen *predictably* combine as water. Unmoderated by Predictability, Efficiency might complicate a citizen's ability to measure time or a denizen's capacity to find food. In personal relations, predictability links with loyalty, trustworthiness, dependability, consistency, reasonableness, etc.

If Efficiency and Predictability alone cannot provide what Valcon and his citizens require, a still higher-ranking law rises to the occasion:

The Third Law of Locedmeda—ADAPTABILITY

Adaptability exploits the same probability laws that Predictability ordains but uses them to provide for *special* creature needs. However, Adaptability's manifold ministration is severely limited here on Planet Earth in this present age for one reason: a higher law, Recompense, restrains Adaptability from ministering as freely to fallen citizens as it does to unfallen beings, wherever such may be. For that reason, the descriptions Scripture gives of Adaptability's special care for Jesus seem so unreal—but only to us. Consider the following three examples.

How a man may walk on water

Predictability allows the surface tension of water to support the weight of an aquatic spider but not the weight of a man. So—if an unfallen citizen genuinely needs to walk on a lake, Adaptability overrules Predictability by *increasing the surface tension* of the water under his feet and balancing that anomaly with an inversely equal *decrease* in the surface tension of water elsewhere across the lake. While the man is walking on the water, aquatic spiders' little foot pads sink a little deeper into the water everywhere else. As long as the *average* surface tension of water is conserved for the entire lake, Predictability, so to speak, 'ignores' the local anomalies Adaptability arranges to meet a special need.

Ergo Jesus, a Man always perfectly subordinate to Valcon, was able to walk on the Sea of Galilee two millennia ago. On another occasion during Jesus' bodily sojourn on Earth, Adaptability overruled Predictability again, this time to render him invisible to enemies.

How Adaptability can make a citizen invisible

People in Nazareth, offended by unwelcome comments Jesus made in their place of worship, angrily resolved to hurl him down a steep slope. Until that moment, Predictability was dutifully scattering photons reflected from Jesus' skin, hair and clothing randomly in *all* directions, rendering him visible to all. If Adaptability—to protect Jesus—temporarily blocks all such photons from being absorbed by his assailants' optic nerves, suddenly he becomes invisible. Jesus simply walks away amid the crowd.

To balance this anomaly, imagine Adaptability making *other* objects more acutely visible to his assailants' optic nerves, an enhancement that they, in the heat of the moment, perhaps failed to notice. Need we explain that by means of Adaptability, Jesus could just as easily change water to wine, still a storm, heal the sick, feed 5,000 people with a few loaves and fishes and even raise the dead, as Scripture affirms he did.

Though Adaptability is able to provide every unfallen citizen's special needs at all times, for reasons I will soon explain, exceptions occur when true citizens intermingle with still unrestored fallen beings. Apart from such exceptions, stones *do indeed* become bread when needed. Tree branches suddenly bear fruit out of season. Thorns refuse to bloody a citizen's brow. Nails cannot pierce his flesh. A thrust spear rebounds from his muscle as from a rock. Famines and droughts do not occur. Childbirth brings momentary discomfort to a woman, but no pain. Denizens do not infect, sting, bite, maim or kill citizens. Nor do citizens age past their prime. As surely as their value loci have *unconditional* existence, even their physical bodies are rendered immortal.

Denizens, having *conditional* existence, *do* know aging and predation. The promise that denizens, at a later time, "will neither harm nor destroy" applies only to a specified "holy mountain" (Isaiah 11:6-9).

Citizens walk about, run or ride; but if special transport is needed, Valcon (who 'wave-moves' sub-atomic particles through the extent continuum] may choose to utilize the extent continuum, à la Adaptability, to *wave-move* citizens—sans machines—from one location to another.

Physicists studying quantum mechanics are already encountering a minimal manifestation of Adaptability. Under certain circumstances, quantum mechanics 'strangely' enables two objects, no matter how far apart they may be, to behave as a single connected entity. This is a phenomenon Predictability alone could hardly ordain.

Applying this principle, if citizens must traverse galactic distances, Valcon, through Adaptability, may afford another kind of transport—*ex-transeo passage.*

How travel, via Valcon, enables citizens to exceed light speed

Consider the following scenario: Valcon, by expanding the above-described feature of quantum mechanics, puts a given citizen's body *in stasis* on his home planet and via Adaptability simultaneously forms a new body for him at a location on a destination planet, wherever it may be. In one instant, Valcon transfers *just the value part* of the citizen's value locus—complete with every self-identifying memory—to a new extent base integrated with the new body awaiting the citizen at his destination, where he wakes simultaneously.

The point is that the value component of a value locus, unlike matter and energy, can "travel"—not only via the extent continuum, wherein velocity is limited, but also *via the Value Continuum himself—where there is no limiting velocity*. The citizen's new body, fully adapted to conditions at his destination, also resembles as closely as possible the citizen's original body lying in stasis on his home planet. When the citizen returns to his original body via "ex-transeo passage," he wakes in it instantly. His interim body, unless needed later, disperses as dust.

The unified field portends ex transeo travel. Thus Paul spoke of being "...away from the body and at home with the Lord" (II Corinthians 5:8). A departed citizen's value locus links immediately to a new heavenly body however many light years separate Heaven from Earth. As the rich man in Hades recognized Lazarus after death (Luke 16:19-31). At the Transfiguration, long-ago deceased Moses and Elijah appeared in distinct forms (Matthew 17:3). Departed citizens do indeed wear heavenly bodies even before the resurrection of their earthly bodies. Add the future privilege of experiencing embodiment on wondrous worlds without needing spaceships to reach them and one begins to envision what Paul might have meant when he wrote, "...no mind has conceived what God has prepared for those who love him" (I Corinthians 2:9). For now, Recompense—the highest Seventh Harmony Law—restrains Adaptability from lavishing mercies such as these even for rebels already restored as citizens. They enjoy partial Adaptability in this age, but bestowing complete adaptive blessing for restored citizens in full view of unrestored abettors of the subversion rampant on this planet puts the unrestored in judicial danger. Adaptability unleashed heightens insight, rendering rebels far more accountable, which in turn hardens the judicial complications awaiting them later under Recompense. More about that later.

Paul, in Romans 8:22-23, sees creation restrained *pro tem* as it waits to 'birth' a new order. He wrote: "...the whole creation has been groaning as in the pains of childbirth.... [And] we ourselves...groan inwardly as we wait eagerly for our adoption as sons [and] the redemption of our bodies." Matter 'groans' as we use it in violation of its dependent meaning. It groans again, longing for the day when it can serve the redeemed freely.

Restored citizens who are denied a reasonable share of Locedmedan mercy due to Valcon's *pro tem* need to suppress the insight levels of obdurate rebels around them are compensated later for every consequent inconvenience—especially if they endure the delay with *patience*.

Adaptability's influence on biology

Evolutionists will recognize that their theory in effect posits only two of the above rules presented here—Efficiency and Predictability—as giving rise to biologic forms. Evolutionists believe that physics and chemistry alone, given eons of time, *predictably* yield the earliest forms of mutating life; thereafter *efficiency* purges those that are unfit, leaving the others to survive if they can.

Efficiency and Predictability work incessantly, to be sure, but the vast range of probabilities they engender are more commonly *adverse* rather than beneficial to life. Even if life could begin under their exclusive rule, Efficiency and Predictability would foster *simple* life forms far more readily than complex entities. Efficiency and Predictability, unaided, would favor organisms that reproduce *asexually*, for example, as far more *efficient* and *predictable* than biological systems that required a fertile male to find and mate with a fertile female capable of gestating, birthing and perhaps nurturing offspring!

The 'Irreducible Complexity Barrier'

Evolution posits simple organisms becoming more complex via randomly successive one-at-a-time by-chance-beneficial mutations. Yet a host of transitions—the already-mentioned transition from asexual to sexual organisms, for example—require several thousand changes, each of which, if it occurred singly, would be pointless if not harmful. Alluding to organisms possessing *both* asexual *and* sexual capabilities does not help. The leap from asexuality to sexuality is still just as complex even if it occurs in a life form that retains asexuality in addition to new-found sexual capacities. Indeed, Efficiency and Predictability cannot originate life itself let alone a vast array of life forms.

Adaptability, conversely, hurdles the irreducible complexity barrier with the ease of a gazelle leaping over a thorn bush. Adaptability even launches "whole new species production runs," resulting in episodes of what biologists call "punctuated equilibria." Large numbers of never-before-seen species appear with relative suddenness in a single epoch.

Why does Valcon, via Adaptability, raise up new genera out of mere dust? Apparently it happens when Predictability has changed an environment so drastically that the world scene needs new genera. Why, then, do researchers attest evidence that one species can change gradually into another? Could it be that Valcon, foreknowing those who argue vehemently against the mere suggestion that he may exist, actually plants ruses to distract such from finding evidence of his existence, evidence that would only exacerbate their accountability in Valcon's eventual court? Dealing with the shrewd, Valcon waxes shrewder.

Under Predictability, organisms adapt as best they can. Adaptability alone fits new organisms to new environments.

The Fourth Law of Locedmeda—ABUNDANCE

Efficiency, Predictability and even Adaptability guarantee only as much food, water, area and material as a citizen or denizen needs. That is why Valcon also ordains *Abundance.* Everything citizens and denizens need is to be bountifully provisioned, Recompense permitting. Apart from Recompense's temporary restraint, Abundance produces more nurture than citizens and denizens can consume and surrounds them with a greater variety of phenomena than all their senses can ever fully enjoy. We, too, as citizens are to manifest abundance via generosity. Jesus said if someone asks for your cloak, give him your tunic also—even if you know he will be unable to return the favor later. Still, it takes two more laws of even higher rank to complete the unified field.

The Fifth Law of Locedmeda—BEAUTY

Abundance—even in a variety of forms—may still feature *plainness*! Thus Beauty, a higher law, adds dash, flourish, color and symmetry to plain entities ordained by the five lesser laws—but not consistently so! Beauty is guaranteed for all citizens (again with certain exceptions in the presence of insubordinates), but Beauty purposefully leaves some denizens and other entities plain and a few even ugly. Why?

If all things were equally beautiful, beauty would equate to plainness. Thus Valcon creates many things beautiful, some things plain and a few things ugly to make beauty stand out even more! Now, at last, I present the sixth and highest Seventh Harmony Law:

The Sixth Law of Locedmeda—RECOMPENSE

First, Recompense rewards Valcon, the Value Continuum, for creating the universe. How does Recompense reward him? It brings him what he most desires—the freewill love of hosts of citizens. Yes, Valcon

—the Threefold One—desires to love and be loved! Mutual love flows within his Three-ness, but all Three Persensions desire something more: to love and be loved by a virtually infinite number of finite value loci.

Second, Recompense guarantees degrees of eternal, glorious reward to all citizens who embrace Valcon. But not all citizens choose him. And that is where the unified field confronts a problem! There are those who hope vainly that punishment for evil may simply be waived. If it were, neither could Recompense ordain *reward!*

Locedmeda's six laws—an example for citizen value loci to emulate

Just as Valcon ministers faithfully to citizens and denizens according to Locedmeda's six laws—with certain exceptions when evil is present—so also he invites citizens to model their interactions with him and with each other according to Locedmeda.

Citizens delight to practice **Efficiency**, doing what is good, saying what is good—preferably without a waste of time and words. Citizens hope not to bore. Nor do they trivialize what fellow citizens deem important. Citizens attuned to the Spirit of Valcon learn efficiency from him as he, the all-efficient one, guides them with whispers in the heart.

Citizens honor **Predictability** by speaking, behaving and relating *consistently*. They are novel and creative but not eccentric.

Citizens honor **Adaptability** by choosing to serve others, as did he who, "being in very nature God…humbled himself" (Philippians 2:5-8).

Citizens also produce and share with more **Abundance** than efficiency, predictability and adaptability alone would require.

Citizens seek to garnish their lives and environment with **Beauty**.

Citizens delight to see efficiency, predictability, adaptability, abundance and beauty *rewarded* in accord with **Recompense**, and the opposite of these reprimanded by the same.

But where are the Ten Commandments, someone may ask. Don't we need prohibitions against specific sins? *We* do, yes. But because all of the unified field's 22 laws existed prior to the emergence of evil, every value locus was upright, meaning that desire and will were everywhere subordinate to reason. Enjoyment under the rule of reason is love, so everyone loved. No one willed arbitrarily. Every value locus, moreover, enjoyed full communion with Valcon, hence no list of prohibitions was needed. Jesus' later summary of the Law and the Prophets prevailed: "Love the Lord your God with all your heart and with all your soul and with all your mind … and…your neighbor as yourself. All the Law and the prophets hang on these two commandments" (Matthew 22:37-40).

With all 22 laws of the grand unified field set forth, note below that the three-sided symmetry of the *pre-creation* unified field, diagrammed earlier, now includes also the 15-law extension of the post-creation unified field. With every series at its 'perfect number,' symmetry reigns over *22* laws in Seven Harmonies.

> With all seven harmonies revealed, behold the *symmetry* of the *extended* unified field! Seven laws of four *pre*-creation harmonies plus 15 laws of three *post*-creation harmonies complete the 22-law grand unified field. Each law except the first is represented by one line of unit length:
>
> P . ← Harmony of Entities: 1 law, represented by a *point*
> R ____ ← Harmony of Dimensions: 1 law, 1 line, unit length
> E ___ ___ ← Harmony of Continua: 2 laws, 2 unit lines
> -- ___ ___ ___ ← Harmony of Persensions: 3 laws, 3 unit lines
> P ___ ___ ___ ___ ← Harmony of Existence-Meaning Combinations
> O ___ ___ ___ ___ ___ ← Harmony of Extent Density Alterons
> S ___ ___ ___ ___ ___ ___ ← Harmony of Locedmedan Ministration
> T

In light of the above symmetry, consider what Judaism's "Star of David," a.k.a. "Solomon's Seal," seems fortuitously designed to signify.

Imagine for a moment that the three sides of the *point-down* triangle in the Star of David symbolize the three Persensions who together comprise the Value Continuum. Imagine also that the *point-up* triangle captures the above-displayed symmetry of the unified field. Interweave the six sides of the two triangles and we have a striking symbolism for the mutual inter-relatedness of the triune God and the unified field. Surround both triangles with a circle to represent eternity and we could hardly have a more fitting depiction of the *eternal inter-relatedness of Valcon and the unified field.* Moderns who identify with David's Star will disagree, yet what they prize as theirs is one of several ancient symbols that read like relics of a possibly antediluvian culture rife with unified field knowledge. Take, for example, a character designating God in ancient Chinese script. God is represented by *three triangles pointing to a common center*:

Another ancient icon that predates whatever use moderns make of it today depicts two entities affecting each other within a circle:

Again, let the circle symbolize eternity. Let the *white* component occupying eternity represent the Value Continuum, white being a fittingly *triune* color embodied by three primary colors. Let the black eternal component represent the uncreated extent continuum, extent by itself being devoid of value just as black is devoid of primary colors. Let the black dot symbolize the extent continuum rendering Valcon eternally omnipresent. Let the white dot symbolize omnipresent Valcon employing the extent continuum as raw material for creation. Harmony Three's two laws could hardly be more fittingly reduced to symbolism.

Unified field precepts are the shoe that fits the foot!

Other ancient designs correspond amazingly to Harmony Five's two categories of existence combining with two kinds of meaning. Note, for example, this recurring pattern from Inca art in South America:

Another timeless symbol honored worldwide ages before the Nazis shanghaied it—the swastika (not shown here)—is found engraved in stone in ancient China and is even etched on the tobacco pipes of stone-age tribes in New Guinea. The swastika's four connected bent arms correspond precisely to the Fifth Harmony's four ways that two kinds of existence combine with two categories of meaning.

Are these correspondences mere coincidence or has mankind, having lost the key to these ancient symbols, been left in some ways confusedly honoring them and in other ways even imposing evil associations upon what was originally given as good?

What if mankind accepts all 22 laws as true?

I bid anyone who doubts that these Seven Harmonies truly are *the* unified field to ponder the following points:

1. As surely as mankind's ongoing extent-related comparisons attest that extent dimensions are real, our ubiquitous value-related comparisons just as readily attest that *value* dimensions exist as well.

2. The fact that four extent dimensions inhere as an extent continuum bodes that three value dimensions inhere as a value continuum.

3. If the extent and value continua are infinite (just try to imagine an 'end' beyond which there is nothing!), "God" can be defined as a triune omniscient, omnisentient, omnipotent Value Continuum who is also omnipresent in the extent continuum.

4. If a unified field is not founded on dimensions and continua, what other entities can it be founded on? Unknowns? Since dimensions and continua—two knowns—serve so well, why posit unknowns?

5. If the physical and cosmological predictions given later in this book are accepted as scientifically confirmed, and if all 22 laws replace whatever was contrary to them in mankind's educational systems, what results may we expect?

If children are taught engagingly about value dimensions, continua, and their personal relation to Valcon, Persensions, existence-meaning combinations, atonement and the six laws of Locedmeda—and if they see parents and teachers revering these concepts—surely they will feel a strong desire to live in ways that honor God, truth and mankind. As surely as math, science, language, government and civic duty are taught as out-workings of these grand concepts, children will grow up eager to gain and apply knowledge in other fields as well. Reason, compassion and justice will increase. Perfection will remain beyond the reach of our inverted value loci—for whom the standards of our faith are so high to begin with—but crime will steadily abate.

Let us all join together in hope and endeavor.

Chapter Seven
How Evil Intruded

As Isaac Newton anticipated, hints of a unified field are found not only in creation but, as we have minimally begun to see, in Scripture also. Finding clues in the natural order of things led us to the Seven Harmonies and their 22 laws. Now we find the unified field and Scripture covered with matching fingerprints—Valcon's!

Comparing the unified field and Scripture for more than four decades, I find them mutually illuminating. What follows now is a tapestry of conclusions based on my perusal of the 22 laws in the light of Scripture and Scripture in the light of the 22 laws. Perusing them together helps us understand the origin of evil.

Why did Valcon create a universe at all, foreknowing that part of his creation would bring forth evil? And—now that evil exists, what is Valcon doing about it? To find answers, we must first understand:

Why creation made evil possible

Recall Harmony Five. It ordains four ways that existence and meaning combine in the unified field. The highest of the four combinations ascribes Unconditional Existence and Independent Meaning to Valcon, mega-infinite Sovereign of all. The second highest EM combination also grants unconditional existence, this time to finite value loci—citizens of the unified field—but only in combination with *dependent meaning of a kind that must be voluntarily chosen*!

Recall also that every value locus possesses a finite measure of Valcon's three inherent value dimensions—reason, emotion and will. Reflect further that the three value dimensions Valcon imparts to value loci are *echeloned,* not only in him, but also *in them*. Thus it is natural for as-originally-created value loci to be guided by what reason approves. Likewise, emotion in as-originally-created value loci *enjoys* only what reason approves and disdains what reason bans. Will, accordingly, acts in conformity with reason and reason-guided pleasure. Thus:

Reason in as-originally-created value loci *agrees* that the highest existence-meaning combination belongs to Valcon. Emotion in as-originally-created value loci *delights* to affirm Valcon's supremacy. Will acts only in submission to Valcon as well. How then can *evil* appear amid so much harmony? The answer: evil emerges only when a value locus affects a *tour de force* within himself by purposely *de-echeloning,* i.e., upside-downing, the three values that are Valcon's gift to all citizens.

An ominous possibility—a value locus can *invert* the Valcon-ordained echelon that honors reason over emotion and will

The fact that as-originally-created value loci must accept their subordination to the Value Continuum means that they *are also capable of choosing insubordination.* The love a value locus offers Valcon gives Valcon no pleasure unless that value locus chooses to love him knowing it is also able to choose *not to love* him. A potential *not to love* gives the choice to love its greatest value, and that greatest value must exist or Valcon surely would not have chosen to extend the pre-creation unified field by even one electron.

A value locus's potential not to love begins as just that—a mere potential; and just as every potentiality in physics yields to governance by a probability law, we deduce a probability law governing this fearful potential associated with freewill as well.

In other words, if Valcon creates *a large enough host* of citizen-value-loci—and he *does* desire to love and be loved by *quintillions* of us—a small but inevitable percentage of those he creates *will* choose, completely on their own, to fall out under the wrong side of what I propose to call "Probability X." Unless a way can be found to reduce Probability X virtually to zero, a small but inevitable percentage of value loci will opt to rebel. Jesus himself declared, "It is *impossible* but that offences will come…" (Luke 17:1, KJV, emphasis added).

At the beginning Valcon created an initial number of field citizens in whom all three values were rightly echeloned. Valcon also displayed for them the wonders of creation and the 22-law unified field that undergirds everything. The awe inspired by that initial infusion of knowledge no doubt diminished the percentage amid that first host who otherwise would have rebelled. But unified field knowledge, though added to the wonders of creation in full display, did not lower Probability X close enough to zero to prevent rebellion from occurring amid that initial company.

As Valcon foreknew, one member of that first host rebelled despite all he knew. Something *more* would have to be added to the wonders of creation and the knowledge of the unified field before Probability X would fall so close to zero that no rebellion would occur even if Valcon subsequently created a host many factors greater in number!

The "fall" that happened in heaven

Scripture attests that evil began when one citizen—a member of that initial host—perceiving the ominous potential freewill entails, chose a dire option by *violating* his dependent meaning. Aspiring to become a *de facto* finite Value Continuum, he—by sheer force of his own will dimension—inverted the three rightly echeloned values Valcon had imparted, thereby becoming a fallen being. Once inverted, he *proclaimed himself as possessing independent meaning* in combination with his already-granted unconditional existence.

This usurper knew that Valcon—having granted unconditional existence to all citizens—had no legal option to annihilate him. Unconditional existence cannot end. The rebel correctly surmised he could continue to exist in the field of truth even while violating it. The moment he chose to be like the Most High by seizing independent meaning, the rebel elevated his will above reason and emotion, wresting for himself a strange new ability—a capacity to act *arbitrarily* without regard for reason, true pleasure or consequence. Evil had begun!

Emotion, ever the middle value dimension, suddenly found itself subordinated in the rebel under a strange new master—arbitrary will. Thus subordinated, emotion became uncannily able to *relish* insubordination to Valcon. *Reason*, enlisted now to justify whatever arbitrary option *will* might impose, became increasingly confused and irrational.

This dread inversion proved irreversible. Granted supremacy, will is released from subordination to reason, hence has no ability to abdicate. A being created to manifest echeloned values becomes anti-value.

Forfeiting all rights as a citizen in Valcon's 22-law field of truth and doomed to moral darkness forever, the usurper tempted others to follow. Some did. He and they thus unwittingly granted Valcon an option that he, the uncreated Creator, foresaw from eternity—the option to exploit this initial cabal of would-be kings as pawns to fulfill his own highest purpose. Exiled to Earth, the rebels found that Valcon had 'carelessly' left two newly created citizens vulnerable to the usurper's guile: our first parents.

The "fall" that happened on Earth

Mankind's subsequent fall differed. The usurpers rebelled out of a state of original purity despite full knowledge of the 22 laws, the wonders of creation and clear warnings of the consequence of rebellion! Valcon offers no redemption for those who sin out of *a state of original purity combined with full knowledge of the unified field and the glory of creation.*

The first man and woman, lacking high levels of insight, sinned against *a faint intuition* of the unified field and only when misled by a being perceived as superior. That is why Valcon offered mercy to our first parents and still proffers redemption to us, their offspring, provided we supplicate him for mercy during this life. Though we age and die until full restoration comes, immortality is ultimately guaranteed for those who 'fall asleep' reconciled to Valcon. For the remainder, there is no restoration.

Alas, a man whose value locus is inverted cannot sire a child with an upright one. His offspring may seem, in childhood, devoid of inclination to do wrong. But a moment comes when the offspring's will, though duly informed and warned, acts arbitrarily. It follows that Adam and everyone descended from him are born with inverted value loci and a bent for evil.

Valcon's servant Paul described mankind's predicament with a lesson from his own childhood: "Once I was alive apart from the law, but when the commandment came, sin sprang to life and I died" (Romans 7:9). Paul's "I was alive" followed by "I died" describes his transition from a childhood state of freedom from condemnation to a state of spiritual 'death'—an event precipitated by his first deed done *with awareness that it rendered him morally culpable.* By saying "sin sprang to life," Paul acknowledges his inverted value locus as waiting in his early years for an opportunity to act arbitrarily—which is exactly what it eventually did.

A child cannot truly request what he does not understand, so redemption based on Valcon's soon-to-be-explained atonement is automatic for little children. Thus if Paul had died *before* first recognizing himself as morally culpable, redemption's atonement-based coverage for young children would have ushered him into Valcon's presence—minus the inestimable privilege of having lived to serve Valcon on Earth.

More than half of mankind is estimated to enter Valcon's kingdom via his *childhood mortality coverage* (CMC). This includes deaths via miscarriages, stillbirths, and abortions. If Valcon foresees his human persuaders failing later to be part of the draw that brings potentially penitent people to repentance post-childhood, Valcon takes the potentially penitent during their childhood, so as not to lose them. That is one reason why, down through history, high infant mortality rates worldwide have ushered away at least two-thirds of mankind.

Saving such persons via infant mortality is *not* Valcon's choicest way of showing mercy. It is, after all, a way that denies Valcon his right to be glorified by those who, if only they could be redeemed post-childhood, would perform significant service for him. Persuaders, recognize how important your work is!

Those who survive *after* Valcon's CMC shield has expired must offer a prayer of true repentance and put their trust in Valcon in order to share in his glory. They must supplicate him—via whichever of his many names they happen to know—at least as Creator, but most especially as Redeemer! As Paul warned, "All [who live past that early period of coverage for children] sin and fall short of the glory of God," hence must "call upon the name of the Lord" (Romans 3:23 and 10:13, respectively). As another author wrote, "He who comes to God must believe that he is and that he rewards those who earnestly seek him" (Hebrews 11:6).

How evil is quantified

Every time a fallen citizen employs matter and energy to do evil, he forces matter and energy to violate its dependent meaning under Locedmeda, Harmony Five's fourth law. If a fallen citizen merely *smiles* with intent to mislead, he forces Locedmeda-ruled muscles and nerves to violate their dependent meaning. Speaking abusively, harboring evil, lying, etc., force neurons and nerves to violate Locedmeda. Stealing, murder, immorality, extortion and slander all incur *indebtedness* to Locedmeda by forcing what Locedmeda controls—matter and energy—to violate their dependent meaning. Once that debt is incurred, fallen citizens can do nothing on their own to free themselves from it. Only Valcon may rid them of that debt, as I explain later.

Recompense rises to punish evil, but Valcon has reasons to delay much of Recompense's inevitable reaction. Valcon's long-range plans require *time*.

The buried "treasure" Valcon 'buys the whole field' to own

As explained above, to be truly free, freewill must be subject to a probability law allowing 'x' violations vis-à-vis 'y,' the number of freewill beings Valcon creates. Freewill with a zero probability of violation is an oxymoron. Valcon, however, is even now working to lower the probability of *future* violations so incredibly close to zero that *none* will occur even if he creates *quintillions* of value loci! Quintillions of us are what he wants! It is like *a manual override* that negates Probability X virtually to zero without negating freewill in a single value locus anywhere. How does Valcon accomplish this incredible feat?

First, Valcon responds to evil's appearance, not by sealing it off on a prison planet but by allowing it to run its tragic but temporary course on this one laboratory world—Earth. Merely sealing evil off on some "hell world" would not lower Probability X as close to zero as Valcon requires.

Second, Valcon—via an atonement explained in a following chapter—provides redemption for mankind in a way that honors the same freewill that enabled some as-originally-created citizens to rebel. In other words, Valcon forces redemption on no one. He also enfranchises those he redeems—provided they consent—to proclaim redemption amid all the chaos evil causes on Earth. There are reasons why Valcon himself must not preach overtly to mankind, as I have already hinted.

Third, redemption must be requested, but with one exception: when Valcon foresees persuader negligence denying adequate persuasion to a potentially penitent person, Valcon offsets the witness's foreseen failure, as explained earlier, by taking the foreknown penitable person as a small child before he or she becomes morally culpable. Read Valcon's servant Isaiah: "…the righteous [*potentially righteous* included] are taken away to be spared from evil" (Isaiah 57:1). "Evil" in Hebrew includes tragedy, disaster and loss, as well as moral failure. Negligent persuaders forfeit their reward, but those they are foreknown to fail are rescued via CMC.

Fourth, Valcon vanquishes evil by utilizing those he redeems from evil here on Earth as story-tellers throughout the cosmos. For ages to come, wherever Valcon seeds habitable planets with unique races of citizens, redeemed citizens of Earth will be there (transported *ex transeo* perhaps) with moving firsthand accounts of Valcon redeeming lost value loci out of the havoc wrought by evil here. As we narrate how Valcon overcame evil, not by omnipotent force but *virtuously* by sacrificing himself, yet-to-be-created hosts will listen in utter awe. As Valcon's story-tellers, we will tell how we—former enemies of Valcon now reconciled—served him, despite temptation, fire and the sword, as messengers of mercy, to draw others from the ranks of his enemies "into the fold."

See at last why Valcon needs to redeem so many from this troubled world! Hosts of yet-to-be-created citizens across the cosmos must have their chance to hear our Great Story and respond by choosing to give evil *no chance to occur where they live!* Impressed by Valcon's power manifest in creation, awed by the wisdom of the unified field and, on top of that, convinced by planet Earth's Great Story, citizens everywhere in the cosmos will reject evil firmly and forever. *Through us* Valcon "manually overrides" Probability X by reducing its dire potential so close to zero that evil is foreknown never to recur anywhere!

How aptly Daniel said, "Those who lead many to righteousness will shine like the stars for ever and ever" (Daniel 12:3). How appropriately Paul wrote that Valcon's "intent" is that "now, through the church, the *manifold wisdom of God* should be made known to rulers and authorities in heavenly realms" (Ephesians 3:10, emphasis added). Indeed, Paul's "manifold wisdom" is but another name for the Great Story—Valcon's way of inspiring the entire moral cosmos to prevent the Fall he permitted in this one laboratory world from recurring anywhere else forever!

Paul inferred the overall cosmic effect of the Great Story again when he wrote: "God was pleased...through him [Christ] to reconcile to himself all things, whether things on earth or *things in heaven* by making peace through his blood shed on the cross" (Colossians 1:20, emphasis added).

Paul's "on earth" aspect of reconciliation signifies atonement-based redemption for those who have already sinned. His "in heaven" aspect of reconciliation inferably is *pre-emptive* as recountings of our Great Atoner overcoming the horrible chaos of evil here persuades yet-to-be-created citizens elsewhere to accept Valcon's rule over all beings forever.

How can we be sure evil will never recur even in the aftermath of Earth's Great Story? Remember that Valcon, omnipresent in time, already exists in the future. He knows because he is already *there*! Reflect also that the quota of story-tellers Valcon requires from Earth may be nearly filled! Choose now to join Valcon's future cosmic missionary task force.

I suggest when quintillions of citizens choose unanimously to love Valcon, each one knowing all the while that he actually *could* choose *not* to love him, *that* is the buried "treasure" Valcon 'bought the whole field' of creation to own and to enjoy forever (Matthew 13:44).

As surely as evil never recurs, redemption need never be procured again. Once evil is fully confined, citizens from across the cosmos—blessed by the Great Story that emerged on our planet, will arrive (*ex transeo*, I infer) to visit Earth sites where Valcon's goodness triumphed.

Some readers may object, "What's so great about the Great Story? Hearing of Jesus dying on the cross has never inspired me. Why should beings on other worlds be charmed?"

I reply: we, inured by viewing reality from the perspective of our inverted value loci, can hardly imagine the shock that the very idea of evil brings to unfallen beings in whom purest reason still reigns. As-originally-created value loci understand and share Valcon's commitment to truth and justice. We, in our finest moments, do not even come close to what unfallen citizens feel.

Beings existing under Adaptability's tender watch-care, moreover, can only gasp at the notion of having mere Predictability as primary caregiver, as tends to be our lot here due to evil. What shock they will feel to hear of Valcon rescuing evil-doers by limiting his power so as to be slain by those for whom he had worked miracles. Finally, Valcon's genius in forestalling Recompense by providing atonement and then using reconciled enemies to proclaim it worldwide, despite hosts of violent censors, will intrigue beings who have never known testing.

Need I continue?

Valcon here and now invites everyone who reads these words but remains estranged from him to be his friend at last! Respond to Valcon and let him prepare you to be another teller of his virtuous Great Story on distant worlds. Take thought, you *others* who still resist Valcon and persecute, slander and oppress his people on Earth. By your deeds you cast yourselves as villains in the Great Story, but as of this moment you have time to switch roles before the cast goes out cosmos-wide.

How, though, was Valcon able to restrain Recompense's otherwise immediate reaction against evil? To do so without violating the unified field obligated Valcon to guarantee three provisos:

A, B and C provisos for delaying judgment

Proviso "A": Valcon must *atone* for mankind's debt to Locedmeda in a way that upholds every requirement of the field of truth. Provided an atonement exists anywhere in the extent continuum, Recompense's reaction to Locedmedan indebtedness may be delayed *legally*.

Proviso "B": Valcon must find a way to offset the evil that still resides in the inverted value loci of those who repent and are restored.

Proviso "C": Valcon must ease the legal 'strain' on Locedmeda by finding a way to reduce the guilt of people who are still actively violating Locedmeda on Earth. The next two chapters explain how Valcon—incarnated as a human—fulfills all three provisos, thus becoming mankind's Redeemer.

Chapter Eight
Atonement!

Honoring proviso "A"—Valcon counter-balances fallen mankind's debt to Locedmeda

Every photon, quark, proton, neutron, electron, atom and molecule in the universe is subject to Locedmeda—the Law of the Conditional Existence and Dependent Meaning of Extent Density Alterons. Thus if citizen value loci rebel by using matter and energy in ways that violate matter and energy's dependent meaning, they are accountable for forcing Locedmeda-bound entities to do what Locedmeda forbids.

Rebel value loci are thus subject to retaliation by Locedmeda's sixth law—Recompense. If a citizen value locus possesses full knowledge of the unified field and its laws at the time he incurs indebtedness, physical death may come quickly. The rebel value locus' unconditional existence is still honored in that value loci survive the death of their bodies. Though 'value locus' can also mean denizens [conscious creatures existing below the citizen level], for brevity I use the term now to denote citizens only.

To cancel fallen humanity's debt to Locedmeda, Valcon found a way to make Locedmeda indebted to him and then used Locedmeda's debt to him to cancel fallen mankind's debt to Locedmeda. To achieve this result, Valcon had to become incarnated as a man. Remember:

Locedmeda controls extent density alterons only—the entities we call "matter and energy." Locedmeda's sovereignty rules nothing else. Hence Locedmeda cannot minister to Valcon directly (nor fail to minister to him!) unless Valcon clothes himself in a body made of extent density alterons. Thus one of the three Persensions—Omnisentience—did exactly that. He as Jesus clothed himself with humanity in the womb of Mary.

It was, after all, humanity's debt that had to be paid.

A Psalm in the Septuagint (40:6-8) declared, "Sacrifice and offering you did not desire. But a body you prepared for me….Here I am, [just as] it is written about me in the scroll. I have come to do your will, O God."

The body the Persension of Omnisentience donned was made for a *perfect* sacrifice, one that mere animal sacrifice could only foreshadow.

Yet Omnisentience donned more than a mere body in Mary's womb. He, a Persension within the Value Continuum, a Being omnipresent in all of space and time, merged a finite human value locus with deity. Thus he who is God became also "Son of God" and "Son of Man." Though Mary's Adamic value locus was inverted, Jesus' value locus was upright, since Joseph was not his father. Thus, "The Word became flesh and made his dwelling among us. We have seen his glory, the glory of the One and Only, who came from the father, full of grace and truth" (John 1:14).

Because the human value locus indwelling the human body of Jesus was rightly echeloned, Locedmeda rightly met his every need and desire. Locedmeda's third law—Adaptability—enabled Jesus to walk on water, still a storm, feed a throng from a few loaves and fishes, cleanse lepers, cause the lame to walk, give sight to the blind, open the ears of the deaf, cause the dumb to speak, and raise the dead. By virtue of Locedmeda's guarantee, Jesus' physical body was indestructible.

Or was it? What if Valcon himself, pursuing a higher purpose, chose to *impede* Locedmeda's otherwise automatic protection for Jesus? What might happen in that event? Could there be a worthy reason for Valcon to deny Jesus the invulnerability that was his by right?

The seven uncreated laws of the first four harmonies cannot, under any circumstance, be impeded. However, the fifteen laws of the creation extension of the unified field may suffer temporary delay provided the delay serves a worthy cause. Valcon did indeed arrange a temporary delay of Locedmeda's Adaptability function for a worthy cause! Jesus, the Second Persension—incarnated in his specially prepared human body—voluntarily submitted to increasingly intense Locedmedan deprivation.

Locedmeda itself has no allowance for failure to protect the righteous. So, though Valcon himself kept Locedmeda from protecting Jesus, by the letter of the law Locedmeda 'failed' Jesus. That 'failure' rendered Locedmeda indebted to Jesus, enabling Jesus thereby to exploit Locedmeda's debt to him to balance mankind's debt to Locedmeda.

How Jesus experienced Locedmedan deprivation

The first deprivation was Jesus' 40-day fast in the wilderness. Only Valcon's power restrained Locedmeda from feeding Jesus by changing stones to bread. Intense hunger left the human part of Jesus sorely tested in what was really only a “dry run” for a greater deprivation to follow. Witness later how easily an unrestrained Locedmeda, from a few loaves and fishes, provided food sufficient to feed hungry throngs!

Recall the wedding feast when Mary advised Jesus about a shortage of wine. He in effect replied, “A problem for you, dear woman, but not for me. My hour has not yet come.” (See John 2:4.) Meaning: “When my final Locedmedan deprivation commences, I will be, temporarily, as helpless to solve such problems as you are now. Because that time has not come, I, via Adaptability, can easily change water into wine for you.”

Another brief moment of Locedmedan deprivation happened when Jesus approached a fig tree, seeking figs out of season. Had Valcon not shielded that tree’s branches from Locedmeda, its branches would indeed have burgeoned with figs ripe and tasty. Instead, Valcon kept Locedmeda from offering that provision so that Jesus could draw a lesson for his disciples from the barrenness of a fig tree.

The ultimate Locedmedan deprivation

Near the end of his sojourn on earth, Judas Iscariot led a posse to arrest Jesus in a dark olive grove. Jesus asked, “Whom do you seek?” They said, “Jesus of Nazareth.” When Jesus said, “I am (he),” they stepped forward to seize him, but—alas—Adaptability was still engaged! To their utter surprise, an invisible ‘hand’ knocked them all to the ground (John 18:6). But in the next moment, Valcon placed Adaptability under restraint. Quite confused, the soldiers got back on their feet and tried again to seize Jesus. This time, to their relief, they succeeded. Jesus placed himself under their power. The ultimate Locedmedan deprivation had begun.

Most of us know what happened to Jesus then. Assailants pierced his brow with thorns and lashed his back, drawing blood. Their taunts and spittle abased him.

Under Hebrew law, sacrifices had to be fastened to the four horns of an altar. Hammer blows drove nails through all four of Jesus’ hands and feet. Lifted between earth and sky, our Lord entered an abyss of estrangement from Valcon—an abyss symbolized by the thickness of the great curtain that barred entrance to the holy of holies.

We sinners, inured to our estrangement from God, barely sense our desolation. For Jesus to experience aloneness was an almost unbearable shock. He cried out, “My God! My God! Why have you forsaken me?”

Locedmeda, restrained at a distance to safeguard Jesus' assailants, vented its frustration by darkening the sky, shaking the ground and splitting some rocks—a mere tithe of the world-shaking paroxysm that otherwise would have struck. Hanging from the nails, Jesus—knowing that his assailants possessed no more than a minimal intuition of a unified field of truth—prayed appropriately, "Father, forgive them; they do not know what they are doing."

Soon thereafter he cried aloud, "It is finished" and died. With Jesus' death, Locedmeda's debt to Jesus matched mankind's debt to Locedmeda. Immediately the great curtain in the temple split, signifying the opening of access to Valcon via atonement. Citizenship in the unified field became restorable—even retroactively—for every fallen citizen who has ever supplicated Valcon while still residing in an earthly body.

Again and again, liberal thinkers—unaware of Locedmeda and their own dire indebtedness to it—scorn the New Testament's strong emphasis that "the shed blood of Jesus" secures salvation. Little do they know that a phrase they disdain here on Earth is esteemed by the rest of the cosmos as the most poignantly meaningful paradox that can ever be, for the simple reason that the blood of someone like Jesus was supposed to be unsheddable, yet was shed! Such a paradox could not possibly happen unless it was the only way to achieve an incredible rescue—ours!

As Paul proclaimed, "In him we have redemption through his blood, the forgiveness of sins, in accordance with the riches of God's grace that he lavished on us with all wisdom and understanding" (Ephesians 1:7). John heard angelic beings sing, "...You were slain, and with your blood you purchased men for God from every tribe and language and people and nation" (Revelation 5:9). Any teacher who denies that divine forgiveness requires atonement is misled and misleading.

Atonement foretold!

Ages before Jesus' suffering wrought atonement, Genesis 3:15 had foretold that a being called "Serpent" would "strike the heel" of a deliverer curiously identified as the Offspring of a woman. Why grant him a title so generically applicable to every human? Birthed by a woman who was not impregnated by a man, Jesus became the Offspring of a woman in a most unique way! As the same prophecy foretold, Serpent—by striking Deliverer's heel—precipitated the crushing of his own head. By instigating the murder of Jesus, serpent 'struck the heel' of God, yes, but unwittingly gave Jesus the moral and legal right to vanquish evil and deliver its victims from bondage.

Another centuries-old text in Psalm 22, as worded in the Septuagint, Syriac and some Hebrew scriptures, even foretold—so strangely at the time—the "piercing" of the "hands and feet" of someone noted for "delighting in the Lord." Isaiah's 53rd chapter also speaks of a blessed Servant "disfigured more than any man," even "marred [almost] beyond human likeness"—a servant with "no beauty or majesty to attract us to him." He would be "despised and rejected . . . a man of sorrows."

Why did grievous calamity befall so blessed a person? Isaiah explains: "He took up our infirmities and carried our sorrows....He was pierced for our transgressions, he was crushed for our iniquities; the punishment that brought us peace was upon him, and by his wounds we are healed. We all, like sheep, have gone astray, each of us has turned to his own way; and the Lord has laid on him the iniquity of us all... He was led like a lamb to the slaughter...The Lord makes his life a guilt offering."

An ancient Vedic text from India foresaw mankind's Blessor as an upside-down tree—a tree rooted in heaven and growing *down* toward the Earth, not up from it; a tree spreading branches in all directions, yielding fruit for mankind. Wait! The trunk of the inverted tree is struck, inflicting a gash. Sap flowing from the gash brings healing to mankind.[1]

A tradition in Thailand names the suffering Deliverer as Phra Aria Metrai—"the Lord of Mercy" who bears *marks* in his hands and feet.

Resurrection!

For three days Jesus lay dead, entombed behind a stone. Then came the moment when Valcon canceled Locedmeda's "restraint order." Jesus resurrected instantly. The stone rolled away.

Centuries earlier, the author of Psalm 16, foreseeing Messiah's return to life, wrote, "...My body also will rest secure, because you will not abandon me to the grave, nor will you let your Holy One see decay." Centuries later, the Holy One's resurrection was prophesied: "After the suffering of his soul, he will see the light of life and will be satisfied" (Isaiah 53:11).

As stated earlier, a fallen value locus is irreversibly inverted. Instead of consistently conforming to reason and emotion's rightfully echeloned counsel, the will factor frequently and arbitrarily overrules good counsel. For Valcon to invade an inverted value locus and undo its inversion by force would require Valcon to undo the freewill choice of the forbear that brought about the original inversion. Rescuing an inverted value locus from its pitiful state is a complex operation, first because it requires Valcon to elicit a plea for help from an intellect that, dominated by will, is pridefully disinclined to plead for help! How then may Valcon rescue fallen citizens who are predisposed to neglect rescue?

Solving problem "B"—the irreversibility of a fallen being's 'invertedness'

First, Valcon surrounds all fallen value loci with his most basic intuitive draw—creation's witness to him and to his law "written on their hearts" (Romans 2:14). Wherever the church provides it, Valcon adds the more reasoned draw of biblical teaching. All the while, Valcon bypasses dominant will, appealing directly to a fallen value locus's subjugated intellect and emotion, both of which still possess intuition of a better way to exist. But why would arbitrary will allow itself to be bypassed?

Will dominates the fallen; but as long as they remain housed in physical bodies, numerous factors counter will's despotism. Instinct for survival, fear of pain, fatigue, hunger, thirst, a need for shelter, rest, sex, recognition, acceptance, enrichment, aid, etc., force dominant will to grant subjugated intellect and emotion some freedom, giving external persuasion some hope! Fallen value loci credit their positive social responses to some of the above external stimuli as virtue, but it is really just a construct. Dominant will still abides at the core. Hence Paul confessed, "…nothing good lives in me, that is, in my sinful nature" (Romans 7:18).

Valcon prefers the construct to its absence; he even grants it some reward, but it cannot be the basis for restoration to his kingdom.

Once an inverted value locus separates from its physical body, bodily restraints no longer counter dominant will. Until then, Valcon exploits every pre-death opportunity to appeal to a fallen value locus's partially free intellect and emotion.

In some fallen value loci, the two subjugated values cease resisting will's dominance. Will's arbitrariness grows increasingly self-destructive. Silly fads are deemed logical. Emotion falls prey to addiction. These value loci rarely respond to Valcon's draw. In others, the two subjugated values, sensing his draw, manage a cry for help, which he never fails to hear. To encourage that cry, Valcon touches just the exterior of the fallen value locus, granting a sense of his presence. Will, the usurper, sensing a threat to its dominance in Valcon's oppositely echeloned values, recoils as from an enemy. Paul wrote, "The sinful mind [i.e., an inverted, will-dominated anti-value locus] is hostile to God. It does not submit to God's law, nor can it do so," (Romans 8:7).

Yet the Apostle Paul still acknowledged his two subjugated value components—reason and emotion—as retaining an intuition of and even a longing for a consistent relationship with truth. He wrote: "What I want to do, that I do not do. But what I hate, I do....I know that nothing good lives in me, that is, in my sinful nature." This is a reference to his prior state as an unrescued—i.e., will-dominated—value locus. Paul then credits his two subjugated value components—reason and emotion—as able at least to know and even to desire truth while dominated by will: "I have the desire to do what is good, but I cannot carry it out. What I do is not the good I want to do; no, the evil I do not want to do—this I keep doing…In my inner being I delight in God's law; but I see another law at work …waging war against the law of my mind and making me a prisoner of the law of sin at work in my members" (Romans 7:15-23).

Thus did Valcon elicit Paul's heart-cry: "What a wretched man I am! Who will rescue me?" (Romans 7:24) It is at just such a moment that the atonement Jesus provided cancels the penitent supplicant's debt to Locedmeda. Still, one thing more is needed. Valcon creates a new, rightly echeloned value locus and attaches it against one side of the unlawfully de-echeloned yet penitent old value locus! The result is "regeneration."

Regeneration!

Just as a physical object has a center of gravity, this newly bi-composited value locus has a 'center of identity.' Rightly echeloned intellect on one side of the bond helps de-echeloned intellect on the other side to shift that single center of identity to the new side of the composite. Moral freedom is immediately revitalized via a *de facto* "new birth." As Jesus told Nicodemus, everyone "born of water"—the main element in the human body—must also be "born of the Spirit," i.e., have a new value locus birthed within him, a gift from Valcon as Holy Spirit.

The two sides of a redeemed value locus are not, however, like Siamese twins. Each of the two twins is a separate value locus. The two sides of a redeemed value locus, conversely, are truly attached, resulting in a *single* center of identity. As long as any two-nature value locus keeps its single center of identity on the new side of its inner boundary, it enjoys and shares goodness and truth almost as naturally as a never-inverted value locus. Valcon's Spirit communes with a two-nature value locus via its new side, offering guidance and enabling grace. As Paul said, "If anyone is in Christ, he is a new creation; the old has gone, the new has come" (II Corinthians 5:17).

The righteousness that the new nature side of a value locus possesses is not something the originally de-echeloned value locus can boast about. It is a gift from Valcon. As Paul wrote, "It is by grace you have been saved, through faith—and this not from yourselves. It is the gift of God—not by works, so that no one can boast" (Ephesians 2:8-9). Still, the transfer of a gift is not complete until it is received.

Valcon as Holy Spirit indwells the new side of redeemed value loci, granting them a special affinity for each other and for him. Wherever they gather in his name, he is present among them. That is why in scripture Valcon describes them corporately as his "body" and "bride."

What does baptism by immersion symbolize? When a person forsakes the "old nature side" of his composite value locus, that side effectively 'dies.' By this token, transiting one's center of identity out of one's old side resembles a 'death.' Entering the new side resembles a 'resurrection.' Jesus' death and resurrection made this transition possible, hence baptism symbolizes the privilege of partaking in Jesus' death and resurrection. So Paul could declare, "I want to know Christ and the power of his resurrection" (Philippians 3:10).

If a redeemed person wills his center of identity back across that inner boundary, sinful habits return. Those who consistently indwell their new side serve God and his kingdom best and engender fathomless blessing. Forgiveness avails for the others, provided they confess their sins and repent. "If we confess our sins, he is faithful and just and will forgive us our sins, and purify us from all unrighteousness" (1 John 1:9).

What happens when a redeemed value locus dies?

Because Harmony Five's second law grants unconditional existence to all citizen value loci, fallen value loci cannot be annihilated. Even so, Recompense ordains that their physical bodies are subject to aging and death. Does this mean that redeemed value loci are fated to carry their "old nature side" with them, tumor-like—even, after death? Not so! Inverted value loci cannot inherit Valcon's kingdom.

What can be done? Because both sides of a redeemed value locus have only one, not two, centers of identity, annihilating the fallen side once the person's center of identity has vacated it does not annihilate the center of identity, i.e., the person! The redeemed side, after the death of the body, survives forever, without that goiterish inverted half. Redemption is complete! True citizenship with full Locedmedan ministration is restored!

What happens when unredeemed value loci die?

Suppressing intuition if not actual knowledge of Valcon to the moment of death is a choice to rue. As surely as fallen value loci abused matter and energy by using it in violation of its dependent meaning, matter and energy will be permitted to force rebels to accept the dependent meaning *they* have violated by usurping Valcon's place. How?

Value loci cannot experience pain apart from being embodied, hence scripture indicates that Valcon will resurrect all his enemies in bodies capable of experiencing pain but not capable of dying (Revelation 9:6). Every rebel—wherever Valcon incarcerates him in his new body—feels stress commensurate with the genocide, murder, thievery, deception, injustice, infamy, betrayals and cruelty perpetrated in this world. That same stress sustains individuals at their personal 'threshold of submission,' the point at which dominant will at last yields fully to reason. And that is as close to 'peace' as beyond-salvation anti-value loci can ever come.

Understand now why Paul declared that "...*every* knee in heaven and on earth and [even] *under the earth* will bow, and *every* tongue confess that Jesus Christ is Lord, to the glory of God the Father" (Philippians 2:10, 11, emphasis added). Where mercy's offer fails to bring the fallen back to dependent meaning, Locedmeda-administered stress enforces perpetual repentance. Nor will fallen value loci blame Valcon for justice meted, or even yearn to repeat any wrongs committed here.

Why does Paul say "under the earth"? Do planets unfit for normal habitation serve as prisons—worlds too hot, too cold, or too dark with gravity too weak or too strong? Will Recompense match hostile environments to the culpability of offenders? John indeed warns of a fiery lake and a 'second death' (Revelation 20:14). Others speak of "blackest darkness... reserved forever" for evil-doers (II Peter 2:17 and Jude 13).

Valcon's people have no part or choice in his inevitable enforcement of Locedmeda. As a long-ago scripture warns, vengeance is God's; *he* repays (Deuteronomy 32:35). Presumption is fatal. Excuses fail in Valcon's court. People indisposed to love Valcon need to know that if they truly supplicate him for mercy in this life, he will impart to them that marvelous gift of a new nature, enabling them to know him forever.

Does Valcon predestine arbitrarily?

An influential man named Augustine, noting that Paul, in Ephesians 2:1, described the unredeemed as "**nekros**" (Greek νεκρός)—dead—even while physically alive, came to a controversial conclusion. Death halts every bodily function, so Augustine assumed Paul meant that unredeemed people are utterly devoid of spiritual capacities.

Reasoning thus, Augustine viewed redemption as not predicated on sinners choosing God because choosing God is something spiritually dead people cannot do. Ergo people can be redeemed only if God, on a whim, chooses them and, having chosen them, irresistibly causes them to be regenerated, at which point they find themselves able to repent and desire God. Other people die unredeemed because God, on a whim, rejects them.

Centuries later, John Calvin codified these two basic precepts as unconditional election and unconditional reprobation. This means that salvation is based primarily on luck and only secondarily on God's grace. Grace operates only for those lucky enough to be chosen by God's whim.

What other basis could there be, Augustine, Calvin and others asked, for God to spare some and reject others? God does not choose or reject people according to inconsequential physical features—hair color, race, etc. Interpreting **nekros** in Ephesians 2:1 as signifying the lost as devoid of spiritual capacity, Augustine thought God's choice of whom to save or reject must be essentially arbitrary (though he avoided calling it that).

As a result, Augustine's influence leads some to insist that urging unredeemed people to repent and believe in order to be regenerated is as pointless as asking dead men to walk. They teach instead that only those whom God, by divine whim, *a priori* selects and regenerates, are able to repent and believe—meaning, of course, that God redeems people *before* they actually repent and believe.

Evaluating Augustine's initial assumption

A more cautious interpretation of Ephesians 2:1 notes that cessation of bodily functions is only the *second of three* things that occur at death.

The primary event is the *separation* of a living soul from its body, from loved ones and from the world. Only then do bodily functions cease. A corresponding third event is the commencement of a process of decay. What if Paul's idiomatic use of **nekros** links with the primary event—the separation factor—rather than with the cessation factor, which is only secondary? If so, Augustine misread Paul.

Comparing Ephesians 2:1 with **nekros**-linked analogies elsewhere in the New Testament yields the following clues as to what first-century New Testament writers meant by such usage. For example Paul, in Romans 6:11, urged, "Count yourselves dead (**nekros**) to sin but alive to God." Did Paul mean, "Consider yourselves no longer able to function in a sinful way"? Elsewhere Paul makes it clear that redeemed value loci do not achieve sinless perfection in this life. Instead, Paul meant *separate* your minds from harboring sinful thoughts, your body from doing sinful deeds. Paul was referencing death as *separator*, not as a function ender.

Again, in Luke's Gospel, it was the prodigal son's *estrangement* (separation) that caused the father to say, "This, my son, was **nekros**..." (15:24). Not until the Prodigal chose to end that separation by returning did the father describe him as "alive again." **Nekros** did not signify the son as lacking ability to repent and return. He demonstrated ability to do both. Clearly, Augustine misled John Calvin, Martin Luther and many others regarding this one particular aspect of Paul's teaching.

The fact that inverted value loci are indeed *separated* from Valcon does not also mean that they have zero potential to choose to return. What, then, does cause Valcon to redeem some fallen loci and abandon others?

How Valcon influences freewill

Fallen value loci, while still alive, divide into three categories—the easily persuaded, the not-so-easily-persuaded and the unpersuadable. Valcon ordains salvation for all who place themselves in the first two categories. He abandons all who choose the third category. Lost people on their own sort themselves out among these three categories as follows.

Easily persuaded value loci are those who, like Job, respond to the beauty and diversity of creation by supplicating the Creator for mercy and favor. The universe itself, they intuit, points to a Creator, Sustainer and Judge who appeals to the consciences of people everywhere. Valcon responds to their plea by placing all such under the atonement Jesus secured at Golgotha. These are his "other sheep" who—though already under the care of Jesus, their incognito Shepherd—have yet to learn his specific name through faithful messengers and thus merge with "one fold under one Shepherd" (John 10:16). When faithful messengers arrive at last, easily persuaded people are the first to sense kinship and respond.

Not-so-easily-persuaded value loci choose to resist natural revelation's basic appeal but remain open to stronger persuasion. For these, a more didactic revelation explaining redemption categorically must be provided or they die in their sins.

Hence Valcon commissioned a special revelation—the Gospel found in canonized Scripture—to be taught across the world. He disseminates this added revelation, not over-poweringly, but through human messengers who model after the likeness of Jesus, be they teachers, proclaimers, translators or publishers.

Valcon supplements the appeal of their proclamation by selecting sequences of cause and effect that combine with the Gospel to draw every middle category person to his or her voluntary threshold of submission. Events, friendships, influences, disappointments, sickness, advantages, crises, setbacks—all are surveyed. If Valcon finds a procurable sequence of cause and effect that leads a lost value locus to believe the Gospel, Valcon guarantees that sequence!

As explained earlier, if Valcon foresees messengers failing to bring the Gospel to not-so-easily-persuaded value loci, Valcon takes those they fail to serve out of this world while they are still covered by the atonement as 'Romans 7:9 children.'

Unpersuadable value loci—third category people—peg their thresholds of surrender so high that even Valcon's most poignant persuasions fail. Warning them of judgment doesn't work either. They refuse rescue under all circumstances. Keep in mind—some persuasions are unusable because they inflict physical death before persuasion dawns.

Some unpersuadables simply ignore Valcon's draw; others are annoyed or even enraged by it. That is why Valcon mercifully reduces rather than increases his persuasions in their presence. Trying to persuade unpersuadables makes them react in ways that increase their already considerable debt to Locedmeda. The judgment awaiting them is austere enough. Why exacerbate their fate by giving them more truth to hate? Still, some persuasions, however reduced, are always there.

When foreseen-to-be-effective persuasions happen, fallen value loci respond by supplicating Valcon of their own volition, yes; but they learn to thank him for orchestrating crucially foreknown persuasions in concert with the witness of creation and/or the Gospel that evoke their freewill response. Unless Valcon selects the right persuasions, no one repents. As Jesus said, "no one comes to me unless my Father draws him" (John 6:44).

Those whom God redeems have no basis to boast about their status. Did they on their own procure atonement for their sins? Were they independently able to attach rightly-echeloned new natures to their inverted value loci? Not at all! We were all quite content to remain estranged until God, by his initiative, sought out effective ways to draw us. Salvation is correctly described as effected "by grace alone."

These divine operations, which I call directive encompassment, signify that Valcon does not overpower a fallen value locus' already partially disabled will. Rather he surrounds those he foreknows to be potentially repentant with external inducements, thus evoking the positive freewill response sinners can render while still in their bodies.

As explained in chapter 7, if Valcon foresees a messenger breaking a crucial sequence of cause and effect by failing to be on message, on time, Valcon has a way to spare second category people endangered by a messenger's failure. He takes those concerned years earlier, while they are still guiltless children. High infant mortality rates on our rebel planet have been a factor in the mercy of God. As for the scourge of abortion, Valcon punishes the aborters but receives those they slay into his presence.

Accordingly, Valcon timed our basic breakthroughs in medicine—inoculation, vaccination, water purification, etc.—to rise concurrent with the reawakening of the church to its largely abandoned apostolic mission. High infant mortality—less needed wherever Valcon's message spreads—diminished steadily as burgeoning medical knowledge spread out worldwide hand-in-hand with the Gospel.

Why Valcon permits unpersuadables to be born

As an omniscient Being, Valcon is able to block fertilizations he foreknows will result in murderous people. Why does Valcon allow another implicit probability law to bring forth both thugs and good citizens from their mothers' wombs?

Positing that freewill is a prerequisite for Valcon to create anything, it follows that blocking fertilizations of a select kind in the womb would violate freewill *a priori*. That being so, Valcon allows Predictability alone to administer what happens in the womb. That is one place where Adaptability is excluded.

Why Valcon permits some evil-doers to live long

Valcon allows evil-doers to be born and live out their lives primarily for two reasons. First, Valcon exploits some evil-doers as "negative shepherds." Ironically the evils that negative shepherds perpetrate cause some people who would otherwise turn away from Valcon to change their minds and turn to him. As for negative shepherds themselves, they receive no reward for unintended service.

Second, Valcon exploits many evil people as breeding stock, plain and simple. Almost every earthborn citizen who inherits Valcon's kingdom is descended from evil-doers who exclude themselves. Forbidding evil-doers to live long enough to procreate would be for Valcon to deny himself the love of their descendants whose repentance he foresees. He endures those wretched forbears—and asks us to endure them with him—for the sake of their descendants who will honor Valcon and share his kingdom of glory with him and with us.

Many who refuse to serve Valcon willingly with reward end up serving him unwittingly, sans reward. Now let us consider how Valcon fulfills proviso "C."

Chapter Nine
The Divine Conspiracy

Proviso "C," introduced earlier, calls for Valcon to ease the legal 'strain' on Recompense by finding a way to *reduce the guilt* of impenitent people even while they are still actively violating Locedmeda. How indeed can people be rendered less guilty while still sinning?

Ben Stein interviewed Richard Dawkins, an atheist, for Stein's film "Expelled." On screen, Stein asks Dawkins what he will say if, after death, he meets God. For an answer, Dawkins quoted fellow atheist Bertrand Russell who, when asked the same question, replied that he would say, "Sir, why did you go to such great pains to hide yourself?"

Russell and Dawkins thus imply that God, if he exists, is so concealed by the cosmos that men are in no way obliged to believe in him. Rather it is God's responsibility, if he wants to be acknowledged, to come out in the open and manifest himself to skeptics like Russell and Dawkins.

The question remains, which manifestation of God would Russell and Dawkins accept as proof? If God appeared to both men as a mile-high man, they could still dismiss him as an unusually large but finite biological form or a fantastic holographic image. Even if God suddenly healed every patient in a thousand hospitals and incarcerated every 'at large' felon in prison, Russell and Dawkins could still say, "This still does not prove that he controls all things." Factual evidence for infinity must itself be infinite, hence more than the finite mind of even a Russell or a Dawkins can grasp.

No physical evidence that a finite mind can grasp can be big enough to constitute proof that something else is infinite. Faith in a "most likely, most desirable" explanation for the cosmos is our only recourse. Finding an infinite Creator at the heart of a unified field that also explains the origin and function of the cosmos is surely a much more convincing proof of God than some merely physical manifestation could ever be.

However, Russell and Dawkins overlook another possibility. Perhaps God, as a mercy to certain people, may actually prefer to *deny* them more overt evidence of his existence than they already have. Being persuaded that God exists, after all, entails surrendering oneself to live in accord with his rule. If God foreknows that persuading a given person will not result in his surrender, the last thing that person needs is for God to give him more proof of God. Dumping more proof on proof rejecters achieves two ill effects: it adds to their guilt and intensifies their annoyance, which in turn causes them to say or do things that add even more to their guilt.

Warnings from Scripture

Let me be clear: Valcon *foreknows* which people will respond wisely if persuaded that he exists. He also foreknows who will reject his rule even if persuaded that he exists. God, by manifesting his presence to foreknown truth responders, induces foreknown response. Conversely, God—magnanimously hiding himself from people he foreknows will reject him no matter what—avoids adding to their guilt by provoking them to greater rebellion now leading to direr judgment later. Call it "a conspiracy of mercy." A state of mind that ignores God announces itself as the best God can do for the individual, present circumstances prevailing.

Insight as to moral responsibility, if violated, heightens guilt. Heightened guilt activates Recompense. If judgment must be delayed pro tem, Valcon must limit the degree of spiritual insight he grants to impenitent value loci. If fallen value loci have only *a faint intuition* of Valcon and the unified field, Valcon justifies delaying or at least moderating Recompense's lawful reaction against the evil they perpetrate. Many Scriptures warn that judicial tension growls behind the scenes of a peaceful Earth when impenitent rebels learn too much.

Matthew 11:20-24—Jesus warned those who witnessed his miracles yet remained obdurate that a correspondingly greater punishment awaited them as a result. How ironic—teaching and miracles that bless and heal become a bane if scorned. Accountability rises with insight.

John 15:22-24—Jesus omened a greater penalty for his enemies when he said, "If I had not come and spoken to them, they would not be guilty of sin. Now, however, they have no excuse for their sin....If I had not done among them what no one else did, they would not be guilty of sin. But now they have seen these miracles and yet they have hated both me and my Father."

Mark 8:11 and 12 and Matthew 12:38 and 39—People who were already arbitrarily hostile to Jesus demanded that he show them "a sign from heaven," as if a sign of that ilk would be more credible than his miracles of healing for needy people. Jesus exposed the irony of their request saying, "A wicked and adulterous generation asks for a sign!"

Evidence cannot assuage *mindless* hostility. Implacable people are best left unconvinced.

Isaiah 6:1-7—Valcon gave Isaiah a vision of Valcon enthroned. *Smoke* billowed up. Why not *mist* with a rainbow? Smoke stings the eye and blurs vision. Reading the smoke as a warning, Isaiah lamented, "Woe to me! I am ruined! For I…a man of unclean lips…have seen the King, the Lord Almighty." The combination of elevated insight added to his until-then unrepented sin placed Isaiah in danger of judgment. Had he not repented, judgment was indeed pending. Had Valcon *foreknown* that Isaiah would not repent, conceivably no vision would have been granted. Coals from the altar of sacrifice touched Isaiah's lips, symbolizing atonement and forgiveness. Coals from Valcon's altar glow also for *us.*

Luke 23:34—Nailed to the cross, Jesus prayed for his murderers, saying, "Father, forgive them, for *they do not know what they are doing.*" This passage and many others certify mankind's relative spiritual blindness as a *de facto* shield insulating evil people from an otherwise active, rumbling, ready-to-strike, sixth law of Locedmeda—Recompense.

Revelation 10:6 and 7—For that era, Valcon forbade John to write what he heard the seven thunders roar. We infer his reason was to keep human insight levels on a lower tier as a proviso for delaying judgment.

The book of Exodus—The sheer number and magnitude of miracles Valcon displayed in Egypt prior to Israel's exodus plunged all who scorned Valcon's display into what may be termed "hyper-evil status," triggering still more plagues. However, some repentant Egyptians escaped with Israel from their devastated nation. Even Israelis who witnessed Valcon's phenomenal display fell prey to swifter judgment if they subsequently offended him. Relatively minor offenses—griping about miraculously provided food, for example—brought dire consequence.

Egyptologists dismiss the Exodus account as fiction, unaware that Valcon, as a favor to impenitent mankind, may hide archaeological evidence that—if revealed only to be scorned—would place more of mankind in greater jeopardy under Recompense. Leaving too much conclusive evidence of miracle-working lying 'out in the open' in archaeological records is contrary to the divine conspiracy, to say the least. Instead, Valcon intentionally makes it easy for anyone so disposed to dismiss the Exodus account as fiction.

Zechariah 5:1-4—Wherever Zechariah's open scroll flies, mankind —accessing what is written on *both* its sides—is either blessed or cursed. Evil-doers who grasp truth revealed by the scroll but remain evil find their habitat destroyed timber by timber, stone by stone. Others are spared.

Psalm 8:2—The Psalmist wrote: "From the lips of children and infants [i.e., through God's redemptive message spoken by 'nobodies' whom the high and mighty dismiss as naive] you have ordained *strength* [Valcon accomplishes his clandestine purpose across the planet without attracting undue attention from unpersuadables] because of your enemies [lest overt operations antagonize truth-rejecters with incriminating insight], to silence the foe [by not forcing unpersuadable people to confront evidence they detest], *and the avenger*" [Valcon averts Recompense's reaction against truth-rejecters by dulling their ability to perceive truth they would summarily reject].

And *that* is the crux of the matter! If Valcon's avenger—Locedmeda's sixth law, Recompense—is to bide its time, the tide in mankind's ocean of guilt must be kept below a critical high water mark, below a kind of 'critical mass.' Lulling his foes *pro tem* with spiritual blindness lets Valcon's 'avenger' postpone the day of reckoning until Valcon achieves his goal.

Hence the genius of Valcon's Gospel

Matthew 11:25—Jesus echoed David's description (Psalm 8:2) of 'children' as wisdom bearers, saying: "I praise you, Father, Lord of heaven and earth, because you have hidden these things from the wise and learned, and revealed them to *little children.*"

I Corinthians 1:20 to 30—Paul explained the clandestine nature of Valcon's proclamation of atonement: "The message of the cross is foolishness to those who are perishing, but to us who are being saved it is the power of God....For since in the wisdom of God the world through its wisdom did not know him, God was pleased through the 'foolishness' of what was preached to save those who believe. Jews demand miraculous signs and Greeks look for wisdom, but we preach Christ crucified, a stumbling-block to Jews and foolishness to Gentiles....For the 'foolishness' of God is wiser than man's wisdom, and the 'weakness' of God is stronger than man's strength" (inner quotes added).

Paul then linked the apparent folly of Valcon's message with the general innocuousness of Valcon's preferred messengers: "Brothers, think of what you were when you were called. Not many of you were wise by human standards; not many were influential; not many were of noble birth. But God chose the 'foolish' things of the world to shame the 'wise' [and] the 'weak' things of the world to shame the 'strong'" (inner quotes added).

Isaiah 45:15—Now we may understand why Isaiah wrote: "Truly you are a God who *hides* himself, O God and *Savior*…"

Evidence that affirms the faith of subordinate value loci *portends disaster* for insubordinates because Locedmeda's sixth law—Recompense—notes how clearly or dimly insubordinates see their own moral reprehensibility. We say "or dimly," because no one after early youth has *zero* awareness of moral accountability. A given rebel's awareness may, however, be minimal. Valcon takes minimal versus heightened levels of awareness into account when he judges mankind.

To this end, Valcon effected a *conspiracy of mercy* by hiding the 22 laws of the unified field (granting *pro tem* that these 22 laws are *it*) from mankind. For judgment to be delayed, rebels must be limited to a mere intuition of the unified field. Releasing Adaptability to manifest miracles in millions of situations would replace intuition with clearer knowledge, thereby precipitating judgment. Hence, for the interim, Valcon subjects the Earth to an almost unmitigated *rule by Predictability.* Why?

When Adaptability—a higher ranking law—overrules Predictability, miracles recede behind seemingly heartless naturalism. Accidents, catastrophes, sickness, aging and death abound, leading some to doubt Valcon's goodness. Yet this is what keeps Valcon from ending this crucial age prematurely by destroying all evil people here and now, overtly.

Sadly, implementing this "conspiracy of mercy" also requires Valcon to restrain Adaptability *pro tem* from rendering full service to already redeemed citizens. Having Adaptability protect the redeemed in full view of rebels struggling under Predictability's sway would give away Valcon's conspiracy and precipitate judgment prematurely. For ages, Job and other sages asked, "Why must good people suffer?" These factors are a major reason! Only as the end of this age draws near may unified field benefits begin to break forth for the redeemed. May it be soon!

Some of us are implacable, others receptive. Some of us are rebels restored. Adaptability 'yearns' always to preserve every restored citizen from harm. Recompense, conversely, 'yearns' to neutralize every rebel. Allowing both laws to "do their thing" in full purview of a world peopled mostly by the unredeemed would render rebel minds more accountable, precipitating direr judgment on greater numbers of people.

As cited earlier, Paul described planet Earth as one extremely conflicted world when he wrote, "Creation waits in eager expectation for the sons of God to be revealed," adding also, "Creation was subjected to frustration [i.e., because Adaptability 'feels' so impeded], not by its own choice, but by the will of the one who subjected it.... [Hence] the whole creation has been groaning as in the pains of childbirth until now, awaiting the redemption of God's children" (Romans 8:19-23).

Paul was quite correct. Keeping higher Locedmedan laws from overruling one of lower rank is hardly normative, but that is exactly what our planet has been experiencing, at least until now.

Does it surprise you that Adaptability unimpeded would transform nature all around you, readying every natural phenomenon to wait upon your every rightful need? Does it surprise you also to learn that Recompense unimpeded can just as readily transform placid nature into an arena wherein finally impenitent people come under attack by nature itself? I suggest we can be just as assured that citizens residing on sinless worlds are just as surprised to hear that Valcon has chosen, *pro tem*, to stultify both Adaptability and Recompense *here!*

Occasional breakthroughs of Adaptability on Earth are what we call 'miracles.' But these are mere 'pop-ups' compared to what Paul called "the glory that will be revealed" when restoration comes (Romans 8:18).

Valcon exploits this present "window" of delayed judgment by using restored citizens as messengers who disperse the "good news" of redemption worldwide. The further the message spreads, the greater the number of special citizens Valcon gathers in for his future purposes. As that number approaches completion, a new era prepares to dawn.

How Valcon limits fallen 'angels'

As for fallen angels, Valcon enforces *one* key proviso: He keeps them physically disembodied lest they incur a higher debt to Locedmeda than they already owe by having formerly misused actual matter. Fallen angels, however, do try to induce mankind to abuse matter and energy *on their behalf.*

If fallen angels, knowing what they know, roamed the earth in bodies of matter and energy, Locedmeda's total reaction against them in full view of mankind would compromise Valcon's conspiracy of mercy for sure! Valcon ensures that fallen angels are disembodied, hence hidden from human eyes.

How judicial tension marks hyper-evil value loci

Judicial tension builds in the proximity of hyper-evil anti-value loci. It is a judicial tension between Locedmeda's second law, Predictability, and its sixth law, Recompense. Recompense—highest of Locedmeda's six laws—gradually, increasingly, overrules Predictability's capacity to keep everything working *normally* in the presence of hyper-evil people. Normally predictable physical phenomena *begin to bend under the weight* of Recompense's escalating judicial takeover.

Even when Valcon keeps the unified field *wrapped* but exposes obdurate beholders to 'miracles,' judicial tension escalates. Allowing Adaptability to array *many* miracles in a brief span of time brings obdurate beholders to the brink of hyper-evil standing by elevating their insight massively. But *even that is nothing* compared to the judicial crisis that results if Valcon unveils the unified field itself to millions of obdurate minds *in combination with a stunning array of miracles.*

Does Valcon ordain spiritual blindness to keep people from turning to him? Never! He blinds only those he foreknows will implacably reject every persuasion arranged for them while they yet live in this world.

To harvest hundreds of millions of redeemed value loci from planet Earth, Valcon had to devise a plan to shepherd redeemable people into the safety of the 'sheepfold' without undoing the spiritual blindness that insulates unredeemable people from otherwise immediate wrath. The Gospel—proclaimed initially by prophets, apostles and now by the Church—is Valcon's ingenious 'under the radar' people harvester.

People may deem me arrogant for suggesting that how they respond to what I have written here may actually affect their standing with God. I reply that Recompense is integral to the 22 laws only if they actually are the unified field. Otherwise reading this book is no different from reading any other. We will wait and see.

Chapter 19, "Valcon's Clandestine Mission on Earth," summarizes how the Church's 2,000-year-long 'all peoples rescue operation' flourished initially, faltered tragically, only now in these more recent times to lock into 'fast forward' gear again. I will show how a glaring omission in Christianity's creeds contributed direly to a costly shortfall.

We turn now to the part of this book that presents the greatest challenge for this author to explain and for an average reader to understand. I intend to demonstrate that even *subatomic physics* and *cosmology* submit to the scope of the 22-law unified field presented here.

Chapter Ten
The Harmony of Extent Density Alterons

For those who cannot accept the seventeen laws already presented unless they are accompanied by scientifically testable propositions, I offer the following five laws of Harmony Six as evidence that matter, antimatter and energy are nothing more than inversely equal alterations—alterons—that Valcon sustains amid the otherwise pristine 'density' of the pre-creation extent [space-time] continuum.

As a time-saver, when I directly derive information from other sources, rather than supplying footnotes that require readers to make trips to a library for further study, I may insert the symbol (W) in my text to suggest that readers needing background can simply look up the subject on the Worldwide **W**eb—i.e., the Internet.

Some thinkers in ancient Greece, crediting a circle as a perfect geometric form, believed a circle is somehow the basis of the physical universe. Plato (W) ventured a guess that something more complex than a circle—a *sphere*—was a more likely motif. But Plato had no clue as to *how* the cosmos could be based upon a sphere. I believe it is possible now to show that Plato was correct. The five aspects of a sphere—spherical *volume,* spherical *surface area, circumference, radius* and *axis* (which is really just a *diameter* of a sphere)—do indeed relate to everything we find, not only in the micro-cosmos, but in the macro-cosmos as well. These five aspects of a sphere, linked with the names they lend to extent density alterons, are manifest in the micro-cosmos in these ways:

Spherical volume → *volons* (quarks, anti-quarks, electrons, etc.)
Spherical surface area → *areons* (concentric 'shells' within atoms)
Circumference → *circons* ("spin" that traces circumferences)
Radius → *radions* (gravity)
Axis, which happens also to be a diameter → *axions* (magnetism)

The unified field's sixth harmony thus ordains five laws requiring all five aspects of a sphere (volume, area, circumference, radius and axis) to be manifest at micro levels of the cosmos and in its macro design also. Valcon achieves this via inversely equal alterations of homogeneous space-time. In all five laws below, the prefix 'exo-' designates ways in which a particular aspect of a sphere presents in an *expanded, outward* or *open* style. 'Eso-' designates the same aspects presenting in a manner that is *contracted, inward* or *closed.* Here are the Sixth Harmony's five laws:

I. THE LAW OF *VOLONS*:

Valcon ordains exovolons and esovolons at micro and macro levels of the cosmos.

II. THE LAW OF *AREONS*:

Valcon ordains exoareons and esoareons at micro and macro levels of the cosmos.

III. THE LAW OF *CIRCONS*:

Valcon ordains exocircons and esocircons at micro and macro levels of the cosmos.

IV. THE LAW OF *RADIONS*:

Valcon ordains exoradions and esoradions at micro and macro levels of the cosmos.

V. THE LAW OF *AXIONS*:

Valcon ordains exoaxions and esoaxions at micro and macro levels of the cosmos.

Part of what follows is already known to scientists. The rest is what I offer attempting to help solve vexing cosmic riddles. Note that the initial letters of volon, areon, circon, radion and axion form the acrostic "VACRA," enabling us to call what follows "The VACRA Hypothesis."

As posited earlier, the extent continuum, prior to creation, was isotropic (the same in all directions), unvaried, uniform, and homogeneous. Isotropic extent thus became Valcon's 'ore,' his 'raw material' for creation. To create subatomic particles, Valcon had only to alter the original uniformity of tiny bits of his own 'hyper-body.' Recall that one way Valcon alters that uniformity is by imparting his own three values finitely to finite parts of the extent continuum, thereby creating individual value loci, i.e., *souls*. This method of creating *personifies* bits of extent while leaving its actual physical 'density' unaltered.

The *second* way Valcon creates is by altering the pristinely uniform 'density' of discrete *volumes* of the extent continuum, thereby creating *volons, areons, circons, radions and axions*. To launch this aspect of the unified field, we begin by asking what are volons and how do *exo*-volons differ from *eso*-volons?

I. Exo- and eso-*volons* in the micro-cosmos

Imagine two spheres of equal volume, A and B, immersed in a tank of water. Consider each sphere as occupying 1.618034 units of volume in the tank. Expanding sphere A by *the square of 1.618034* increases its volume to 2.618034, thus raising the level of water in the tank by unit 1 in volume. To return the water in the tank to its original level, simply divide sphere B's 1.618034 units of volume by 1.618034 and then divide the result by that same factor *again!* Sphere B's volume reduces to 0.618034 (a reduction of unit 1 in volume). Sphere B's contraction and sphere A's expansion are inversely equal, all by means of a single factor—1.618034!

Readers may recognize 1.618034. It is *the golden mean.*

Harmonic Origin Cosmology proposes that Valcon, utilizing this same single factor, creates esovolons and exovolons by means of inversely equal alterations in homogeneous space-time. The result is what physicists call "particle-antiparticle pairs." As you may guess, the contracted particle is an **esovolon**. The expanded one is an **exovolon**—nomenclature pertaining to spherical *volume*. We will now see how the inverse equality that forms them also explains their mass and charge.

The basis of charge, mass and conservation laws

It follows that entities thus created have opposite *charge* because the expanded component can never return to homogeneity apart from its inversely equal contracted counterpart. Such entities also have equal *mass* and thus are able to achieve mutual annihilation, as particle-antiparticle pairs famously do, because the contraction embodied in the one matches the expansion in the other. Finally, as surely as all forms of matter and energy consist of inversely equal departures from originally isotropic extent, **conservation laws** (W) are sure to arise as *guarantors* of inverse equality for alterons throughout the cosmos.

So—creating an esovolon necessarily entails creating an equal-mass exovolon with it. That is why energy can never convert to a particle of matter by itself. If energy (or homogeneous extent, for that matter) is to be converted to mass, particle-antiparticle pairs must result.

The volumes of isotropic extent from which Valcon creates exovolon-esovolon pairs are their *spheres of origin*, or what I call *orispheres.* Exovolons and esovolons derived from equal orispheres are particle-antiparticle pairs. If they are not separated effectively at their creation, exovolon-esovolon pairs 'seek' each other, mutually 'wanting' to be restored to a normal state, which is isotropic homogeneity.

Exovolon-esovolon pairs derived from equal orispheres 'feel' the strongest attraction for each other, because each has *exactly* what the other needs to return to homogeneity. If we call an exovolon's attraction for an esovolon *positive* charge, an esovolon's reciprocal draw must be labeled *negative* charge. Any exovolon also 'feels attracted' to any proximal esovolon that is *not* its antiparticle—i.e., an esovolon derived from an orisphere of a larger or smaller size. This attraction, though, is weaker because each such volon 'knows' that the other has either too much or not enough of what is needed to return both volons to homogeneity.

It follows that exovolons *repel* other exovolons and esovolons *repel* other esovolons because two volons of a kind hold *the opposite* of what either one of them needs to return to homogeneity.

What happens when particle meets antiparticle

When an electron, for example, encounters its antiparticle—a positron—both particles want to restore each other to homogeneity. They fail only because Valcon maintains the *quota* of physically altered extent he requires for the cosmos. Alterons are needed to fulfill the fourth existence-meaning combination, LOCEDMEDA (law of the conditional existence and dependent meaning of extent density alterons). So, when particle-antiparticle pairs collide, rather than letting them return each other to homogeneity, Valcon converts them instead to another form of alteron—*photons.* The energy of the resulting photon burst is, of course, equal to the mass of the two colliding particles, via Einstein's famous formula $E=mc^2$ (W). Matter may convert to energy or energy to matter, but matter/energy cannot be destroyed as long as Valcon requires it to exist under the fourth existence-meaning combination.

How volons *move* across the extent continuum

Volons and all other alterons are of *one substance* with unaltered extent around them. Hence a volon does not move through unaltered extent the way a fish moves through water. A volon moves through the extent continuum the way a *wave* moves through water, water and wave being of one substance.

Yet there is a difference: the momentum of a wave in water constantly disperses and diminishes, whereas the momentum of volons wave-moving through the extent continuum is ever conserved, even if by way of transfer to another form of alteron.

Why volons have mass and photons do not

Also unlike a wave, the motion of a volon is facilitated within a cylindrical 'sleeve' of fluxing extent, called "energy." Ahead of the volon, the sleeve fluxes outward or inward to accommodate the altered volume of the passing volon. Once the actual volume of the volon has passed, the 'sleeve' fluxes back to homogeneity, but not before. Because flux is sustained inside the actual volume of the volon as it wave-moves, mass is being transported inside the energy sleeve. It's as if a wave of water is shifting a surfboard along but the surfboard is nothing more than a 'firmer' part of the wave. That is why physicists say a moving particle can be called a "wave" and a "particle" at one and the same time.

Whereas a mass-bearing energy sleeve is limited to *sub*-light speed, a photon is an energy sleeve experiencing flux at *every* point (i.e., it is a wave with no surfboard to push); hence a photon flies at light speed. No central spherical volume of altered extent is sustained at a constant density change, hence no mass is involved. As stated above, a moving particle can be called a particle or a wave, but a photon is only a wave.

This is why the Michelson-Morley experiment (W) failed to find an *ether*—a substance that impedes the motion of light in some directions but not in others. "Light" is simply an alteron in the form of a volon-less "energy sleeve" wave-moving at velocity '*c*' in its own substance of origin—the extent continuum. Physicists who describe 'the vacuum' as teeming chaotically with 'virtual particles' that pop in and out of existence are really detecting only the ordered passage of myriad "energy sleeves" wave-moving through in their substance of origin, the extent continuum.

II. Exo- and eso-*areons* in the micro-cosmos

As volons emphasize *spherical volume*, areons emphasize spherical *surface area*. Again, whereas volons come as exovolons or esovolons, so areons also are of two kinds—exoareons and esoareons.

Esoareons in the micro-cosmos are hollow spheres of interlocked *nucleons*. Esoareons—when enough nucleons are present—manifest as *solid*, *closed* concentric spheres; hence the eso- prefix. **Exoareons** in the micro-cosmos are *open* spheres that form as orbiting electrons crisscross at discrete distances *outside* atomic nuclei, hence the exo- prefix.

In the nuclei of heavy atoms (W)—as scientists now know—protons and neutrons do not clump like golf balls in a bag. Instead, they "lock arms" contiguously, forming concentric hollow spheres. Nuclei of the heaviest atoms may contain enough protons and neutrons to form *multiple* concentric spherical shells. The closed nature of esoareonic spheres lends stability to atomic nuclei.

Electrons orbiting around atomic nuclei (W) do not "lock arms"; but when enough electrons are present, the *virtual* spheres they describe by orbiting at discrete distances from atomic nuclei emphasize surface area just as surely as do the solid spheres of nucleons in the nucleus itself.

The open nature of electron shells facilitates the ease with which electrons can be added to or subtracted from atoms, making electrical currents possible. If spheres of nucleons in atomic nuclei were open, atoms would be less stable. If electron spheres were closed, electricity could not flow. The above principles also describe the structure of anti-atoms consisting of anti-protons, anti-neutrons and positrons. Thus does

July 16, 2012 New third paragraph for page 89 (after "as follows":)

Whereas a wave-moving *spherical volume* maintained in an 'energy sleeve' is a *volon*—a particle—energy sleeves that expand or contract merely to manifest *circumferences* are *circons*, i.e. *photons*. Volons—obliged to feature spherical volume only—move at sub-light speeds. Circons, linked only to circumferences, move at light-speed. Photons—featuring their circumferences *continuously*—qualify as *eso*-circons. Another kind of circon—by manifesting circumference *interruptedly*, serves as an *exo*-circon. Here's how:

Valcon sustain esoareons and exoareons in the micro-cosmos. Their namesakes in the macro-cosmos will be explained later.

III. Exo- and eso-*circons* in the micro-cosmos

Volons denote spherical volume. Areons emphasize spherical surface area. Circons describe spherical *circumferences.* Circons also appear in eso- and exo- categories, as follows:

Picture a subatomic particle suspended in the extent continuum. It appears to spin on an axis, but in fact it does not spin like a rubber ball in air or water. A rubber ball is not of one substance with air or water; but the surface of an electron, for example, is of one substance with the surrounding extent. True spin would require the electron to *shear* from the unaltered extent around it, which is impossible. How then can an electron spin?

Instead of an entire electron spinning, a point of *maximum* extent density alteration wave-moves around a circumference of the electron. On its opposite side, a point of *minimum* extent density alteration wave-moves to maintain the average extent density alteration required for an electron. "Wave movement" around a circumference of an *eso*volon is an ***eso*circon**. "Wave movement" that describes a circumference of an *exo*volon is an ***exo*circon**.

IV. Eso- and exo-*radions* in the micro-cosmos

Radions are spherical force fields that attract or repel mass-bearing alterons—volons—regardless of their electrical charge or lack of the same, on radii *toward or away from the centers of the fields!* Again, an eso/exo duality exists. Fields that draw mass-bearing alterons radially *toward* centers of mass are **esoradions**, otherwise known as *esogravity* or just *gravity*. Fields that propel mass-bearing alterons radially *away* from centers of mass are **exoradions**, otherwise known as *exogravity* or *negative gravity*. Currently some scientists are returning to the idea that negative gravity has its place in the cosmos. In my later chapters on cosmology I explain why it must exist and how to recognize its manifestations in the cosmos at large.

Drop two balls from opposite ends of a lofty precipice. The balls appear to fall on parallel lines; but, in fact, each ball is falling *on a radius* toward the earth's center of mass. The further they fall, the more their trajectories converge. Earth science views the fact that the balls are falling on radii as coincidental to the earth's gravity attracting them. Seven Harmonies science avers that *the only reason the earth is here to attract the balls at all is because gravity was a radius-based force to begin with!*

V. Eso- and exo-*axions* in the micro-cosmos

Whereas radions attract or repel alterons *radially* relative to the *center* of a spherical field, axions attract or repel charged particles only relative to *the ends of a diameter of a* sphere, i.e., to opposite ends of an *axis* linking the center of a sphere with two points on opposite sides of its surface. Thus we encounter *magnetism*—a force that moves charged particles vis-à-vis *the ends of an axis of a sphere*; hence the term *axion.*

Whereas radions attract or repel every kind of alteron according to its *mass*, axions exclusively attract or repel only those alterons that bear *positive or negative electrical charge.* In order words, axions selectively guide particles known to physicists as *ions* and *anions*.

Again, eso and exo features pertain. The end of a magnetic axis that attracts ionized exovolons is an **esoaxion**. The end of a magnetic axis that attracts esovolons is an **exoaxion**. Both kinds of axions *ignore* electrically neutral volons, leaving such to be guided solely by radions.

Axion fields tend to be superimposed over radion fields. For example, while the Sun's radion field (gravity) draws all matter within its reach toward the *center* of the Sun, the Sun's axion (magnetic) field largely overrules gravity by directing charged particles toward the Sun's magnetic *poles* as opposed to its center.

Key differences between axion and radion fields

Since radion fields are spherical, if two or more radion fields impinge upon each other, their conjoined shape may become elliptical, but the radius-of-a-sphere principle is still basic. The upper and lower ends of axion (magnetic) fields resemble spheres too—spheres that are cratered at their poles, like pumpkins! The pumpkin analogy breaks down at the *equator* of an axion field. Axion lines of force at greater distances from the axis lie almost parallel to the equator of the field, then angle steeply up or down until at last they arc into the field's polar depressions.

Unlike radion fields, axion fields are not designed to direct matter on *ever straightening* trajectories toward a common center. Electrically charged particles follow lines of force that prefer *oblique* approaches to the attracting pole. Only on the final arc of their journeys do charged particles swarm directly toward a magnetic pole.

Our Sun helps us understand another major difference between radion and axion fields. The Sun's radion field ignores the fact that the Sun itself rotates on its own axis. Hence neutral particles attracted radially toward the center of the Sun feel no lateral pull from the rotation of the Sun, at least not until they enter the Sun's actual heliosphere and are swept along by swift-moving gas.

The Sun's magnetic field, conversely, tends to rotate with the Sun! Magnetic fields are sometimes described as semi-solid. Ergo charged particles following lines of force toward the Sun's poles also begin sharing the Sun's own rotational momentum. This unique feature of axions becomes outstandingly important in our later study of cosmology.

Chapter Eleven
From Atoms to the Cosmos

Something Einstein overlooked about gravity

Failure to see gravity as radius-based caused Albert Einstein to err. In one of his 'thought experiments' (W), Einstein imagined a man waking to find himself *weightless* inside a door-less, windowless, box-shaped container. The man guesses immediately that he is weightless because he and the "box" are falling, but falling where? Toward what? Hearing no sound of air rushing by outside, the man assumes he and the cubicle are out in space. Because no one side of the enclosure feels hotter than any other side, the man surmises he is either very distant from radiant stars or else he and the capsule are hidden from the Sun in the shadow of a not-so-radiant body like the Earth or the moon.

Unable to see outside the box, the man gasps. If he is falling under the pull of gravity toward the moon, for example, at any moment he and the cubicle may be destroyed on impact. But wait! On second thought, the man finds an alternate way to explain his weightlessness: *perhaps he is weightless because he and the cubicle are merely in orbit or are simply moving in interstellar space by inertia alone, apart from gravity?*

Einstein averred there is no test the man inside the cube can perform to verify whether he and the cube are falling or orbiting in a gravity field or simply moving solely by inertia, i.e., with zero influence from gravity.

Einstein thus thought he was proving what physicists call 'the fundamental equivalence of gravity and inertia' (W). But in fact the man in Einstein's thought experiment **can** easily ascertain if he and the cube are falling in a gravity field or moving along solely by inertia.

Let the interior of the cube be airless. The man (wearing a spacesuit for survival) takes eight objects, be they dice, buttons or bits of paper—which of course are also weightless—and carefully places one item just inside each of the eight corners of the cubicle. The man then measures and records the exact lateral, vertical and diagonal distances separating each object from its seven neighbors. After a few hours, the man records a second set of measurements and compares them with the first set. Why?

If gravity is the dominant force moving the cube, the man knows that all eight apparently motionless objects are actually not motionless, but are falling, as he and the cube are, *on radii* toward the *center* of that external esogravity field. Radial trajectories are not parallel! Esogravitational trajectories *converge*! Hence objects falling on radii toward a common center of gravity *move toward each other as they fall!* If exogravity dominates, objects repelled on diverging radii will separate. If the distances between all eight objects remain constant, inertia is the prevailing force. If the cube happens to be *orbiting* around another body, inertia is prevailing over gravity, hence no objects converge.

Because objects *accelerate* as they fall in a gravity field, successive hourly measurements will show those falling on *adjacent* radii to be converging more *rapidly*, enabling the man inside the cube to estimate how much time may remain before impact. *Einstein's theory that gravity and inertia are equivalent is thus erroneous.* Gravity is intrinsically radial and can be measured as such, whereas inertia is not a radial force!

Astronomers cannot deny that Einstein overlooked this refutation of his thought experiment, but many still accept the equivalence of gravity and inertia because of Einstein's supposed "proof" that gravity is simply inertia affected by *curvature in space-time.* Let's examine *that* "proof."

Is gravity only inertia affected by space-time curvature?

In 1919 astronomer James Eddington (W), observing starlight passing near a limb of the Sun during a total eclipse, saw stars shift their apparent positions just as Einstein, believing the Sun's gravity *bends* starlight, had predicted! The scientific world was agog. Space is the medium light travels in, so light could not change direction in that medium apart from curvature in the medium itself, scientists thought. By inference, the mass of the Sun could curve the surrounding medium such that starlight passing by the Sun is slightly re-vectored.

Thinkers thus reasoned that gravity is not a force that acts at a distance, as scientists had thought, but is simply an effect due to the *curvature* of space-time around concentrations of matter. In other words, gravity is nothing more than inertia guiding photons, in this instance, to follow curves in space. Einstein's 'principle of equivalence' seemed "confirmed." One could of course posit gravity *as a force that curves space-time* near the Sun rather than as an effect of supposed curvature. That would allow viewing gravity as a uniquely radius-related force, unlike inertia, which is linear. But still another question must be asked:

Does re-vectored light prove space curvature?

Absolutely not! Light passing through transparent matter—a prism, a lens or even just a glass of water—is re-vectored. Light traveling horizontally via miles of air over hot sand becomes re-vectored as a *mirage*. We call *that* re-vectoring of light *refraction.* No one takes *that* re-vectoring of light as evidence of a curvature in space.

Starlight passing close to the Sun *penetrates more than one million miles of hot gas enveloping the sun like an atmosphere.* We call the inner part of the Sun's hot gaseous envelope "the chromosphere" (W). The chromosphere alone is nearly 1000 miles in radial depth. Encompassing the chromosphere is a 5,000-mile deep layer of gas called the "transition zone." Outside the transition zone we find a third ocean of gas called the "corona." And *it* is some 440,000 miles deep!

Strangely—in spite of its lower density and greater distance from the Sun—the corona measures *125 times as hot* as the transition zone, even though the latter lies much closer to the Sun's actual surface!

Could it be that Eddington and his team observed starlight that was bent, not by curved space, but simply by *refraction* in the solar corona?

Check scholarly opinion on the Internet! Several scientists fault Einstein and Eddington for failing to posit *refraction* in a million miles of solar corona as the real starlight bender. Some suggest that Eddington, an Englishman, was eager to confirm a theory posed by Einstein, a German, as a way of promoting reconciliation after World War I (W). Physicist Simon Singh's 26-page adulation of Einstein and Eddington in *Big Bang: The Origin of the Universe*, (pp 118-144), makes no mention of the likelihood that Eddington had merely confirmed starlight as refractible!

Von Kluber (1960), Bertotti, Brill and Krotov (1962) cite refraction of light (and especially of radio waves) in the Sun's corona as *limiting the accuracy* of all attempts to verify starlight as re-vectored by gravity alone.[1] Despite using *two* frequencies—2.3 and 8.4 GHz respectively—"propagation in the solar corona [i.e., refraction] remains the major factor limiting accuracy." They add, "One must model this additional bending to correct the data."[2]

But is it really "additional" bending? What were the other "factors" besides refraction, if refraction was only a "*major*" complication? The scientists do not say *how much* observed bending was due to refraction and *how much* to space curvature. Does one have to accept Einstein's prediction about space curvature *a priori* in order to have a "model" for "correcting the data"? If so, we are left with circular reasoning.

Some scientists who agree that refraction by the corona happens promptly dismiss it as "probably not significant."[3] They cite no tests as evidence for that supposed improbability.

Why solar refraction of starlight is significant

When the Sun shines down upon us at noon, its light penetrates *only a few miles* of atmosphere with minimal refraction. Conversely, the light of the rising or setting Sun reaches us *obliquely* via several hundred miles of atmosphere with noticeable refraction. Due to evening and morning refraction of sunlight in our atmosphere, we actually see the Sun rise a few seconds *before* it actually rises! For the same reason, we see the Sun set a few seconds *after* it has already set.

How great is the potential for nearly one million miles of extremely hot corona gas to re-vector a beam of starlight passing close to the Sun? Surely that much hot solar gas must have a significant refractive effect on starlight! Does the corona's refractive effect just happen to match Einstein's theory that the Sun's gravity bends starlight by 1.75 degrees?

Starlight re-vectored close to the limb of the moon (seen from earth) would be more persuasive, *since the moon has no atmosphere to refract light.* Or is the moon's gravity too weak for such a test to be viable?

Positing bent starlight as due simply to refraction conforms to a principle of logic called Ockham's Razor, so called because it was formulated by William of Ockham (W), a 14th-century English scholastic philosopher. William taught that the simplest of two or more competing explanations for a phenomenon must have its day in court first! If something already known can explain a mystery, one is ill-advised to prefer an exotic explanation instead. Exotic explanations are last resorts.

"Lensing" of light around galaxies (W) is also offered as proving Einstein correct. Light from a distant galaxy that is hidden from us behind a nearer galaxy is believed to be "lensed" as it passes through the gravity field of the nearer galaxy, enabling us to see the hidden galaxy 'doubled,' meaning that the hidden galaxy appears as if it were two galaxies located on opposite sides of the nearer object. Cosmologists credit the gravity of the nearer galaxy as causing this remarkable "lensing" effect. *Plus!*—because gravity linked with *visible* matter is never enough to achieve so pronounced a lensing effect, cosmologists take lensing as "proof" that an enormous quantity of a theoretical something they call *dark matter* [more about that later] co-exists with visible matter in all galaxies.

Still the question remains: is light from a hidden galaxy re-vectored by the gravity of a nearer galaxy, or is it merely *refracted* as it passes through *thousands of light years of gas clouds amid billions of stars in the nearer galaxy and its halo?* Once again, refraction in galactic halo gas is almost certainly the real light bender, in which case a major evidence for both space-time curvature *and* dark matter vanishes!

The same caution applies to still another "proof" linking space-time curvature to the bending of radiation. Earth's gravity supposedly bends beams bouncing back and forth between global positioning satellites and ground transmitters. However, because every such beam completes a return trip through the Earth's atmosphere, refraction is inevitable. The more oblique the angle of transit and the greater the number of transits, the greater the refraction! Could that be the cause?

Astronomers now credit "gravitational lensing" as aiding the discovery of "exo-planets," i.e., planets orbiting distant stars. If an exo-planet's orbit takes it across the disc of a distant star, the exo-planet's gravity temporarily "lenses" the star's light, theoretically concentrating more of the star's photons per unit of space than would otherwise be received on Earth. Result: for perhaps just a few hours, the star—as seen from Earth—brightens and then fades back to its usual luminosity.

Clearly, exo-planets as large as, or larger than, Jupiter, Saturn, Uranus and Neptune almost certainly have gaseous atmospheres capable of rendering a lensing effect by refraction alone. "Gravity lensing" should not be posited unless it can be proved that a given luminosity-enhancing exo-planet has no atmosphere.

Solving the precession of Mercury's perihelion

Some scientists ignore the above objections on grounds that the same theory of gravity that enabled Einstein to predict the bending of starlight near the Sun also enabled him to explain a strange anomaly related to planet Mercury's orbit around the Sun.

Mercury's orbit around the Sun is not a perfect circle; so once in every orbit, Mercury reaches its *perihelion* (the point in its orbit when it comes as close to the Sun as it ever gets). Strangely, Mercury's perihelion *shifts.* On each orbit, Mercury reaches it perihelion slightly earlier than Newtonian mechanics predict. Astronomers refer to that variance as "the *precession* of Mercury's perihelion." (W) Einstein's theory of gravity is credited for explaining *both* the bending of starlight near the Sun *and* Mercury's strange orbital precession as well.

Again, a simpler explanation is overlooked. Mercury's orbital precession may be linked to the fact that Mercury is deeply embedded in the Sun's magnetic field. The Sun rotates on its axis once every 25.38 Earth days. As the Sun rotates, magnetic lines of force encircling the Sun barely lag. They rotate too, trying to keep pace with the Sun's spin! Because Mercury takes *88 Earth days* to orbit the Sun, the Sun's faster-moving magnetic lines of force are constantly 'bumping Mercury in the behind,' so to speak, easing it ever so slightly ahead of its otherwise standard orbit, like a parent nudging a child forward as a queue moves.

The Sun's magnetic field links Mercury to the Sun like an umbilical cord. Little by little, the Sun feeds some of its own angular momentum via that umbilical cord to baby Mercury, resulting in the precession of Mercury's perihelion. Call it 'magnetic nudging.'

This theory implies that if Mercury's orbit *opposed* the Sun's rotation, the perihelion of Mercury's orbit would *regress.* So, then, launch a satellite into an orbit similar to Mercury's except that it moves *opposite* to the direction of the Sun's rotation, and the perihelion of that satellite's orbit should regress! If indeed the perihelion of that satellite's orbit shows *regression* instead of precession, the above explanation regarding Mercury's orbital precession triumphs over Einstein's math.

Explaining the precession of Mercury's perihelion as linked with the rotation of the Sun's magnetic field is another example of "Ockham's Razor." If already known principles explain a phenomenon, let them! Inventing exotic theories for the sake of novelty is a disservice to science.

Another problem re: Einstein's view of gravity

Seven Harmonies logic indeed agrees that space can be contracted or expanded, but only in connection with the VACRA principle, as explained earlier, not in connection with gravity, which is radial. Einstein erred by linking altered space with gravity. For example:

Dozens of astronomy textbooks use a well-known diagram to explain gravity. The Sun is shown *depressing* a graph of the space around it, like a bowling ball indenting the middle of a trampoline. Objects passing near the Sun, according to the diagram—far from being drawn *radially* toward the *center* of the Sun—are spiraling toward the lowest part of a funnel somewhere *under* the Sun, much as a golf ball rolling across a trampoline spirals down into the 'funnel' created mid-sheet by the greater mass of a bowling ball. Ergo the diagram really does *not* show gravity as a radial force guiding planets relative to the *center* of the Sun in regular space. Gravity in the diagram is simply good-old inertia guiding planets in conformity to 'funneled' space. Or so Einstein is interpreted.

Logically, objects do not roll into a depression just because the depression is there. Release a bowling ball on the edge of a depression on a small asteroid that has virtually no gravity and the bowling ball will not roll anywhere. The above-described diagram begs us to ask, "But *what* is pulling the Sun *down* to create that 'funnel' in space?" Those who draw such diagrams supply no answer.

Suppose indeed that the Sun is that inexplicably 'heavy' bowling ball and space around the Sun is like an indentation in a trampoline. If the Earth is like a golf ball that is supposed to orbit around the bowling ball, the funnel shape of the indentation around the Sun *will not allow* the golf ball to orbit on a plane even with the *middle* of the bowling ball! All the golf ball can do to avoid falling *on* the bowling ball is to orbit on the wall of the funnel *above* the bowling ball! The further out the golf ball orbits, the *higher* its orbital plane will be *above* the bowling ball!

Planets, we all know, orbit—not *above* the equator of the Sun but on planes extending out from its approximate equator. The oft parroted 'gravity as an indented trampoline' analogy is ludicrous. Gravity is a *radial* force facilitating *circumferential* orbits, not orbits haloed above a pole like an aurora borealis. Inertia, conversely, is merely a *linear* force.

More on Einstein's principle of equivalence

If gravity is the same as inertia, stars and planets could hardly form at all. As surely as inertia makes bits of matter bump together; *conservation of momentum* makes them rebound! Entities that rebound after every collision can hardly congregate enough to begin warping space around them, even if space could be warped. Gravity, conversely, works constantly to reduce the degree of rebound that inertia permits as a given.

When inertia bumps *chemically bondable* entities against each other—two hydrogen atoms and an oxygen atom, for example—they accrete as a molecule of water. Still, that accretion is due to the laws of chemistry, and only coincidently to inertia. Inertia alone *cannot* enable one water molecule to attract another at a distance. Hence there may be water, but never dew, rain, clouds, lakes or oceans. Gravity accretes matter *apart from chemical bonding*. If gravity is by nature identical to inertia, cosmologists would be at pains to explain how merely inertial collisions between primeval hydrogen, deuterium and helium nuclei could accrete to form stars, galaxies, quasars, planets, moons and asteroids.

Other contrasts separate gravity from inertia

It takes more momentum in one's arm to overcome the inertia in a stationary bowling ball and send it rolling toward the ten pins than it takes to toss a stick for Fido. Not so for gravity! Gravity moves a stick or a bowling ball with equal ease. Dropped at the same instant in a vacuum, even a feather and a bowling ball fall at the same speed. Clearly, gravity and inertia are two *very* different forces.

The same physicists who accept Einstein's view of gravity as facilitated by curvatures in space also believe by consensus that every atom in the universe continuously attracts every other atom in the universe gravitationally. If both precepts are correct, every atom or group of atoms in the universe has to have its own unique space curve *connecting it all the way across the universe* to every other atom or group of atoms, no matter how many billions of light-years separate them. How many septillion to the *n*th degree space *curvatures* crisscross the continuum if that is true? How enormously less convoluted space is if we just let Einstein's idea of gravity-as-curved space fall away by its own inertia.

How the extent continuum's four sub-continua may relate to certain subatomic anomalies

1. What do physicists mean by 'strings' and 'membranes'?

Some physicists, positing something called "string theory," envision still more extent dimensions added to length, breadth, height and time. Strings linked are termed "membranes," or simply "branes." I propose that what *appear* to be other dimensions are really only length, width, height and time embedded in the extent continuum's four sub-continua. Four by four could even appear to be sixteen extent dimensions, but there are really only four. The extent continuum's four sub-continua, thus constituted, could indeed be called "membranes," if one so wishes.

String theorists also posit the possibility of "parallel universes" aside from the one we experience. Each of the four sub-extent continua is indeed 'parallel' to the other three, but the physics presented here differs from string theory in that we experience all four sub-continua as one!

2. Physicists credit sub-atomic particles called quarks with odd qualities called 'strangeness,' 'color,' 'up' and 'down.' Why?

In earlier stages of their discipline, physicists—to categorize sub-atomic particles—had only to designate them according to their respective mass, charge and spin. An electron, for example, has mass 1 with *negative* charge. A positron (antiparticle of the electron) also has mass 1 with *positive* charge. A proton has mass 1836.12 with *positive* charge. Other particles, such as neutrons and neutrinos, have neutral charge.

Later, when physicists discovered that protons, neutrons and their respective antiparticles consist in turn of smaller entities called *quarks* and *anti-quarks,* they assumed at first that categorizing quarks and anti-quarks in terms of their mass, charge and spin would be sufficient. It was not to be. Quarks, it turns out, manifest undefined anomalies not found in other particles. New names were needed, but how does one name what is still undefined? Physicists solved the problem rather whimsically by assigning tongue-in-cheek *pro tem* names—*color, strangeness, charm, up* and *down* (W)—to designate qualities that somehow differentiate one kind of quark/anti-quark pair from its fellows.

If indeed the extent continuum consists of four sub-extent continua, as posited here, linking each quark/anti-quark pair known to science with *just one,* or perhaps with *just two* or even *just three* of the four sub-extent continua may suffice to explain what makes each category of quark different! Matching *charm, color, strangeness, up* and *down,* etc., with sub-continua "A," "B," "C" or "D" or combinations of the same will, I propose, actually enable physicists to replace their *pro tem* terms with objective definitions.

It follows that any two quarks with opposite charge—regardless of which of the four sub-extent continua they derive from—attract each other electro-magnetically. But that is by no means the whole story.

3. Physicists find something *odd* about the way unlike quarks (not just quarks with opposite charge) attract each other.

Baffled scientists find that quarks having not just opposite charge but 'color,' for example, are attracted to quarks manifesting features such as 'strangeness,' 'up' and 'down' with a force that transcends mere electro-magnetic attraction by far.

Other attractive forces in the cosmos—gravity, for example, or magnetism—*weaken* with distance. Conversely, the force that glues one kind of quark to other kinds of quarks grows *stronger* if the distance between any two such quarks increases. As a result, it is virtually if not actually impossible for physicists to extract one quark out of a proton or a neutron, or one anti-quark from an antiproton or an antineutron, and keep them apart! In this present work I designate this unusual intra-quark attraction as *hyper-bonding* in contrast with what may be called *hypo*-bonding attractions, those that *weaken* with distance.

Why is the bond between unlike quarks so strong? Why does that force strengthen rather than weaken if the distance between any two or three unlike quarks increases? Positing the extent continuum as consisting of four sub-continua enables me to offer the following premise.

Each lone quark that derives its mass solely from just one, two or three of the four sub-extent continua is 'haunted,' so to speak, by a 'sense' of extreme incompleteness due to the absence of one or more missing sub-extent continua in the mix. Incompleteness is an 'abnormality' that translates physically into a force that strongly 'prefers' completeness. But—let three unlike quarks form a proton, for example, and their 'three-ness' reduces their 'sense' of incompleteness proportionately. The 'urge' to add still another unlike quark for full four-part restoration is weaker than the attraction that 'glues' three unlike quarks together initially. The same principle applies to unlike anti-quarks forming an anti-proton.

It follows that increasing the distance between already 'glued' quarks or anti-quarks *heightens the abnormality*, so to speak, triggering an urge to bond that, not so mysteriously after all, *increases* with distance.

If the force that hyper-bonds unlike quarks as nucleons were no stronger than a hypo-bonding force, like the "strong force" that glues protons to neutrons or like electro-magnetism, nucleons—a primary building block of atoms—would be far less stable than a billions-of-years-old cosmos requires. Quarks 'glued' in the above manner are guaranteed to stay bonded no matter what. Hyper-bonding stabilizes the enormous numbers of nucleons needed for the cosmos. Read the preceding sentence again, substituting 'anti-quarks,' 'anti-protons' and 'anti-neutrons' to see the same effect at work in antimatter.

I predict that physicists in time will recognize my four-sub-extent-continua premise as the only viable way to fit quarks, strings, membranes, color, strangeness, charm, up, down and the force that increases with distance into a single working theory. Until then, I will listen bemusedly to terms such as color, strangeness, etc.

Why electrical charge, unlike quark hyper-bonding, *weakens* with distance

Volons derived from *all four* of the extent continuum's sub-continua do not *hyper*-bond as do quarks. Their mutual attraction, called *hypo*-bonding, is merely *electrical,* i.e., an attraction that *weakens* with distance. An electron paired with a proton is an example.

Physicists find a proton to be an aggregate of three quarks, two with positive charge and one with negative. The proton's net charge is thus positive. Whereas the proton's three quarks are *hyper-bonded* by an attractive force that increases with distance, an electron—a volon derived from complete extent—though drawn by the proton's net positive charge, does *not* hyper-bond with the proton, opposite charge notwithstanding. Protons 'like' electrons enough to want to keep them hypo-bonded in orbit, but not enough to 'marry' them, so to speak.

If quarks in neutrons and protons were only *hypo*-bonded, neutrons and protons would be less stable. Hyper-bonding assures enough of them to form all the elements, light and heavy, that a cosmos requires. Conversely, if protons hyper-bonded with electrons, electrons would be unable to flow from atom to atom, making electrical currents impossible.

These rules apply also to anti-quarks and positrons in antimatter.

Honing Ockham's Razor for a crucial 'shave'

I contend that Einstein, Eddington and others violated the efficiency principle called Ockham's Razor by conjuring space-time curvature and the 'principle of equivalence' to explain gravity. Designating gravity as a radial force is much simpler and quite adequate. The same thinkers violate Ockham's Razor *again* by ignoring *refraction* and offering re-vectored starlight as evidence for gravitational lensing. They sideline Ockham's Razor a third time by substituting arcane math for 'magnetic field cradling' to account for the precession of Mercury's perihelion.

The scientific community's premature endorsement of these multiple violations of the principle of Ockham's Razor initiated a trend that continues today. Scientists, convinced that curved space could re-vector starlight sans refraction and confirm gravity as inertia revisited, raced to find still more novelties to explain still more exotic unknowns.

Prosaic explanations of natural phenomena became passé. Prosaic explanations may be too dull to grace the cover of a scientific journal. Prosaic explanations tend to *bore* the media, the public and grant-bestowing foundations. Pseudo-plausible theories that should be rigorously critiqued before publication are rushed into print to generate sales and perchance enhance the name recognition of a theorist. Mere plausibility is credited as *proof.* Worse yet, pseudo-"proofs"—spermed by premature media praise—beget more of the same over time.

As a snowball rolls, it grows. If one universal natural law can be demoted as no longer universal, but time and place dependent, why not others? Soon 'charge parity violation' (W) replaces conservation of charge. Cosmologists posit space, as my next chapter explains, initially violating conservation of momentum and gravity by 'inflating' the entire universe many times faster than the speed of light. Then, just as suddenly, mysteriously and conveniently, space brakes itself back down to sub-light velocity. 'Dark matter' jumps in to bolster enfeebled gravity, only to have 'dark energy' rise up and accelerate the expansion of the universe in spite of dark matter's heavy foot on the gravity brake.

These and many similar cosmic exotica blended together afford modern man one of science's biggest flights of fancy: Big Bang Cosmology! As Steady State cosmologist Eric Lerner opined:

> The most unfortunate effect of the Einstein myth is the enshrinement of the belief...that science is [so] incomprehensible that only an initiated priesthood can fathom its mysteries. ...Soon...the most popular science books became those that presented...insults to common sense [as science]...The limit between science and pseudo-science began to be erased.[4]

Another author, Roy C. Martin, Jr., echoes Lerner, claiming, "Big Bang Cosmology has raised imaginative invention to an art form

[with]...a ready willingness to surrender and ignore fundamental laws, such as the second law of thermodynamics and the speed of light."[5]

Lerner's own Steady State Cosmology is also a myth—it's just less fanciful. Nor should we dismiss *all* of Albert Einstein's research as untenable. For example, $E=mc^2$ still works.

I thought refuting Einstein's principle of equivalence would suffice. Little did I know that I would soon find myself drawn to the task of deconstructing Big Bang Cosmology itself and offering a superior system in its place! I think readers will be stunned to learn in my next chapter how many complications popularizers of Big Bang Cosmology do *not* reveal about their purportedly credible Big Bang.

I have yet to explain how the five features of a sphere also provide a unifying motif for the *macro*-cosmos. To accomplish that, I must introduce a system that is far superior to Big Bang Cosmology. I call it Harmonic Origin Cosmology (HOC). It traces VACRA's five features motif across billions of years from creation to today's cosmos. I have much to explain about this great cosmos Valcon shares with us.

Chapter Twelve
Critiquing Big Bang Cosmology

My goal in the following chapters is to help readers grasp the problems and paradoxes of cosmology. I will try to explain cosmology so clearly that people who have never 'talked cosmology' before will be eager to introduce the issues it raises to their friends. Let's begin!

Modern science's most popular current theory as to how the universe began is called "Big Bang Cosmology" (BBC). Scientists cite two major astronomical findings as evidence for it:

1) The universe is *expanding*. Cosmologists thus infer that everything burst out billions of years ago from an explosion called "the Big Bang." As a result everything—even the extent continuum itself—is still expanding.

2) The universe is flooded with microwave energy radiating with almost perfect uniformity in all directions. It is called "cosmic microwave background" or CMB (W). Cosmologists regard that unique radiation as a by-product, a *residue* from the Big Bang—a kind of 'forensic evidence' that the universe exploded out of an incredibly compact 'singularity.'

Earlier, I urged readers to reject as an oxymoron Big Bang Cosmology's notion that the extent continuum itself had a beginning. Recall—if time and space did not already exist, there was *no moment* for an event to occur in, *nor even a place* for it to happen. However, Big Bang Cosmology is riddled with other problems largely unacknowledged in the media. In this chapter I explain why we need a far more rational cosmology than BBC. In following chapters I offer a cosmology that fits the universe! I call it *Harmonic Origin Cosmology* (HOC) because it conforms on a cosmic level to the five laws of Harmony Six.

Twelve enigmas a viable cosmology must solve

Big Bang Cosmology and Harmonic Origin Cosmology agree as to which enigmas a cosmology must solve but are at odds when it comes to solutions. Both cosmologies agree on the approximate age of the cosmos:

1. **A viable cosmology must explain why the cosmos is 12 billion or more years old.**

Some of my fellow Christians believe God made the entire cosmos a few thousand years ago but gave it an *apparent age* spanning billions of years. Light arriving from distant galaxies, they claim, did not originate in them. Rather, God created photons arriving everywhere from every light source in all galaxies from Day One. He created supernova debris spread across light years of space, but the supernovas really didn't explode.

Averring the Hebrew word for 'day'—*yôm*, as in *Yom Kippur*—means a 24-hour day, young-cosmos advocates believe Genesis describes God creating the entire cosmos in six 24-hour days. Yet *The New Strong's Concise Dictionary of the Words in the Hebrew Bible* (page 55) grants that *yôm* [spelled *yowm*] can mean "a space of time defined by an associated term…age."[1]

Brown-Driver-Briggs' Hebrew Lexicon grants *yôm* a dozen meanings, three of which are a "time," a "period" and a "year," as in Ezekiel 4:5 and 6, where God is quoted as saying, "I have assigned you forty days, a day for each year" (translation based on Textus Sinaiticus). Similarly, Psalm 90:4 reveals a poetic propensity to use brief periods of time—a "yesterday" or a "watch in the night"—as symbolizing a millennium, for example.[2]

Even if proponents of a young cosmos are correct, their own phrase '*apparent age*' implies processes consuming billions of years in real time. Exploded supernovas imply process. Anyone tracing cosmic process may be unwittingly analyzing the plot of a *de facto* cosmic novel where God replaces fiction with real events only on the final page. Even so, those implied processes, even if fictional, are still awesome to analyze.

As surely as an infinite Being must have a *large* capacity for patience, the universe really is billions of years old and God is by no means bored shaping it from age to age. Valcon, "the God of *all* truth," can hardly be, when it comes to creation, a God of 99.99999999 to the nth degree *fiction*!

So then, Big Bang and Harmonic Origin Cosmologies agree as to the approximate age of the cosmos. What else do they have in common?

2. **A viable cosmology must explain how creation could begin with *equal quantities of matter and antimatter* but end up with *only matter* in evidence.**

Big Bang cosmologists have two valid reasons for positing creation as beginning with equal quantities of matter and antimatter.

(A) Tests in particle accelerators affirm what a law called *conservation of charge* requires: energy cannot convert to a charged particle unless that particle's equally-massive-but-oppositely-charged antiparticle appears with it. Big Bang cosmologists, positing the energy of the Big Bang as producing subatomic particles, are thus obliged to regard the Big Bang as yielding equal quantities of *antiparticles* as well.

Once a particle-antiparticle pair has formed, its particle component cannot revert to energy unless a matching antiparticle is there to revert with it! If a positron, for example, were to revert to energy apart from an electron, the cosmos would be left with an imbalance of positive versus negative charge. Conservation of charge forbids any such imbalance. We will soon see if Big Bang cosmology honors that requirement.

As surely as particles and antiparticles must be *paired* at creation, just as surely they must *fly apart* the instant they are created. If a particle remains near its antiparticle, their opposite charges draw them together in mutual annihilation, sometimes called *co-annihilation*. In other words, both the particle and the antiparticle convert entirely to energy as per Einstein's $E=mc^2$ equation. Nothing remains but a burst of photons.

Since half the mass of the cosmos had to consist originally of antimatter, a viable cosmology must explain what happened to the antimatter. Was the initial separation of matter from antimatter so effective that both categories still exist with equal mass and opposite charge but remain far enough apart to avoid co-annihilation?

Harmonic Origin Cosmology (HOC) matches matter with antimatter at creation, not only because of what particle accelerators reveal but also because the second law of the Harmony of Continua *forbids* a matter/antimatter imbalance. Creating volons (electrons, quarks, etc.) means creating them as volon/antivolon pairs because the alterations of homogeneous extent that birth them must always be inversely equal.

As Big Bang cosmologists admit, particle-antiparticle pairs—unavoidably intermixed in Big Bang Cosmology's point-initiated, expanding fireball—*could not avoid co-annihilation.* If an electron, for example, evades co-annihilation with its own co-created positron, it is still destined to collide in the surrounding plasma with another positron that has just separated from a different electron. If matter and antimatter were as thoroughly mixed at the beginning as Big Bang cosmology inherently requires, how could *any* matter survive to form our cosmos? Yet the massive inefficiency of requiring enormous quantities of newly formed matter and antimatter to revert immediately back to energy does not trouble Big Bang cosmologists at all. Why not?

(B) The energy released by the co-annihilation of so much matter and antimatter is what Big Bang cosmologists think they need in order to explain why cosmic microwave radiation still floods the cosmos billions of years later. *How much* intermixed matter and antimatter do Big Bang cosmologists posit was formed only to co-annihilate as microwave energy in the aftermath of the Big Bang? Prepare to be shocked.

According to Big Bang Cosmology, our entire universe with its billions of galaxies—most of which contain hundreds of billions of stars and enormous clouds of gas—is a mere *one-billionth* of the mass of *antimatter alone* that formed out of energy only to be promptly converted back to energy in concert with a billion times as much matter as still exists! Our present cosmos is thus only *one part in two-billion* of what supposedly had to form and immediately co-annihilate as energy so this relatively tiny filament of matter, our cosmos, could survive.

Hold on! According to the law of conservation of charge, if a billionth part of Big Bang matter survived re-conversion to energy to form the cosmos, surely a matching billionth of Big Bang antimatter must also have survived. If antimatter equal in mass to this cosmos still exists, beware! What if that unfinished co-annihilation resumes again?!

But no, Big Bang cosmologists assert that if matching quantities of matter and antimatter are sufficiently enormous at the beginning, conservation of charge is flexible enough to annihilate *all* the antimatter while leaving one-billionth of the matter conserved.

What could possibly motivate scientists to posit something so implausible? Big Bang cosmologists are well aware of conservation of charge, of course, but Big Bang theory paints them into a corner. If you believe a Big Bang happened and find that it conflicts with conservation of charge, redefine conservation of charge and the problem is solved. Or is it? Could a theory adverse to one universal law soon find itself in disharmony with others? As we will see, that is exactly what happens.

Big Bang populists tend not to mention the above quandary. For example, Simon Singh's engaging 532-page treatise titled *Big Bang: The Origin of the Universe* (New York: Harper Perennial, 2005), made it to the *New York Times* bestseller list. Surprisingly, Mr. Singh says nothing in his own entire text about how Big Bang Cosmology grapples with the antimatter conundrum. In fact, the word 'antimatter' is not listed in Mr. Singh's index. I found it, but only in miniscule print on page 475, not in his own text but in a diagram copied from a feature in a United Kingdom newspaper (*Independent,* April 24, 1992).

That small print reads: "10 to the 15th degrees. More matter than antimatter in cosmos," implying that antimatter and matter *at some point existed in equal amounts*. Symbols for antimatter also appear equally intermingled with symbols for matter wherever the same diagram depicts an earlier stage of the posited Big Bang.

Thoughtful readers, if they choose to read the small print, will wonder: *What is antimatter? Why was Big Bang-generated antimatter diminishing faster than Big Bang-generated matter? Does antimatter still exist somewhere?* And, finally: *Why does the author of a best-selling book about the Big Bang fail to tell us more about its antimatter component?*

Michael Lemonick, in "How The Stars Were Born" (one of *Time* magazine's many Big-Bang affirming cover stories), also says not a word about the awkward 'matter' of a billion universes' worth of antimatter plus *almost* a billion universes' worth of matter co-annihilating yet somehow leaving our universe of matter surviving so *biiiiiiig* a bang![3]

Singh and Lemonick are mute (at least in the above-cited publications) on the presence of antimatter in the Big Bang; but two other popularizers, astronomer Neil deGrasse Tyson and journalist Donald Goldsmith, freely mention the antimatter problem. They even credit the Big Bang as requiring a "matter-antimatter suicide pact." Just as freely, they accept the idea that a billionth of the matter—our cosmos—somehow reneged from the "suicide pact" by violating conservation of charge. Consider the following quote from their book *Origins: Fourteen Billion Years of Cosmic Evolution*:

> …an episode in the very early universe…endowed the cosmos with a remarkable asymmetry, in which particles of matter outnumber

> particles of antimatter by only about one part in a billion—a difference that allows us to exist today. Without the imbalance of a billion and one to a mere billion between matter and antimatter particles, all the mass in the universe (except for the dark matter whose form remains unknown) would have been annihilated before the universe's first second had passed, leaving a cosmos...[of] photons and nothing else—the ultimate let-there-be-light scenario.[4]

Note Tyson and Goldsmith's subtle obfuscation. Calling that matter-favoring imbalance "a remarkable asymmetry" avoids outing its real name—*charge parity violation* (W). Authors eager to popularize a theory as a virtual dropdown from heaven are not eager to let the public know that it violates a natural law. People in general believe in the immutability of natural law. Why rouse questions by overtly admitting that one's favorite cosmology negates that long-established immutability?

Big Bang cosmologists *must* rescind conservation of charge at the moment of origin or seek another cosmology, something they as yet are unwilling to do. Beware any claim that an infinitesimally tiny charge parity violation of one-billion-or-more-to-one has been detected in a particle accelerator. Any measurement that miniscule is highly suspect, especially when the claim is so direly needed to buttress a favorite theory.

How ironic—Big Bang Cosmology violates conservation of charge to facilitate a universe that somehow later learns to *honor* conservation of charge. Stephen Hawking once asked, "If the laws of physics could break down at the beginning of the universe, why couldn't they break down anywhere?"[5] Author William Carroll echoes, "Why should the beginning of the universe be exempt from laws that apply to other points?"[6]

Harmonic Origin Cosmology, conversely, does *not* require two billion extra universe-size masses of matter and antimatter to be created only to co-annihilate so our one universe of matter may exist and be flooded with microwave background radiation. Nor does Harmonic Origin theory require conservation of charge to be violated at all

3. A viable cosmology must explain why some 99 percent of the cosmos consists of *hydrogen* and *helium*.

Stellar spectra reveal hydrogen (H) and helium (He)—the two lightest elements—to be vastly more abundant across the cosmos than all the heavier elements combined. Hydrogen alone comprises some 90 percent of all matter. Helium adds approximately 9 percent; hence the two lightest elements account for some 99 percent of all the elemental mass of the universe. Heavy elements—oxygen, carbon, silicon, iron, *et al.*—comprise only about 1 percent of everything "material." (W) (Neutrinos, almost massless, are also extremely abundant but are not an element.)

Of course Big Bang cosmologists credit their Big Bang fireball as sourcing all the hydrogen and helium but almost nil of everything else. With good reason! Spectrographic analysis credits *exploding stars*—"novas" and "supernovas" (W)—as primary heavy element 'factories.' If heavy elements formed in *both* the Big Bang fireball *and* in stars that exploded billions of years later, heavy elements would comprise far more than 1 percent of the universe! Thus hydrogen and helium had to be virtually the only elements a Big Bang fireball produced.

How then do exploding stars add heavy elements to the cosmos? Astronomers credit gravity pressure in stellar cores as fusing hydrogen nuclei to make helium. This fusion—known as *nuclear synthesis* or *nucleo-synthesis* (W)—releases the energy that enables stars to shine. Low-mass stars, 'burning' hydrogen slowly, shine for billions of years with little change in their composition. Faster-burning middle-mass stars and fastest-burning *massive* stars eventually deplete their hydrogen fuel and collapse. Amplified heat and pressure due to the collapse causes a middle-mass star to explode as a *nova.* Extremely massive stars, once collapsed, rebound again as *supernovas.*

Whereas pressure in the core of a nova fuses hydrogen and helium nuclei into middle-weight elements (nitrogen, carbon, oxygen, silicon, *et al.*), far greater pressures in supernovas fuse smaller atomic nuclei into the heaviest elements (iron, lead, gold, platinum, uranium, plutonium, etc.). Blasted into space, weighty elements fused in the cores of exploding stars coalesce again, forming still more massive stars enriched with more heavy elements than their predecessors. This means, of course, that novas and supernovas did not begin forging heavy elements *until at least a billion years after the Big Bang!*

What, if anything, is *wrong* with the above picture?

In light of the above, surely one may surmise that *the Big Bang fireball itself*—at some stage of its hundreds of thousands of years as an expanding yet still ultra dense, ultra hot mass—*must have replicated the heat and pressure that would later fuse light nuclei as heavy elements in novas and supernovas. The Big Bang fireball itself—if there was one—assuredly would have strewed incredible quantities of heavy elements everywhere long before novas and supernovas had time to begin adding their heavy element quotas to the cosmos!*

A Big Bang fireball, due to its immensity, would sustain heavy-element-production *over tens of thousands of years and across a vast girth*, unlike the brevity of a supernova that explodes in a relative speck of space and begins cooling in days. Stellar spectra would show even the oldest stars (those that coalesced from clouds of gas relatively soon after the supposed Big Bang) to be heavy-element-rich, not heavy-element-poor. Hydrogen and helium, accordingly, would be less abundant than stellar spectra show them to be. Subsequent nova/supernova fusing of hydrogen and helium into heavy elements would be *a mere supplement* to the Big Bang fireball as the universe's *primary* heavy element source.

Big Bang cosmologists, pressed to explain why their primordial supernova-like fireball failed to fuse enormous quantities of hydrogen and helium as heavy elements, resort to one of the strangest artifices in the history of science. I explain that artifice in connection with Big Bang Cosmology's next problem, below. Harmonic Origin Cosmology, conversely, needs no artifice to explain why hydrogen and helium are naturally so much more abundant than heavy elements.

4. A viable cosmology must explain why gravity fails to inhibit the present expansion of the cosmos.

Big Bang cosmologists posit that "black holes" exist, i.e., that gravity can become so strong that it compresses the mass of *an entire star* down to the size of a walnut. Not even photons of light traveling 300,000 kilometers per second can escape from a "black hole." Scientists also believe paradoxically that all the mass in the universe nonetheless escaped from the ultimate concentration of mass—the Big Bang—where a mass equal to *billions* of galaxies and quasars emerged in a space tinier than a walnut. Big Bang cosmologists had to grapple with a daunting question:

If a Big Bang produced that much mass at one tiny point, what kept gravity from morphing the site of the Big Bang itself into a voracious, universe-swallowing black hole from which not even that ubiquitous cosmic microwave background energy could escape?

Another rule of physics establishes **c**, the speed of light, as the top rate at which anything in the cosmos can move. Thus, in early Big Bang theory, nothing emerged from the Big Bang faster than **c**. Quandaries arose. Limiting the cosmos' initial expansion to **c,** let alone a sub-light velocity, enabled gravity to keep the cosmos from expanding! Forced to choose between Big Bang theory and gravity, Big Bang cosmologists sacrificed the latter by accepting Alan Guth's notion that the Big Bang began with an "inflationary epoch"—a period when, inexplicably, space instantly catapulted everything outward at *10^{45} times the speed of light!*

There was no gradual acceleration by the application of a force, as conservation of momentum would require. Instead, according to Alan Guth, if space itself expands, any mass in it, no matter how enormous, accelerates instantly and—theoretically—to any speed *sans propulsion by any known force, sans interference by gravity!*

Later, of course, that inexplicable expansion of the entire material universe just as inexplicably *slowed*—apart from braking by any known physical force—to its current sub-light speed. Thus do Big Bang cosmologists, hard-pressed to match theory to reality, assign *virtual omnipotence* to inert space!

Time's aforementioned cover story, "How the Stars Were Born," references Alan Guth's "inflationary epoch" (W) obliquely, saying: "...according to the widely accepted 'standard model' of cosmology, our entire cosmos had swelled from a space smaller than an atom to something 100 billion miles across."[7] *Time* avoids mentioning that the 'swelling' had to race along trillions of times faster than the speed of light. Readers are not told that conservation of charge, gravity, **c** and conservation of momentum are simply brushed aside to make room for an artifice contrived to justify Big Bang Cosmology's troubled premise.

Big Bang theorists need Alan Guth's 'inflationary epoch' because it instantly eased and cooled the Big Bang's incredible heat and pressure before it had time to cook up and add every heavy element in the periodic table to the recipe for the first stars that formed! Ever since, books and magazine articles promoting Big Bang Cosmology keep emphasizing the "rapid cooling" of the Big Bang fireball. Now you know why.

To show why "rapid cooling" is so essential to Big Bang Cosmology, I quote again from Tyson and Goldsmith's book *Origins*: "...If, for example, a single anti-star annihilated with a single ordinary star, the conversion of their matter and antimatter into gamma ray energy....would produce an object so luminous that it would temporarily out-produce all the energy of all the stars of 100 million galaxies."[8]

With that staggering comment in mind, consider that in the Big Bang *far more than the mass of two stars* was converted to energy via matter-antimatter annihilation. Instead, one billion times as much matter as now exists in the universe—plus *slightly more* antimatter—blazed out in mutual annihilation. How hot, how capable of synthesizing enormous quantities of heavy elements must that primeval fireball have been *during at least one era* of its hundreds of thousands of years of expansion!

BBC theorists seem unaware that the gamma radiation released by annihilating mass equal to two billion universes is problematic. Radiation that intense exerts enough pressure to blast BBC's surviving billionth of matter to the far reaches of space long before gravity forms stars. Guth's inflation slows but BBC's matter is long gone faster than at present!

"Rapid cooling," even if it requires space to expand at 10^{45} times the speed of light, was needed for sure, but look at the price tag! Conservation of charge, **c** as top velocity, gravity, conservation of momentum and now the laws of nuclear synthesis are all altered to satisfy BBC theorists. Why not surmise that heavy elements are rare in the universe simply because there never was a primeval fireball to synthesize them? With that conclusion, we can begin to seek a better way to explain the predominance of hydrogen and helium over heavy elements.

However many exotic terms Big Bang cosmologists conjure to justify Alan Guth's "inflationary epoch" notion—scalar fields, phase transitions, etc.—the fact remains that all such terms and Big Bang Cosmology rely upon reciprocal justification, otherwise known as *circular reasoning.* Harmonic Origin Cosmology, conversely, needs no artifice to keep gravity from crunching everything into a black hole eons ago. Simply by discerning how the five features of a sphere manifest in the cosmos, Harmonic Origin Cosmology affords a winsomely unproblematic alternative to Big Bang Cosmology's wrangle of conundrums spiced with artifice. Not that I've shown you the last of its artifices. There are more!

5. A viable cosmology must explain why some 90 percent of the hydrogen and helium in the cosmos is *ionized* rather than *atomic*.

The universe would look very different if the opposite were true—if 90 percent of the two lightest gases (which comprise 99 percent of everything) were atomic instead of ionized. Electrons orbiting around protons and neutrons (nucleons) in the nuclei of *atomic* hydrogen and helium have an ability protons and neutrons lack. Electrons are able to snag passing photons, delay them a while and then release them randomly. End result? Clouds of *atomic* H and He are rendered *opaque*. Clouds of *ionized* H and He enjoy *transparency* because they consist of nucleons only. No electrons are present to stall and then redirect the flow of photons. Ionized helium, even if it lacks only one electron, is still more transparent than atomic helium, where each nucleus has *two* electrons.

The transparency of clouds of ionized hydrogen and helium enables us to see billions of stars, galaxies and quasars that would otherwise be hidden. That is why captions under photos of opaque clouds hiding distant star fields invariably name *dust*, not hydrogen, as the light blocker. We can thank Valcon for causing 90 percent of cosmic hydrogen and helium to be ionized. The views are great! But BBC theorists have a problem:

Protons and electrons intermixed in BBC's fireball (assuming there was one) could not possibly fail to combine as *atomic* hydrogen and helium! This means that the first stars that formed had to consist exclusively of *atomic* hydrogen and helium, the *opaque* kind. For Big Bang thinkers to conjure their primeval fireball as proton-sated but electron-starved would only add still another violation of conservation of charge to their already straining theory. Even if Alan Guth's theoretical hyper-inflation *delayed* protons from finding electrons in the primordial mass, as soon as inflation slowed, they still would combine with electrons as opaque hydrogen! Yet some 90 percent of the hydrogen and helium in space is *ionized,* hence transparent.

Obviously BBC launches the cosmos on its age-long journey with the wrong star fuel in the tank. *Could the first stars* (or any stars, for that matter) *shine at all if they consisted entirely of* ***opaque*** *H and He, the kind that retards the flow of energy from stellar core to surface?* Stars are able to shine for billions of years because they consist primarily of *ionized* hydrogen, the ***transparent*** kind, the kind BBC's fireball totally lacked.

In stars comprised primarily of transparent hydrogen, energy generated in the stellar core meets relatively little resistance as it rises to the stellar surface and escapes as radiation. Granted, 10 percent or so of the hydrogen and helium in stars is atomic; but radiation pressure tends to force that less permeable component away from the core toward the surface, where it is so attenuated it impedes escaping radiation minimally.

Conversely, millions of kilometers of *opaque* hydrogen—especially in very large stars—would so *retard* energy generated in stellar cores from rising to the surface and escaping as light that there can be only one result. Thermo-nuclear energy growing exponentially while trapped deep, deep, deep inside an insulating mass of opaque hydrogen can only speed a star right through to its final nova or supernova stage, perhaps within only a few months or years after its thermonuclear reactions begin.

Let's take another moment to ask BBC cosmologists the following questions about that supposed one-billionth of the original mass of matter that—helped by 'charge parity violation'—evaded co-annihilation with antimatter in Tyson and Goldsmith's above-mentioned "suicide pact."

(A) Since the only kind of hydrogen and helium BBC's fireball provided for star-making was atomic, how did we get from a cosmos where 100 percent of the gas inside and outside stars was atomic to our very different cosmos now where some 90 percent of the hydrogen and helium inside and outside stars is *ionized*?

What a quandary! But BBC experts remain undaunted. Astronomer Dr. Wei Zheng of Johns Hopkins University comments, "Most of the diffuse matter [hydrogen and helium gas] in the early universe is highly ionized. The electrons are removed from the atoms. That means in the early universe there [had to be a] very strong radiation that ionized everything, and we would like to know…what could have produced it."[9]

So how did this transition from neutral to ionized hydrogen occur? That is, what force was able, after the fact, to strip electrons from some 90 percent of that enormous quantity of opaque hydrogen and helium?

(B) Just as important, though not mentioned, is an adjoining question: what prevented banished electrons from returning later to make transparent hydrogen opaque once more? Followed by:

(C) Where are all those banished electrons hiding out *now*?

Accepting *a priori* the notion of a Big Bang, BBC theorists have no choice. They *must* posit post-Big-Bang energy sources powerful enough to ionize 90 percent of the diffuse gas in the early cosmos and then keep all those banished electrons from returning! Astronomers call their posited period of intense electron banishment *the epoch of decoupling* (W).

If an alternate cosmology—one that violates no natural laws—exclusively provides for 90 percent of newly minted hydrogen and helium in the primeval cosmos to appear *already ionized*, rendering a subsequent 'decoupling epoch' unnecessary, what would you say? If that same theory also explains why 90 percent of that hydrogen *remains ionized* billions of years later, would you perhaps prefer that alternate cosmology to one that first weds all the hydrogen and helium to electrons and then conjures up a temporary irradiation to enforce a massive cosmic decoupling?

Vexing cosmological evidence drives BBC theorists to artifice *again.* Despite the fact that the oldest stars visible in space consist primarily of ionized gas, BBC theorists have no choice but to posit a still older generation of stars that no longer exist. These long-ago vanished hypothetical stars of course had to be large enough and bright enough—despite consisting of *opaque* hydrogen—to emit ultraviolet radiation intense enough to expel electrons, not only from within their own mass but also from the remainder of opaque hydrogen that had not yet coalesced as stars. Only thus could subsequent generations of stars—the very old stars still shining today—consist primarily of ionized gas.

BBC thinkers concede that darkness prevailed because the energy emitted by each massive hypothetical star could shine only a relatively short distance via the encompassing fog of opaque hydrogen. That is why they dub that early phase "The Dark Era" (W). Note the admission that even ultraviolet radiation could shine only a short distance despite the diffuseness of the surrounding opaque gas.

I dare to comment: If clouds of *diffuse* opaque hydrogen could block intense ultraviolet rays *between* the first stars, surely millions of kilometers of *extremely compacted* opaque hydrogen *inside* the first stars would stifle the core-to-surface movement of that radiation even more! Surely the following scenario describes what would have happened:

One moment the surface of a posited opaque star is dark despite the fact that thermonuclear reactions have already begun deep inside its core. Rather than all that energy breaking the bond between electrons and protons and shooing the former out of its way from core to surface, the insulating resistance caused by so much opaqueness (plus gravity's drag) would have rushed the star through to its supernova stage almost immediately. Opaque hydrogen in the stellar core would have fused promptly as heavy elements replete with still-present electrons!

Whatever part of the star was blasted into space would still be as opaque as ever and could serve only as grist for another generation of stars made of opaque hydrogen. The notion that stars made of opaque hydrogen can emit intense UV radiation at all, let alone over millions of years, is quite illogical. No matter; Big Bang cosmologists posit generations of UV-radiating-though-opaque stars—while full of electrons themselves—somehow banishing most of their own electrons and those in the surrounding cosmos far off to a who-knows-where electron limbo, leaving almost all the hydrogen transparent forever.

With the above in mind, note the naïveté of the following article.

Time magazine's September 4, 2006, cover story popularizes Big Bang Cosmology's assumption that all the primordial hydrogen and helium became atomic (i.e., opaque) as the Big Bang cooled. It then had to be "re-ionized" by intense UV radiation from the above-mentioned special kind of stars that no longer exist so that later generations of stars could shine out via mainly *transparent* hydrogen, as they do today.

Author Michael D. Lemonick explains:

> …These first stars were, on average, gigantic—at least 25 times as massive as the sun and ranging as much as 100 times as massive, if not more. A star that big burns very hot, shining perhaps a million times brighter than the sun….
> Because they were so hot, the first stars…poured out…copious amounts of high-energy ultraviolet radiation [which was able to] knock apart hydrogen atoms [i.e., it changed hydrogen *atoms* into hydrogen *ions* by stripping electrons away]...thus destroying their ability to block light. That process is known as re-ionization… It's this radiation…that many theorists suspect…re-ionized the remaining hydrogen, making it transparent again and bringing the Dark Ages to a close.[10]

I protest again: massive stars comprised of opaque hydrogen can only explode as supernovas. Only if they first ionize their own innards can they shine powerfully enough to ionize vast *external* clouds of opaque hydrogen over millions of years. Even then, another problem remains: any electrons such stars expel from their own mass have only one place to go—out into those external clouds of opaque hydrogen, where of course they *replace* the very electrons they are supposed to have banished from the external clouds!

I have one thing to say for cosmologists who believe the first stars had to consist briefly of opaque hydrogen so later stars could subsist much longer on the transparent kind: they bravely offer a prediction whereby their premise can be verified or disproved. Michael Lemonick asserts that astronomers, using the next generation of very large radio telescopes, will soon be able to do the following:

> . . . map cosmic hydrogen at, say, 50 million years after the Big Bang—before the first stars had a chance to form—then at 100 million, 200 million or half a billion years later, [like] a series of snapshots. Combine them, says [Avi] Loeb, and "you'll be able to make a 3-D picture of hydrogen gas as the universe evolves. At

> some point, you'll start to see holes, like Swiss cheese," as the gas clouds become ionized and transparent. Precisely how the holes grow and merge over time will help determine whether the clearing out is being done by small galaxies, big black holes or something entirely different—and depending on which it is, some theorists could be vindicated and others refuted. But astronomers will at last have an answer to a mystery they have puzzled over for a decade and a half.[11]

In Harmonic Origin Cosmology—presented in a later chapter—precisely equal numbers of protons and electrons appear in a way that kept almost all of them apart from creation until now. Opaque hydrogen was relatively rare. Transparent hydrogen prevailed from the outset, enabling the first stars and all stars ever since to shine at full radiance.

I predict: Avi Loeb will find no 'Swiss cheese holes' of transparent hydrogen because there was no dark fog of opaque hydrogen for holes to form in because there was no Big Bang to produce an opaque cloud!

6. A viable cosmology must explain the cosmic microwave background radiation and its amazingly *omni-directional* nature.

As explained earlier, Big Bang theorists see the cosmic microwave background (CMB) radiation which floods the cosmos as a kind of forensic residue from a co-annihilation of matter and antimatter equal in mass to two billion universes. Hardly a month goes by without the media touting that ubiquitous radiation as affirming Big Bang Cosmology. Still, a few cosmologists disparage their claim. Quasi-Steady State cosmologist William C. Mitchell states in "Big Bang Theory under Fire" that the *"omni-directional"* nature of CMB renders CMB *defunct* as an evidence for Big Bang Cosmology.[12]

By "omni-directional," Mitchell means *approaching any one place from all directions*. The roar of a crowd cheering at a football game in a packed 360-degree stadium is *almost* omni-directional relative to a player at center field. For the roar to be truly omni-directional, it would also have to come up to him from the ground and down to him from the sky.

Microwave background radiation is truly omni-directional because it reaches the Earth from every direction in space. It is precisely the omni-directional nature of CMB that refutes Big Bang Cosmology's assertion that it originated at one point. To explain why that is so, I paraphrase William Mitchell's comments regarding *space curvature*:

All cosmologists agree that empty space across the cosmos must be either ***linear*** or ***curved*** (W). If space is *linear*, conservation of momentum dictates that photons of energy radiating *outward* over billions of years from the site of the Big Bang—unless subsequently absorbed, reflected or refracted—must continue moving outward *unveeringly* as long as the cosmos endures. Conversely, if space is *curved,* its curvature may be positive or negative. **Positive** space curvature, over billions of eons, keeps photons *arcing* around the cosmos on vast circumferences. **Negative** curvature keeps seemingly parallel trajectories diverging. Recent cosmological observation has convinced astronomers that space is neither positively nor negatively curved, but *linear*. Alas for Big Bang Cosmologists, *linear* space is not what their theory needs.[13]

In a *linear* universe, microwave background radiation—if indeed it radiated from one point billions of years ago—could not be reaching us *omni-directionally* today. Photons of that radiation, dispersing from one point of origin on straight trajectories in *linear* space, would already have traveled far beyond us (and even far beyond every galaxy and quasar) into some vast external void.

Only positively curved space—something physicists now say does not exist—could cause radiation emitted from one point eons ago to veer back omni-directionally toward us today. Even then, why would radiation emitted billions of years ago reach *us* omni-directionally? Why would *our* part of positively curved space be so special?

The cover story of *Time* referenced earlier describes the cosmic microwave background radiation as "…a faint whisper of microwaves streaming from all directions in space. The discovery of those microwaves in 1964 confirmed the existence of the Big Bang."[14] Author Lemonick fails to mention that space is now known to be linear; hence CMB, if it originated from one point, must still be on its way *out!*

If CMB originated at one point yet still reaches us *omni-directionally* despite the linear nature of space, then conservation of momentum, as it relates to photons of energy, is violated! Conservation of momentum decrees that mass-bearing bodies and photons of energy moving in *linear* space, unless acted upon by a natural force (friction, gravity, magnetism, refraction, etc.), must keep moving on straight trajectories at constant velocities. No moving mass or photon can inexplicably speed up, inexplicably slow down or inexplicably *veer*.

One moment Big Bang cosmologists have CMB radiating *outward* from a single source. The next moment they admit that CMB is radiating *in* from an all-encompassing source. Millions accept this self-contradiction uncritically, exempting Big Bang Cosmology from the intensive scrutiny it merits.

Harmonic Origin Cosmology's universe, conversely, begins with a full constitution of natural laws plus the right percentages of hydrogen and helium with the right percentages of atoms versus ions. It also explains the expansion of the universe and the origin of the microwave background radiation with no Big Bang, no Dark Era and no hyper-inflationary epoch.

7. A valid cosmology must explain why *neutrinos* are so abundant.

Cosmologists know that microwave background radiation is not the only omni-directional entity flooding the universe. Swarms of nearly massless particles called *neutrinos* crisscross the cosmos almost at the speed of light. Neutrinos, along with neutrons, protons and electrons, *are the four most abundant forms of matter detected.* Whereas neutrons, protons and electrons combine to form ions and atoms, neutrinos interact with almost nothing. They pass easily through stars and planets.

The fact that neutrinos are plentiful is a major clue to the origin of the cosmos because we know their primary source. Curiously, a primary source for neutrinos is also able to source protons and electrons. What does that suggest? Aha! Could it be that protons, electrons and neutrinos are co-abundant because they sprang co-equally from a common source?

Which single source was capable of yielding three of the four most plentiful forms of matter? If you've already guessed, give yourself an A.

Neutrons!

As every atomic physicist knows, free neutrons enjoy a remarkably productive 12-minute half-life. Count any number of free neutrons (those not linked with protons in atomic nuclei). Wait 12 minutes. Count again. By then *half* of your sample of free neutrons will have 'decayed.' 'Decay' means that a proton, an electron and a neutrino emerge from what *was* a neutron. The protons and electrons and remaining undecayed neutrons combine as hydrogen and helium, but the neutrinos leave and keep going.

Here is the crux of the matter: if free neutrons supplied the cosmos with its primal quotas of protons, electrons and neutrinos, free neutrons had to be the first form of matter to exist! Big Bang Cosmology, failing to take the super-abundance of neutrinos as a clue, fails also to posit a mega-abundance of free neutrons as a source for the other three most abundant forms of matter.

Harmonic Origin Cosmology does not ignore this vital clue, as you will soon see. My comments regarding the last five crucial cosmological issues, listed below, will be found in the following chapters.

8. A viable cosmology must explain why some stars assemble *elliptically* while others spread out on *planes*, as in galactic spiral 'arms.'

9. A viable cosmology must explain why spiral arm stars *far* from galactic nuclei defy gravity by orbiting around galactic nuclei *faster* than close-in stars.

10. A viable cosmology must explain why globular clusters and halo stars do not share the angular momentum of galaxies they orbit.

11. A viable cosmology must explain why the arms of some spiral galaxies are *barred.*

12. A viable cosmology must explain why some galaxies, despite gravity's inability to slow the expansion of the cosmos, actually *collide* while others form clusters which may align as "*walls.*"

There are, of course, many other features of the cosmos that require explanation; but any cosmology that fails to explain the above 12 enigmas has little hope of solving whatever other conundrums remain.

Refuting Einstein's 'man inside the windowless cube' analogy took very little time and thought. Refuting Big Bang Cosmology and replacing it with a cosmology that actually fulfills the above 12 demands and more has occupied me for decades of careful reading and research. You will find what I offer in the next few dozen pages.

Chapter Thirteen
Harmonic Origin Cosmology

According to English geneticist J. B. S. Haldane (1892-1964), a new scientific theory passes through four stages to be accepted:

1. **This is worthless nonsense.**
2. **This is an interesting but perverse point of view.**
3. **This is true, but quite unimportant.**
4. **I always said so.**[1]

At last, Harmonic Origin Cosmology stands primed and ready to survive the above gauntlet. In BBC, matter, antimatter, dark matter and presumably *anti*-dark matter all exploded from a tiny point. In BBC, even the space-time continuum itself originated at that same miniscule size and ever since has been expanding from it as a finite entity. Thus the expansion of the universe is due, first, to a gigantic explosion pushing everything in all directions and, second, to the expansion of space itself ushering everything along.

Harmonic Origin Cosmology (HOC) agrees that *part* of space is indeed expanding, but denies that currently expanding space is all the space there is. In HOC, if one part of space expands another part *must* undergo an inversely equal contraction. Think of it as a conservation law balancing spatial alteration on a cosmic scale. What's more, an expanding region in space, over eons, may reverse and begin contracting. If it does, a contracting region must also reverse and begin expanding.

Harmonic Origin Cosmology thus avers that Albert Einstein's space-time continuum always existed before matter, antimatter and energy popped up in it. Einstein at one time pondered the possibility that the stellar universe may be "a finite island in the infinite ocean of space."[2] That is what Harmonic Origin Cosmology affirms! The primary yet-to-be-answered question is—according to which *format* did matter, antimatter and energy appear amid already existing homogeneous extent?

In Big Bang Cosmology, almost two billion universes of excess mass emerged at one point only to co-annihilate. One billionth of the original mass, spared by charge parity violation, dispersed to form the cosmos. This theory of creation, as we saw, suspends several natural laws long enough to get the cosmos launched. Crediting so counter-intuitive a notion yields no advantage. Conundrums abound.

Harmonic Origin Cosmology, unlike Big Bang Cosmology, does not require two billion universes of excess matter and antimatter to be created and annihilated to get one universe jump-started. Locedmeda's first law—Efficiency—forbids so untenable a notion. *One* universe of matter balanced by an equal mass of antimatter was quite enough.

In Harmonic Origin Cosmology, only *part* of the original mass of matter and antimatter co-annihilated, yielding the cosmic microwave background. But HOC's matter and antimatter were never co-mingled in a fireball with charge parity violation sparing the matter that became our universe. Under Locedmeda's second law, Predictability, natural law cannot be altered unless Adaptability, a higher law, overrules Predictability as a service to citizens and/or denizens.

How then did matter and antimatter co-appear? Again, as Isaac Newton anticipated should be possible, I find subtle hints in Scripture. Genesis credits creation as spanning six "days." My comments here relate only to curiously-described events that transpired on "days" one and two.

The three "separations" in Genesis 1

> **"And God said, 'Let there be light,' and there was light. God saw that the light was good and he *separated* the light from the darkness"** (v. 3, emphasis added).

> **"God set [the stars] in the expanse of the sky to give light *on the earth*, to govern the day and the night, and to *separate* light from darkness"** (vv. 17-18, emphasis added).

Note that verse 18's separation of light from darkness distinguishes day from night *only for the Earth.* The prior separation of light from darkness in verse 3 is thus apparently something much grander. From the viewpoint of the 22 laws, let verse 3 denote Valcon separating 'light' from 'darkness' by *demarcating* a finite part of his infinite 'hyper-body,' the extent continuum, to be his light-filled 'creation room.'

Only in that appointed sector of the extent continuum would energy, matter and antimatter appear. Only there would thermonuclear fusion enable stars to shine. So, figuratively, that one favored sector of the extent continuum became the domain of *light*. Call that sector "DZ" for "demarcated zone," i.e., a site for the universe.

The already-existing but un-demarcated infinity surrounding the DZ on all sides is designated 'darkness,' not in any moral sense but simply because energy, light, color, etc., would not occur in that infinite outer zone. Poetically, the DZ's transition from a prior state of 'dark' to a new state of 'light' is likened to a transition from an 'evening' to a 'morning'—the first "day"!

Inside that singular domain of 'light' demarcated amid 'darkness,' verses 6 and 7 describe another major 'separation' denoting "day two":

> **"And God said, 'Let there be an *expanse* between the waters to separate water from water. So God made the expanse and *separated* the water *under* the expanse from the water *above* it"** (vv. 6-7, emphasis added).

The Hebrew word rendered 'expanse' (or 'firmament' in some translations) is transliterated *râqîya*—"visible arch of the sky." *Râqîya* derives from the primary root *râqa,* signifying something spread or stretched out, as a thin layer.[3] Genesis thus describes creation happening *on a kind of arcing plane* rather than at a point, as Big Bang Cosmology requires. We are left to ask: What then was the *shape* of that expanse? Could it be an 'arcing plane' in the shape of a sphere?

Also, if 'water' in verse 6 was literal H_2O, surely the text would speak of water finding its own level *on opposite sides* of something rather than *above* versus *below* it. Note also that what is separated is designated as already a plurality—'waters'—*before* the separation occurred, not *after*, suggesting perhaps that *one kind* of figurative 'water' had to be separated from another kind of figurative 'water.' The text thus prompts us to ask: What was the expanse? What were the 'waters'? Why did the water above the expanse have to be separated from the water below?

Consistent with the sixth Harmony's requirement for the cosmos to conform to the five features of a sphere, Harmonic Origin Cosmology posits the Genesis 1:6 'expanse' as a spherical plane that Valcon drew inside the DZ—a spherical plane with a diameter spanning several billion light years. HOC also posits that the 'water' *under* the expanse was a thin layer of *matter* that Valcon created on *just the inner side* of that immense spherical plane. The 'water' *above* the expanse was a matching layer *of antimatter* created on just the *outer* side of the same plane. In other words, Valcon created the cosmos in the form of perhaps several million particle-antiparticle pairs on every square millimeter of an incredibly vast spherical plane and then immediately split every pair apart. The immediate result was two concentric spheres, a cosmic 'double bubble'!

Let's call that enormous plane of origin the *orisphere* and its hollow core *the cosmic center.* Space *inside* the orisphere is 'matter-space,' the realm of matter. Space between the orisphere and the outermost perimeter of the demarcated zone is 'antimatter-space,' the realm of antimatter.

Initially, the two concentric spheres—a sphere of matter inside an outer sphere of antimatter—were both incredibly *solid!* For reasons that will soon make amazing sense, the inner sphere at first consisted solely of *neutrons* comprised of their component quarks. The outer sphere consisted entirely of *antineutrons* comprised, of course, of anti-quarks. Thus the inner sphere was a "neutron bubble." Its exterior counterpart was an "antineutron bubble." All the positive, negative and neutral charge plus all the mass and radiation that would ever exist were initially contained in those two concentric spheres. Big Bang Cosmology's theoretical "dark matter" was not present, nor would it ever be needed.

If, at creation, neutrons were the only kind of matter (ignoring antimatter for the moment), the three other main constituents of matter—protons, electrons and neutrinos—were also sure to appear, as explained at the end of the previous chapter. But how did we get from an ultra-solid, ultra-*thin* neutron bubble to billions of galaxies and quasars spread across billions of light-years? Consistent answers will emerge as Valcon, in accord with Locedmeda's first and second laws, Efficiency and Predictability, transforms that inner sphere—the neutron bubble—into a cosmos wherein Locedmeda's four higher laws reveal the power and goodness of Valcon to myriad field citizens.

The neutron bubble's immediate separation from its antineutron counterpart was the first manifestation of *energy.* The neutron bubble separated uniformly from the *inner side* of the orisphere at Velocity X—a sub-light velocity. Antineutrons departed from the *outer side* of the orisphere, also at Velocity X. Hence each neutron and its co-created antineutron receded from each other at Velocity 2X (Velocity X inside plus Velocity X outside). The ever-widening gap that Velocity 2X rifted between the two 'bubbles' is called the "Great Cosmic Gap," or GCG.

Diagram 1

Creation began with antineutrons O separating above and neutrons ⦿ separating below the plane of a cosmic "orisphere." Each nucleon departs from the orisphere at 'Velocity X' ↑↓. *Two* concentric cosmic 'bubbles' resulted—an outer 'antineutron bubble' and an inner 'neutron bubble' separating concentrically at Velocity 2X:

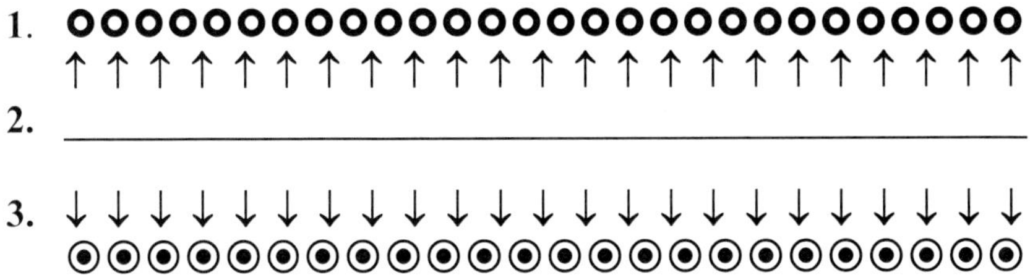

Legend for Diagram 1:

1. A tiny segment of the *antimatter 'bubble*,' comprised of antineutrons
2. A tiny segment of the "sphere of origin"—*orisphere*—a cosmic plane billions of light years in diameter.
3. A tiny segment of the *matter 'bubble*,' comprised at first of neutrons only. The space between the bubbles became 'the Great Cosmic Gap.'

Neutrons attract antineutrons but only at very close range, so Velocity 2X easily kept neutrons from co-annihilating with antineutrons, leaving the cosmos initially *cold* with zero entropy. That state was soon to be altered as two other cosmic motions partnered with Velocity 2X. One of those other motions was a bilateral motion *in space itself*:

Space flexed laterally away from the orisphere

Inside the orisphere, matter-space itself began contracting at sub-light velocity toward the cosmic center, thereby gradually accelerating Velocity 2X, the neutron-antineutron separation velocity mentioned above. *Outside* the orisphere, antimatter-space matched the matter-sphere's cosmic-centerward contraction with an inversely equal expansion *out toward* the perimeter of the demarcated zone (DZ), thereby adding still more impetus to Velocity 2X. That added impetus would soon vary.

Billions of years of contraction toward the cosmic center eventually *slowed to zero* as space near the cosmic center reached maximum compaction at the factor explained earlier—1.618034 times pre-creation density. By then, space at the orisphere had attained maximum *stretch,* whereupon the initial contraction gave way to a steadily accelerating *expansion.* Imagine matter space as a soccer ball shrinking to become a softball and then returning to soccer ball size. Concentric antimatter space, conversely, is like a soccer ball swelling to basketball size and then reversing to become a soccer ball again.

Our part of the matter cosmos, in this present eon, is being swept along as expanding matter-space accelerates toward restoring pre-creation space density at the orisphere. Now you see how Harmonic Origin Cosmology explains why the expansion of the cosmos is accelerating. "Dark energy" is thus redefined.

During these same eons, the inversely equal *expansion* of space in antimatter's exterior domain also maxed and has reversed. Besides these spatial expansion and contraction factors, Valcon gave each of the two bubbles their own individual rotation vectors:

The opposite rotations

Valcon also gave the neutron bubble a '*clockwise*' *rotation* as it compacted cosmic centerward. Conversely, he gave the antineutron bubble a matching *counter-clockwise rotation* as it expanded *out* toward the perimeter of the zone demarcated for creation.

Because the angular momentum of both bubbles is conserved over time, the closer the neutron bubble compacted toward the cosmic center, the *faster* everything in it rotated. The further the antineutron bubble expanded out and away from the orisphere, the *slower* it rotated. The quickening rotation of the neutron bubble as it neared the cosmic center plays a major role in shaping features of today's cosmos, as we will see.

Now that the matter bubble is in its expansion phase, its rotation is slowing even as its expansion accelerates. Take that as a prediction of harmonic origin cosmology.

No natural law is violated in the Harmonic Origin model. There was no charge-parity violation, nor any need for conservation of momentum and **c** to be overruled by an "inflationary epoch." Gravity was not threatening to trigger premature heavy element synthesis let alone crunch everything into an all-consuming black hole. Nor would thermodynamically inert (hence undetectable) "dark matter" be needed to *strengthen* gravity or "dark energy" required later to counteract strengthened gravity.

Gravity, like every other natural law, was totally present and ready to work, but matter was not yet concentrated enough *anywhere* for gravity to manifest its power. That would come later. Now I have the task and privilege of following Efficiency and Predictability's traceable long sequence of cause and effect to demonstrate how the above starting point leads directly to the cosmos that surrounds us today.

As readers know by now, processes occurring in the contracting neutron bubble have their corollaries in the expanding antineutron bubble. For now, I describe only what occurred in the neutron bubble, leaving readers to imagine parallel occurrences amid outbound antineutrons.

Entropy appears

Entropy, defined as random motion leading to a state of increasing disorder, appeared immediately after the separation of the well-ordered neutron and antineutron 'bubbles' from the inner and outer 'surfaces' of the orisphere. How did entropy begin?

Despite their neutral charge, neutrons repel each other, though only at close range. Even then, their mutual repulsion is not as strong as the mutual *repulsion* exhibited by two particles with like positive or like negative charge. Nor is it nearly as strong as the mutual *attraction* that particles of *opposite* charge manifest for each other.

Predictably, neutrons—created 'shoulder to shoulder' just inside the orisphere—engaged in brusque 'nudge matches,' with every neutron trying to make every nearby neutron 'keep its distance.' Crowding prevented neutrons from separating laterally. The only option was to separate from each other *at right angles* to the surface of the bubble itself. Predictably every second neutron—sharing a given polarity and spin—popped *in* from the plane of the neutron bubble. Every neutron with *opposite* polarity and spin popped *out*.

Imagine you are holding a chessboard that suddenly disassembles. Dark squares repel white squares *up*. White squares push dark squares *down*. So it was with *like-polarity-and-spin* neutrons repelling *opposite-polarity-and-spin* neutrons "off plane." As a result, the neutron bubble, initially ultra-thin, began to *thicken* and simultaneously became more *fluid*. It was indeed beginning to resemble 'water.' This initial thickening of an originally ultra-thin neutron bubble was, however, only a prelude to far more remarkable changes.

Free neutrons' threefold gift to a baby cosmos

Note that each of the two 'bubbles,' at the moment of separation, consisted only of neutrons and antineutrons respectively. Charged particles—protons, antiprotons, electrons and positrons, for example—were still totally absent. Why is this important?

It matters because (1) neutrons are designed to bond with protons to form atomic nuclei, and (2) the neutron urge to bond with protons is so strong that if neutrons find no protons to bond with, some of them actually go 'pop,' thereby changing the major part of their mass into protons for other still-intact neutrons to bond with! Two accessory gifts—an electron and a neutrino—are also released at each 'pop.' Keep in mind also that *neutrons and protons attract each other*, though only at very close range.

Physicists find that free neutrons have a 'half-life' that *predictably* subjects 50 percent of them to the subatomic equivalent of a 'gender change' in each 12 minute period. That is why protons—plus electrons and neutrinos, the two other byproducts of 'neutron decay'—began appearing at once in enormous numbers as newly minted neutrons all across that vast sphere—the neutron bubble—began going 'pop.'

Note: if protons and electrons appeared apart from neutron decay, neutrinos would not exist in great quantities!

The generous self-sacrifice of vast numbers of 'bachelor' neutrons gave the newborn cosmos exactly what it needed to form hydrogen and helium in guess which ratio? Yes! Ninety percent or so hydrogen to 10 percent or so helium! Just as amazingly, the same provision guaranteed that 90 percent of the hydrogen and helium would be *ionized* and only 10 percent *atomic*! How so? I will now explain why Harmonic Origin Cosmology's above-described *planar* model of creation readily guaranteed these essential cosmic ratios—numbers that Big Bang Cosmology's *fireball* model strains the brain in vain to explain.

Picture an imaginary 360-degree cosmic protractor straddling the plane of the neutron bubble at creation. One hundred eighty degrees rises above; 180 degrees drops below. Visualize 1000 neutrons decaying along the protractor's diameter in the cosmos' first 12 minutes. As they decay, the 1000 neutrons randomly scatter 1000 protons, 1000 electrons and 1000 neutrinos *on, above and below* the neutron bubble plane. Dividing

360 degrees into 1000 decay events reveals an important average. For every 1000 decay events, an average of 2.7 protons, 2.7 electrons and 2.7 neutrinos will move on or away from the neutron bubble on each of our cosmic protractor's 360 degrees. 1000 newly-minted protons—each one 1836.12 times as massive as an electron—dawdle randomly away from the 1000 decay sites. 1000 lightweight electrons depart swiftly. 1000 nearly massless neutrinos, conversely, depart from the site of each decay event almost at the speed of light.

Since neutrons and protons attract each other only at close range, Harmonic Origin Cosmology avers that the small percentage of protons expelled a few degrees *above and below* the plane of the neutron bubble —where undecayed 'bachelor' neutrons were still abundant—bonded in their slow flight with just enough neutrons to make heavy hydrogen, tritium, light helium and finally *helium*, by a natural, four-step energy-emitting process known to physicists, as in Diagram 2 on page 133.

That, then, explains why only 10 percent of all expelled protons became bonded with neutrons as helium nuclei. Also, the energy released by the latter three stages of the above four-stage process helped disperse newly-minted hydrogen and helium ions even further 'off-plane,' thickening the neutron bubble still more.

The other 90 percent of protons, expelled *at steeper angles* all the way up to 90 degrees above and below plane, easily avoided bonding with neutrons. That 90 percent dispersed above and below the neutron bubble *as hydrogen only*, requiring us to answer an extremely important question: *which kind of hydrogen did that 90 percent become—ionized or atomic?*

Why *ionized (transparent)* hydrogen prevails

Big Bang Cosmology's protons and electrons, intermixed in BBC's expanding fireball rather than departing from the inner and outer surfaces of a spherical plane, certainly would find each other, forming electrically neutral hence opaque hydrogen in cosmic abundance. Electrons flying for ages through a proton-rich cloud cannot avoid capture by protons. In HOC, the preponderance of ionized hydrogen was automatic because protons—1836.12 times as massive as electrons and moving proportionately slower—captured a mere 10 percent or so of swift electrons, i.e., those released on or just a few degrees above or below the neutron bubble. The high velocity that popping neutrons gave to ejected electrons enabled the other 90 percent of them to evade dawdling protons.

A large majority of protons were thus abandoned to spend the next few billion years as ionized, hence transparent, hydrogen! By the time protons outnumbered the diminishing quota of undecayed neutrons remaining on the neutron bubble, most ejected electrons had escaped much too far to be captured by protons.

Commentary on Diagram 2 on the next page

Neutrons and antineutrons (when not conjoined with protons and antiprotons) begin 'decaying' under their 12-minute half-life. Focusing only on neutrons, we find that every decaying neutron releases three new sub-atomic particles:

A Proton ●: Each neutron decay expels a proton across or away from the plane of the neutron bubble. Protons attract neutrons at close range, ergo HOC estimates that +/- 10 percent of expelled protons got close enough to still-intact, on-plane neutrons to bond, making in succession 'heavy' hydrogen ●⦿, tritium ⦿●⦿, 'light' helium ●⦿● and helium ●⦿⦿●. This occurs via the four steps of 'cold nucleo-synthesis' known to physicists (W). Neutrons, once bonded with protons, no longer obey the 12-minute half-life. The other 90 percent of protons, expelled at *acute* angles, escaped 'neutron-less' above and below the neutron bubble as hydrogen ions. This process changed the neutron bubble into the 'ionized hydrogen bubble' (IHB) depicted in Diagram 2.

An Electron ✧: Each neutron decay also expels an electron. Much less massive than co-birthed protons, electrons depart so rapidly that only 10 percent (5 percent over plane, 5 percent below plane) are bagged by protons dawdling close to the neutron bubble. That is why only 10 percent of the primeval hydrogen and helium became *atomic*. The other 90 percent of the hydrogen and helium remained *ionized* (45 percent over plane, 45 percent below plane). Farther from the neutron bubble, hydrogen ions outnumber deuterium, tritium and helium ions by far. Further still off-plane, swift electrons and, of course, even swifter-moving neutrinos (not shown in Diagram 2) predominate.

A Neutrino ✷: Each neutron decay also expels a neutrino (not shown in Diagram 2) at near light speed. Neutrinos do not interact with any part of the neutron bubble. Those expelled *outward* do, however, begin co-annihilating later with antineutrinos (as depicted later in Diagram 3).

Diagram 2

The 12-min. half-life governing the decay of free neutrons⦿ floods the plane of the neutron bubble with protons● and electrons✧, 10% of which combine on plane as *atomic* H. As 45% of electrons escape above plane and 45% flee below plane, leaving 90% of all protons as *ionized* hydrogen●. 10% of the ionized H, via successive neutron bondings, soon becomes heavy hydrogen●⦿, then tritium⦿●⦿, then light helium ●⦿● and finally helium ●⦿⦿●, as depicted below:

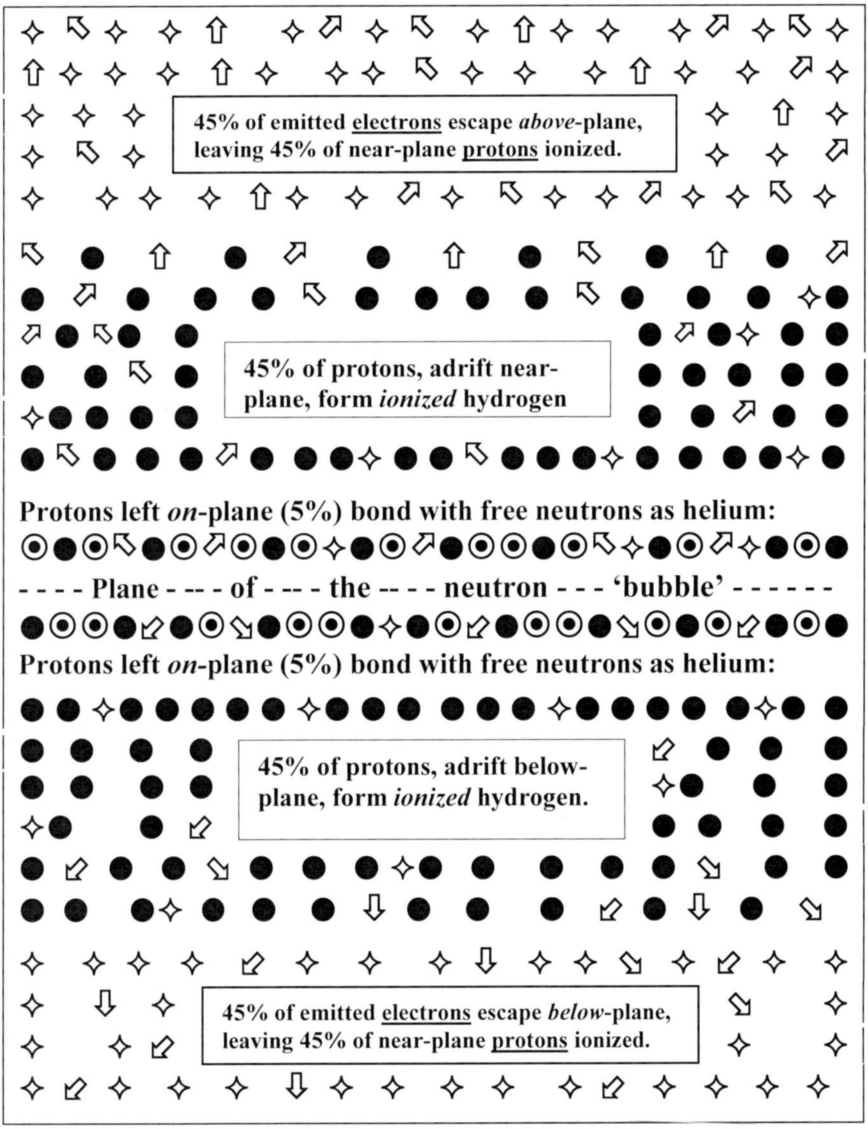
45% of emitted electrons escape above-plane, leaving 45% of near-plane protons ionized.
45% of protons, adrift near-plane, form ionized hydrogen
Protons left on-plane (5%) bond with free neutrons as helium:
- - - - Plane - -- - of - -- - the -- - - neutron - - - 'bubble' - - - - - -
Protons left on-plane (5%) bond with free neutrons as helium:
45% of protons, adrift below-plane, form ionized hydrogen.
45% of emitted electrons escape below-plane, leaving 45% of near-plane protons ionized.

Why cosmic microwave background is omni-directional

Antineutron 'decay' similarly ejects antiprotons, positrons and *antineutrinos*. Neutrinos and antineutrinos—almost massless—leave their respective 'bubbles' omni-directionally at nearly the speed of light. Neutrinos that vector *out* toward the antineutron 'bubble' almost at light-speed eventually collide with antineutrinos vectoring *in* toward the matter realm at near light-speed. When they collide, their mutual annihilation emits cosmic microwave background, half of which vectors *away* from the cosmic center, half *toward* it (see Diagram 3 on the opposite page).

Because we are located somewhere *inside* the Great Cosmic Gap where the microwave radiation originates, the latter reaches us on Earth omni-directionally, i.e., almost equally from all directions. Despite the obvious evidence that its source encompasses us, many cosmologists mistake the cosmic microwave background as originating in a "Big Bang" at what, in Harmonic Origin Cosmology, was simply a *vacant* cosmic center.

Why, then, is it elegantly logical to posit creation beginning with neutron/antineutron pairs separating in the form of two concentric bubbles rather than as a mix of already existing protons, antiprotons, electrons and positrons all blasting each other and several natural laws to smithereens in a Big Bang fireball? By way of summary, here is why:

Provided quark-comprised neutron-antineutron pairs separated effectively at creation, the 12-minute half-life of free neutrons was sure to yield an adequate supply of protons and electrons in minutes—with neutrinos serving as intrinsic evidence of how it happened! Why not let primeval free neutrons provide what free neutrons were obviously designed to bestow?

Of course all this had to happen in a context that permitted some 10 percent of newly-minted protons to bond with 20 percent or so of the remaining neutrons before *all* the neutrons were forever demolished by that otherwise unstoppable free neutron half-life. Ergo, neutrons must have ejected those other three 'gift particles' while aligned on a plane, rather than intermixed with antineutron byproducts in a fireball.

Just as logically, separating neutrons from co-created antineutrons had to happen in a way that enabled byproduct neutrinos and antineutrinos to find each other and co-annihilate, emitting microwave radiation. All this, and not even one law of physics lies bloodied! Thus reads my main premise for positing creation beginning as described above.

Diagram 3

Depicting neutrino✱ antineutrino ☼ co-annihilation ✹ as the source of Cosmic Microwave Background▲▼:

50% of antineutrinos☼ released by antineutron decay on the external 'bubble' vector *in* toward the matter 'bubble.' Over time, midway in the Great Cosmic Gap, they co-annihilate with outbound neutrinos✱, spraying microwave radiation in all directions.

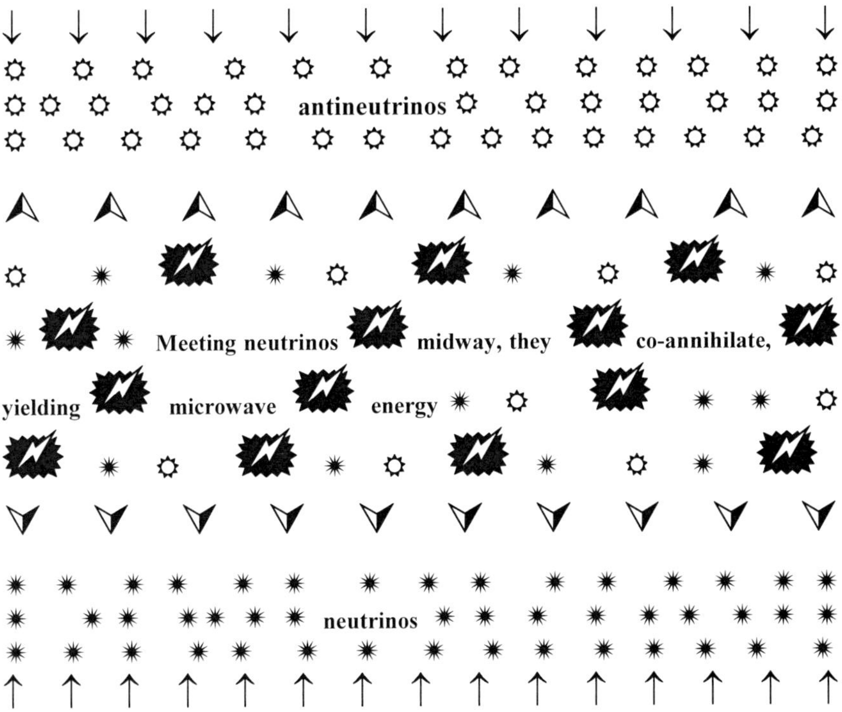
antineutrinos
Meeting neutrinos
midway, they
co-annihilate,
yielding
microwave
energy
neutrinos

50 % of neutrinos released by decayed neutrons on the <u>matter</u> 'bubble' vector *out* toward the <u>antimatter</u> 'bubble.' Colliding with anti-neutrinos anywhere in the Great Cosmic Gap, they co-annihilate, yielding the cosmic microwave background that reaches us omni-directionally billions of years later.

Chapter Fourteen
The Five Features of a Sphere in Cosmology

Just as VACRA's five aspects of a sphere—spherical **v**olume, spherical surface **a**rea, **c**ircumference, **r**adius and **a**xis—manifest as "eso" and "exo" *volons, areons, circons, radions and axions* at the sub-atomic level, so also do they appear on a cosmic scale.

How a cosmic *esovolon* and *exovolon* appeared

When Valcon separated the neutron bubble from its antineutron counterpart at the moment of creation, he also caused the entire volume of extent *inside* the orisphere to begin *contracting.* That entire contracting region of space was Valcon's **esovolon**. He also caused an equal volume of extent *outside* the orisphere to *expand* away from the sphere of origin to an inversely equal degree, yielding a cosmic **exovolon**. The two 'bubbles' thus departed from each other at a rate surpassing Velocity 2X, which, you may recall, was Velocity X separating matter from *inside* the 'orisphere' *added to* Velocity X moving antimatter away *outwardly*.

The contraction of the cosmic esovolon, combined with the neutron bubble's already centerward motion, over time helped magnetism first and gravity second to coalesce ionized hydrogen and helium gas as stars and stars as galaxies, etc. Hence gravity, in HOC, needed no assist from hypothetical "dark matter." Conversely, the *expansion* of the cosmic exovolon, combined with the antineutron bubble's initial velocity of recession *away* from the cosmic center, *retarded* coalescences of antimatter to such an extent that antimatter failed to coalesce as anti-stars. Antimatter still exists but only as an all-encompassing, relatively attenuated sphere of *plasma* far beyond the limits of the matter cosmos.

By the time galaxies, globular clusters, etc., had time to form and then be combined (as explained later), the cosmic esovolon's contraction had slowed, maxed at 1.618034 times its original density and *reversed*, resulting in the current back-toward-the-orisphere expansion that we now observe. That present accelerating expansion is Harmonic Origin's answer to Big Bang Cosmology's "dark energy." Correspondingly, the expansion of the antimatter domain—maxing at 1.618034 times its original density near the perimeter of the demarcated zone—is now steadily contracting back toward the orisphere and will be for a long time.

In the micro-cosmos, esovolon-exovolon pairs spring complete from equal but separate orispheres in the extent continuum. In the macro cosmos, a *single* billions-of-light-years-wide esovolon-exovolon pair contract and expand *concentrically* in relation to the same orisphere.

How a cosmic *esoareon* and *exoareon* emerged

The two ultra-thin concentric spherical 'bubbles' that emerged at creation—one inside, one outside the orisphere—were cosmic areons. Of these, the inward-contracting neutron bubble was a cosmic **esoareon**. Its outward expanding antineutron counterpart was a cosmic **exoareon**.

How cosmic *esoradions* and *exoradions* formed

The descent of every neutron and its subsequent byproducts following *inward* radii toward the cosmic center was Valcon's cosmic **esoradion**. The ascent of every anti-neutron and its byproducts on *outward* radii toward the demarcated zone (DZ) was his **exoradion**.

How a cosmic *esoaxion* and *exoaxion* appeared

As the cosmic esoareon (the neutron bubble) *contracts* toward the cosmic center, it also *rotates* on the orisphere's axis, thereby providing the cosmos with its macro **esoaxion.** As the cosmic exoareon (the antineutron bubble) expands *away* from the cosmic center, it provides the universe with its oppositely rotating macro **exoaxion**.

How a cosmic *esocircon* and *exocircon* emerged

Esocirconic 'spin' requires two points—one of maximum extent density *contraction*, the other of maximum extent density *expansion*—to wave-orbit around a circumference of a volon. This happens on a cosmic scale as well. A region of maximum extent density *contraction* measuring tens of millions of light years across keeps 'wave-orbiting' around a circumference girding the cosmic esovolon. That is the cosmic **esocircon**.

A region of inversely equal extent density *expansion*—a cosmic **exocircon**—also wave-orbits on the cosmic esovolon's opposite side. These two cosmic circons—chasing each other around a circumference of the matter domain—serve as **cosmic *churners***. Galaxies were evenly distributed until these two massive cosmic esocircons and exocircons—wave-moving among billions of galaxies—tilted many on end, caused a few to collide, crowded others into clusters and even left clusters arranged as galactic 'walls' on either side of cosmic 'halls' or 'voids.'

Please note that gravity and magnetism have nothing to do with this extra motion of galactic clusters affected by either of the two cosmic circons. Just as the expansion and contraction of the cosmic eso- and exo-volons is nothing more than concentric motion that Valcon ordains in the extent continuum itself, so also expansion and contraction of the cosmic eso- and exo-circons is circumference-linked motion in the extent continuum only.

The "wake" of the cosmic eso- and exo-circonic orbits around the cosmic center can be traced by noting where galactic roiling has occurred. That is how Harmonic Origin Cosmology explains why some galaxies, after the even dispersion that enabled all of them to form originally, still managed to collide or crowd together despite their current rapid recession from each other.

I wrote the above for the first time many years ago, only now to find —as I write—an article dated yesterday, September 23, 2008, on the *Universe Today* Web site, declaring that astronomers have just detected what they call "dark flow":

> Just as unseen dark energy is increasing the rate of expansion of the universe, there's something else out there causing an unexpected motion in distant galaxy clusters. Scientists...are calling it "dark flow" ..."The clusters show a small but measurable velocity that is independent of the universe's expansion and does not change as distances increase," said lead researcher Alexander Kashlinsky at NASA's Goddard Space Flight Center in Greenbelt, MD. "The distribution of matter in the observed universe cannot account for this motion. We never expected to find anything like this," he said.[1]

The article implies that "hundreds of galaxy clusters" are being deflected *away* from trajectories consistent with the already-measured, basic expansion of the cosmos. Their noticeably different vectors, researchers find, are carrying them toward a 20-degree-wide sector of the sky located, line of sight, between two constellations: Centaurus and Vela.

I predict the above researchers will eventually find a second region undergoing similar disturbance. It will be located approximately 180 degrees away, cosmically speaking, from the above described roiling, and VACRA will be confirmed by the discovery of Valcon's cosmic circons. Keep in mind that VACRA cannot be confirmed alone. If VACRA is confirmed, the body of laws which enabled us to posit VACRA stands confirmed with VACRA.

Chapter Fifteen
Magnetism First, Then Gravity

Why 'dark matter' is integral to Big Bang Cosmology

Big Bang Cosmology relies exclusively on *gravity* to accomplish two major achievements despite impossible odds. Gravity alone must somehow reverse the continuous *attenuation* of Big Bang Cosmology's very rapidly expanding clouds of atomic hydrogen and helium in order to compact them as stars. Second, gravity alone must single-handedly persuade clouds of stars, once formed, to congregate as galaxies and globular clusters but still have them all rushing away from each other once formed!

Harmonic Origin Cosmology agrees—gravity has a severe 'initial weakness syndrome'! But proponents of Big Bang Cosmology have no choice. They *must* contrive a way to explain how weak gravity triumphed over their from-day-one ultra-explosive cosmic expansion. Two problems dog their efforts.

First problem: By the time Alan Guth's posited 'inflationary epoch' braked to sub-light speed, all of Big Bang Cosmology's big-bang-generated atomic hydrogen and helium were *thinly dispersed.* Gravity is even weaker when it comes to compacting *thinly dispersed* matter, especially if it consists of the two lightest elements, hydrogen and helium. Gravity is even weaker if the two lightest elements *are expanding rapidly*!

Hence Big Bang Cosmologists absolutely *must* posit physically undetectable dark matter to act as a kind of cosmic 'steroid,' enabling gravity to accomplish what gravity unassisted simply could not do. Big Bang cosmologists even claim that dark matter *constitutes as much as 90 percent of the universe!* Some steroid!

Was Big Bang Cosmology's *dark* matter created *after* the Big Bang? Was there a *second* Big Bang for dark matter only? Or was *dark* matter created 'banglessly'? If the answer is "yes," why not posit that *visible* matter was created 'banglessly'? BBC theorists prefer to leave all such questions unasked, let alone unanswered.

Second problem: Gravity acts *radially*, drawing both atoms and ions toward any place where mass happens to be more concentrated. However, when matter is evenly dispersed on a vast scale, gravity works against itself, pulling from everywhere toward everywhere, achieving nothing. Gravity works best if some accessory force has already made matter denser in some areas, leaving it less dense elsewhere, providing gravity with 'mass centers' it can attract more matter to, with a steadily increasing pull.

Big Bang Cosmology, lacking ionization in its primeval mass, cannot cite magnetism as gravity's initial auxiliary matter compactor. BBC has no choice, so it must invent "dark matter" to fill that role. However, unless something *else* compacts dark matter more in some areas than in others, would not BBC's strengthened gravity still work against itself, pulling from everywhere toward everywhere, achieving nothing?

Alas, dark matter's undetectable nature relieves Big Bang theorists of having to explain why that did not happen.

Harmonic Origin Cosmology replaces Big Bang Cosmology's undetectable "dark matter" with two far more logical "gravity assistors":

Matter Compactor #1: the initial *contraction* of the ionized hydrogen bubble (IHB)

The neutron bubble was being steadily *compacted* as it closed toward the cosmic center at Velocity X. That primary compaction was supplemented by the rate at which matter-space itself was contracting. However, as neutron decay changed the neutron bubble into an ionized hydrogen bubble (IHB), Velocity X quickly became only the IHB's *average* rate of approach to the cosmic center.

Protons and electrons ejected *ahead* of the IHB were now moving at Velocity X *plus* the space contraction rate *plus* the centerward momentum they gained from the neutron decay that sourced them. Call this new range of *accelerated* centerward velocities Velocity X+. Protons and electrons ejected from *the aft surface* of the ionized hydrogen bubble had their centerward motion reduced to Velocity X *minus* the 'away momentum' they inherited from the neutron decay that sourced them. Call this range of *reduced* centerward motion Velocity X-. Particles ejected *laterally* on the IHB of course still moved virtually at Velocity X.

It follows that clouds of IHB hydrogen and helium, converging radially toward the cosmic center at speeds in the range of Velocity X+, were being *compacted* far more rapidly than sibling clouds lagging behind at speeds in the range of Velocity X-. Later we will discover how remarkably these consequent diverse compaction rates—coordinated with matter compactors #2 and #3 below—divided stars, once formed, into the variety of stellar communities we observe in the cosmos today.

Matter compactor #2: *magnetism!*

In Harmonic Origin Cosmology, magnetism *preceded* gravity by clumping *ionized* matter around magnetic poles while gravity was still mulling what to do with matter as a whole. Big Bang Cosmology's primeval absence of ionization forces it to focus on gravity, gravity, gravity, whether it is gravity linked to dark matter or to the ordinary kind.

How easy for earthlings, scientists included, to virtually ignore magnetism as a major cosmic force. Here on Earth, virtually every proton is balanced by an electron; hence ionization and magnetism are less imposing factors here than in the cosmos at large.

Natural phenomena related to magnetism—static electricity or lightning—are obvious, of course; but it is gravity that keeps our feet on the ground, rain falling on our crops and rivers flowing. Even magnetism's benefits are relatively insignificant. Sea captains, pilots and boy scouts appreciate compasses; but most of us find our way without them. Based on our own experience, we unwisely project out into the cosmos our mistaken perception of magnetism as relatively insignificant.

In the vast domain of stars, globular clusters and galaxies, the opposite is true. Ninety percent or so of *everything* out there is ionized; hence magnetism dominates. BBC theorists, by emphasizing gravity and failing to discern magnetism's primary role, in effect resemble a man trying to run a two-cylinder engine on one cylinder. What then must we know to understand magnetism's power as a major player in the cosmos?

First, keep in mind that magnetism ignores atoms. Magnetism manages ions (electron-less protons) and anions (proton-less electrons) and nothing else. Henceforth when I say "ions" and "ionization," know that "anions" are implied; but for simplicity I will say "ions" and "ionization" because stars consist mainly of ionized protons. Stars do not coalesce from clouds of electrons!

Reflect also that magnetic fields move ionized matter thousands of times more efficiently at relatively short range than same-mass gravitational fields can move any kind of matter. A small bar magnet, for example, lifts a nail despite the gravity of something as large as the Earth.

Big Bang Cosmology's atoms-only fireball of course had no ions for magnetism to manage; thus magnetism played no part in Big Bang Cosmology's primeval cosmos. That explains why Big Bang cosmologists *must* make total use of gravity—even if gravity has to be abetted by undetectable dark matter—to shape the early cosmos.

Whereas gravity attracts both atoms and ions radially toward a *single* center of mass, magnetism overrules gravity by attracting *ions* toward one or the other of two poles equidistant from a common center and located on an axis running through the common center. One magnetic pole attracts anions only. The other pole attracts ions only.

Gravity is a ratio of mass vis-à-vis volume of space. Raising the ratio of mass to a given volume of space strengthens gravity. **Magnetism** is a ratio of *ionization* vis-à-vis a given volume of space. Even raising the ratio of *ions* vis-à-vis *atoms* in a volume of space strengthens magnetism. A mass consisting almost exclusively of ions generates a stronger magnetic field than an identical mass of ions mixed with atoms.

Nor does it take a great mass of ions to generate a strong magnetic field. In fact, the force a magnetic field exerts on nearby ions is several thousand times stronger than the gravitational influence the same mass exerts. When ionized protons first appeared among neutrons in the neutron bubble, magnetic fields formed at once but remained weak as long as chargeless neutrons outnumbered protons. Though able to draw slow-moving protons to their negative poles, early magnetic fields were still far too weak to nab speedy electrons.

By the time the neutrons' 12-minute half-life generated stronger magnetic fields by making protons far more numerous than neutrons, 90 percent of all the electrons that would ever be were *long gone,* escaping inside and outside the plane of the neutron bubble. Billions of years later, those fugitive electrons fulfill a special destiny, as a later chapter explains.

Protons and electrons that would have formed *neutral atomic* hydrogen if only they could find each other failed to find each other due to the initial weakness of magnetic fields. 'Electron flight' left a large majority of pre-stellar hydrogen and helium ionized, hence transparent. The resulting high levels of ionization brought *all* the primeval magnetic fields to 'full strength,' thus *elevating magnetism far, far above gravity* as ***the*** dominant matter handler in the early cosmos.

With full-strength magnetic fields clumping ionized hydrogen and helium at myriad negative poles, widening gaps opened between clumps. More important, magnetism's crowding of ions at negative poles, abetted by the age-long contraction of the entire ionized hydrogen bubble, eventually gave gravity the *concentrations of mass* it needed to fuse myriad globules of hydrogen into larger concentrations called 'globes.'

As gravity's continuing draw kept fusing ever larger 'globes' together, eventually more and more globes attained the critical mass gravity needed to trigger thermonuclear reactions, transforming spheres of largely transparent gas into glowing stars. Stars began to shine everywhere on the vast expanse of the ionized hydrogen bubble.

Still, stars were largely confined to one great spherical plane. Which force later removed stars off-plane into their present-day distribution? Even more crucial, which force lifted many stars from the IHB's flat plane to form *elliptical* structures—galaxies and globular structures—leaving others, known as 'halo stars,' thinly dispersed?

Magnetic field reversals—a phenomenon strangely absent in Big Bang Cosmology

Cosmologists in general ignore magnetic field reversals (**MFR**s) as a major factor shaping the cosmos. A few researchers at last are beginning to use expressions such as "polar electric discharge," "plasma discharges" and "plasma gun"—apparently without crediting such phenomena to magnetic field reversals. The US Navy's new weapon called a "rail gun" (W) unwittingly harnesses magnetic field reversals to hurl projectiles as far as 300 miles at speeds exceeding Mach 7! Yet magnetic field reversals occur naturally in nature too. For example:

Evidence "A": magnetic field reversals on the sun eject solar flares into space at enormous velocities. HOC avers that the reversed polarities detected *after* a flare are not a mere effect, but the *cause* of the flare!

Evidence "B": Geologists find that the Earth's magnetic poles reverse—by some estimates—every 70,000 years or so.

Evidence "C": Harmonic Origin Cosmology posits magnetic field reversals in heavily ionized clouds as triggering lightning bolts.

Evidence "D": Harmonic Origin Cosmology credits alternating magnetic field reversals for *adding lenticular disks and spiral arms* to some elliptical galaxies (W). In each reversal, a galaxy's negative magnetic pole, turning positive, expels an enormous volume of positively ionized matter directly above the expelling pole. Positive ions on the galaxy's opposite side, finding a negative pole suddenly planted in their midst, converge upon it until a second reversal expels them as well. A later chapter will explain why matter ejected by alternating magnetic field reversals over tens of millions of years bends around a diameter of the expelling galaxy in various ways.

Search online for photographs of large elliptical galaxies ejecting columns of stars and gas from their nuclei. You will see what VACRA posits as soon-to-be "spiral arms" launched on their way. As subsequent reversals reduce its mass, an elliptical galaxy downsizes until it becomes the relatively diminutive nucleus of a spiral galaxy. In still other photos, an elliptical giant's *second* MFR has already launched a second proto-spiral-arm from what HOC posits is its opposite magnetic pole.[1]

Evidence "E": Magnetic field reversals are still happening amid nebula expelled from exploding stars. Unidirectional, finger-like projections of gas and dust depicted photographically in numerous recent books and periodicals on astronomy are obviously denser than and secondary to the more diffuse gas and dust clouds that form the main mass of the nebulae.[2] Prominent columns of gas and dust in one photo are dubbed "pillars of creation" (W). Use the Internet to view photos of the Eagle Nebula (M16), the Rosette Nebula (NGC 2237), the Keyhole Nebula (NGC 3372), the Lagoon Nebula (NGC 6523), The Trifid Nebula (NGC 6514), the "Bug" Planetary Nebula (NGC 6302) and many others.

Commonly, astronomers credit the stellar wind and intense radiation from nearby stars as "etching" or "hewing" these fingers, towers and columns out of the more diffuse nebulae. That theory does not, however, explain why the towers are both linear in form and denser than the intervening nebula gas. HOC explains their greater density as due to their mass being concentrated initially at magnetic poles amid the more diffuse material and their linear form as due to magnetic field reversals hurling them across or out of the parent nebulae. More about this later.

What causes magnetic fields to reverse?

Scientists are not sure what causes magnetic field reversals (those they recognize as such, that is). Harmonic Origin Cosmology offers the following explanation: Positive ions (protons)—ions that a negative magnetic pole attracts—repel *each other* even while being drawn together at a negative pole. The same applies to anions; they repel each other even while massing at a magnetic field's positive pole. Even so, magnetic fields retain ions and anions at their respective poles despite mutual repulsion.

Harmonic Origin Cosmology posits one exception. If one pole in a magnetic field attracts a massive quantity of ions while the opposite pole finds virtually no ions to attract, the magnetic field becomes awkwardly imbalanced. Magnetic fields 'dislike' polar imbalance so intensely that they solve the imbalance problem by *reversing their poles!*

At the instant a magnetic field reverses, the mutual repulsion that myriad protons, for example, already have for each other is amplified exponentially when the pole that drew them together suddenly becomes a repelling force. Protons massed at a pole that is suddenly even more positive than all of them put together are summarily ejected into space 'at the speed of lightning,' so to speak. See Diagram 4 on the next page.

Just as remarkably, if a reversed field finds that its new negative pole is pointing *away* from the nearest mass of still resident protons, rather than waiting for the protons to migrate to it, the field flips its negative pole straight back toward them, drawing, expelling and flipping only to draw, expel and flip again—like a reversible cosmic machine-gun shooting one proton mass after another in virtually the same direction. This continues until no protons remain *or* the magnetic poles are no longer imbalanced.

How MFRs split the IHB in two concentric spheres

Behold the predicament facing myriad magnetic fields on and near the neutron bubble. Minutes after creation, positive ions were everywhere but electrons could hardly be found. Every magnetic field was both massively imbalanced and at full strength virtually as soon as it formed. However, it is important to observe that magnetic fields closely aligned on a plane take opposite orientations. Imagine ranks and files of soldiers with every second soldier standing on his head! Even so, every second magnetic field had its positive pole oriented toward the cosmic center.

Diagram 4

Magnetic field reversals initiate star formation

1.

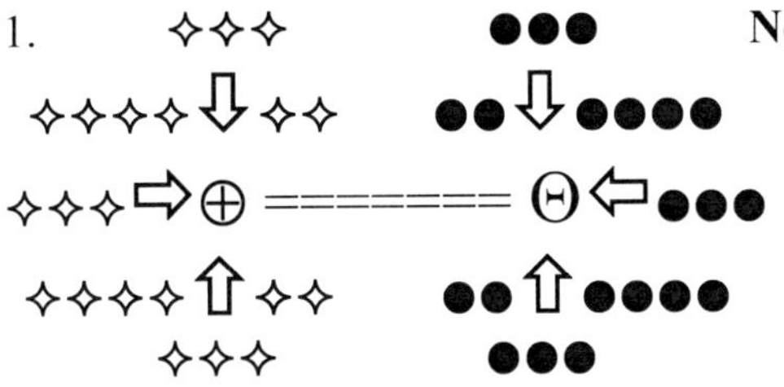

Normally anions ✧ and ions ● converge at *both* poles, as in the *balanced* magnetic field at left.

2. Early IHB fields, hyper-saturated at *negative poles only,* reversed forcefully, hurling globes of ionized hydrogen ● and helium away from the IHB. Some were hurled cosmic center-ward, hastening the overall contraction of the matter cosmos. Others were hurled away.

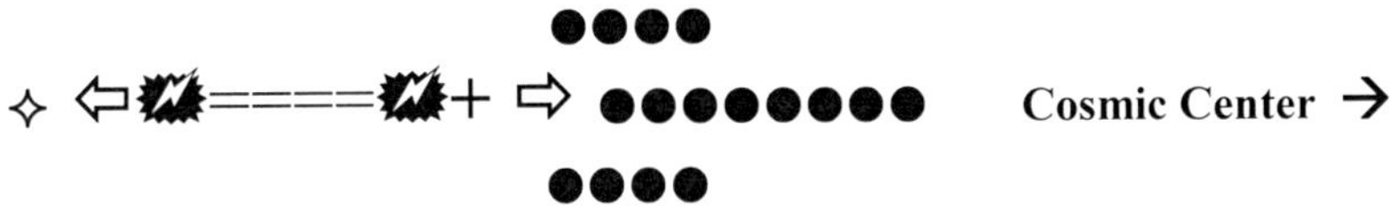

3. Expelled ions ● re-converged around *new* negative poles, only to be expelled oppositely by further imbalance-triggered reversals:

4. As globes of expelled hydrogen and helium, colliding and merging, achieved critical mass, gravity precipitated *nuclear synthesis* ☼. Myriad Population II stars blazed at last inside the plane of origin.

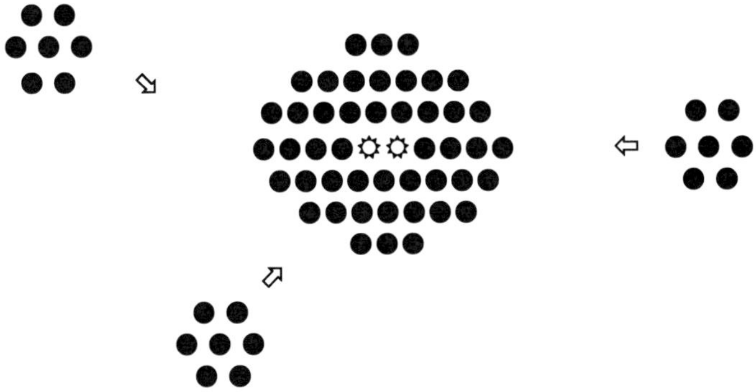

Every other field showed the cosmic center its negative pole! Thus when *all* the fields began reversing more or less simultaneously (as do solar flares) every other globe of magnetically clumped gas took flight at 90 degrees or so *inward.* Every remaining globe flew *outward* relative to the cosmic center. The mass ejected cosmic centerward *equaled* the mass ejected toward the orisphere. Thus the IHB split into two concentric spheres (which is as close as HOC comes to positing a "Big Bang"!).

As explained earlier, neutron decay had already accelerated some protons *ahead* of the IHB at Velocity X+ and decelerated other protons left *outside* at Velocity X-. It follows now that globes of ionized hydrogen hurled cosmic centerward by powerful magnetic field reversals were approaching the cosmic center at a still greater velocity—Velocity X++! Those hurled back toward the orisphere, though still approaching the cosmic center, were slowed to what may be called Velocity X- -.

Globes of hydrogen in the above magnetically separated concentric spheres were now divided by a steadily enlarging spherical *rift* of empty space. Call it 'the Great Magnetic Rift.' This 'Great Magnetic Rift' (GMR) is distinct from the Great Cosmic Gap (GCG) mentioned earlier. The GCG separates matter from antimatter (neutrinos and antineutrinos excepted), whereas the Great Magnetic Rift merely separates the swifter-compacting inner half of the IHB from the slower compacting outer half.

Now we must ask what further divided these same stars *again* into globular clusters, galaxies and halo stars.

Introducing "Population II" stars

Diagram 5 (page 150) depicts the first stars—known to astronomers as "Population II stars"—forming as a byproduct of myriad magnetic field reversals everywhere on the inner and outer shells of the ionized hydrogen bubble (IHB). When at last Population II stars were born and began to shine, another "evening" of darkness was superseded by a spectacular "morning," corresponding perhaps to another primeval creation "day."

Population II stars, the *oldest* stars shining, differ notably from the relatively *young* stars astronomers call "Population I." Population II stars far outnumber their Population I counterparts, which exist mainly in the arms of spiral galaxies and in galaxies disrupted by collisions. Population II stars, conversely, are virtually the only stellar category found in four major cosmic entities: (1) elliptical galaxies, (2) the nuclei of both spiral and dwarf galaxies, (3) globular clusters and (4) galactic "haloes."

Although they exist in these four different contexts, Population II stars share features implying a common origin: (1) The spectra of Population II stars favor *redness*. Population I stars favor *blue*. (2) Less massive hence cooler-burning and long-lived, Population II stars—unlike their Population I counterparts—rarely explode as novas or supernovas. (3) Population II stars contain mere traces of elements heavier than helium. Population I stars are comparatively rich in heavier elements.

In Diagram 5 on page 150, Harmonic Origin Cosmology credits Population II stars as sharing a common origin in the two halves of the IHB that magnetic field reversals had opened shortly after creation. Next we examine how already divided Population II stars became further sorted into globular clusters, elliptical galaxies, dwarf galaxies and halo stars.

Matter compactor #3—*gravity!*

As consecutive magnetic field reversals caused more and more hydrogen globes to collide and merge, more hydrogen globes achieved star-mass, enabling gravity to 'turn on the lights' by triggering nucleosynthesis. Population II stars blazed!

Whereas matter in Big Bang Cosmology—*attenuating* from day one—leaves gravity helpless to coalesce stars without the help of "dark matter," gravity in Harmonic Origin Cosmology, conversely, has no difficulty compressing matter into stars for two reasons: (1) the cosmos—for its first few billion years—was *contracting*, and (2) prolific magnetic fields (not available in the Big Bang Cosmology model) did the initial coalescing and then turned its results over to gravity.

Magnetism's work was not over, however. No sooner had magnetism enabled gravity to become a major matter compactor than gravity reciprocated, giving magnetism *its* next assignment.

How gravity and magnetism played 'tag'

As Diagram 5 depicts, myriad Population II stars formed from MFR-caused collisions. But a relative few collided and fused, forming a larger, hotter-burning stellar minority designated in HOC as *Phase 1 Population I stars*. These at that time relatively rare stellar giants are not to be confused with *Phase 2 Population I stars*, described later. Unlike Population II stars, Population I stars are much more prone to explode as novas or supernovas; hence they are relatively short-lived.

Diagram 5

How magnetic field reversals (MFRs) aided star formation

In a fragment of the IHB depicted below, initial magnetic fields concentrate hydrogen ions at their negative poles as globules of virtually liquid hydrogen. MFRs ✷ expel globules of liquid hydrogen ⌖ away from the IHB, initially at 90^{0} above ⇧ and 90^{0} below ⇩ plane, leaving an empty space—the 'Great Rift'—where the IHB had been. Subsequent MFRs re-expel globules but at increasingly random angles (⬀⬁, ⇨⇦ and ⬃⬂), causing globules to collide and merge ↱↰, whereupon an even greater excess of positive charge triggers ever stronger MFRs. When a critical mass of vectored globules becomes sufficiently proximate or merged, gravity takes over, fusing multiple globules together despite their mutual repulsion and 'turning them on' as Population II stars ☼.

Above-rift Population II stars

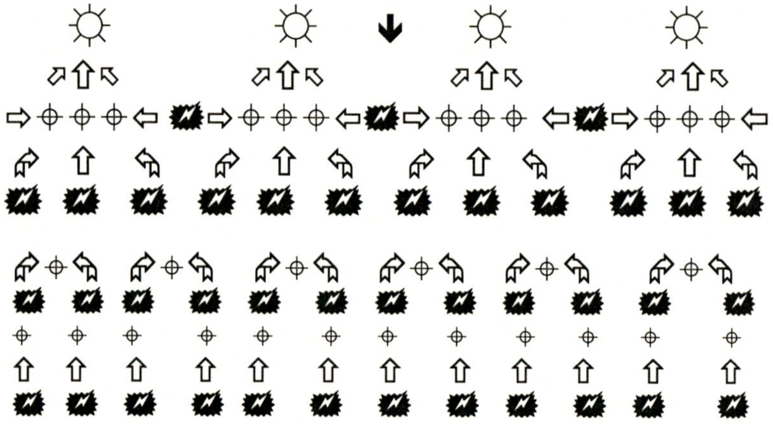

Initial MFRS opened a Great Rift of space between the outer half of the IHB and the inner half, not shown here. Simply invert the above diagram and you have Population II stars forming below rift. Above-rift Population II stars still moved toward the cosmic center, but at slower rates designated in Diagram 5 above as Velocity X- -, or simply as 🡇. Below-rift Population II stars, already moving toward the cosmic center at Velocity X, gained the additional velocity imparted by center-aimed MFRs. That greater center-ward velocity is termed Velocity X++.

The immense clouds of ionized debris blasted into space by exploding Phase 1 Population I stars were gravity's means of reciprocating a cosmic favor to magnetism. Clouds of strongly ionized supernova debris gave magnetism the expanded magnetic centers it needed to fulfill its next assignment. Call it gravity-magnetism 'tag.'

Why did on-plane stars congregate *elliptically*?

Shepherding myriad Population II stars *off* the relatively flat inner and outer planes of the ionized hydrogen bubble to fill out the elliptical shapes of *globular* clusters and *elliptical* galaxies required a 'stellar congregator' that favors *elliptical* shapes. What was that congregator?

In Big Bang Cosmology, elliptical galaxies form when two *gravitational* influences interact. One is a point-like *black hole* at what is destined to be a galactic center. The other is a for-some-reason-elliptic-shape-favoring outer halo of 'dark matter.' Globular clusters are also elliptical, but BBC theorists seem not to posit dark matter helping to structure *them*.

For reasons yet to be explained herein, HOC rejects the theory that 'dark matter haloes' and gravitationally powerful black holes alone are able to gather stars into the elliptical shapes we call galaxies and globular clusters. *As black holes pull stars in from the galactic plane, consuming some but keeping others in orbit, surely their gravitationally determined orbits would tend to conform to the galactic plane!*

Astronomers posit that approximately 70 percent of observed galaxies are elliptically shaped. Even most of the other 30 percent—galaxies with spiral disks or lenticular rims—still tend to have elliptical nuclei. HOC, which posits all Population II stars as originating on the outer and inner planes of the ionized hydrogen bubble, accepts the obligation to explain how stars born on two initially flat concentric planes were drawn off plane to fill elliptical structures.

Here is HOC's answer. Magnetic fields by nature are inherently elliptical except for the depressions around their poles and the widening spread of lines of force at their equators. Thus HOC posits super-strong *magnetic fields* forming in the debris of Phase I Population I stars as drawing stars off the IHB's two flat planes to form the ovoid shapes known as elliptical galaxies, spiral galaxy nuclei and globular clusters.

Astronomers currently acknowledge stellar and interstellar magnetic fields as capable of shepherding nothing much more than tiny ions and anions, i.e., protons and electrons. Gravity and momentum alone are credited with governing the motion of entities as large as stars. Harmonic Origin Cosmology reaches far beyond magnetic micro-herding of mere particles by positing large magnetic fields as capable of macro-herding *billions of stars* far more effectively than mere gravity and momentum!

How *magnetism* herded stars elliptically

Because they consist primarily of ionized hydrogen, stars are markedly subject to magnetic influence. Recall also that a magnetic field surrounding a given ionized mass moves other ionized matter within its reach thousands of times more effectively at relatively short range than a same-mass gravitational field moves *any* kind of matter. A small bar magnet, for example, lifts and holds a nail despite the gravity of something as massive as the Earth.

So as surely as ionization generates magnetic fields, magnetic fields are sure to encompass groupings of stars made almost entirely of ionized gas. When the first globes of ionized hydrogen were still evenly spread on the relatively flat inner and outer planes of the ionized hydrogen bubble, their attendant magnetic fields remained approximately equal in strength. With powerful magnetic field reversals disrupting that uniform distribution, Population II stars birthed from colliding globes of gas ended up *unevenly* dispersed. Strong magnetic fields formed around *larger, closer* groupings of stars. Weaker magnetic fields attended the balance.

By far the strongest magnetic fields formed where crowds of Population II stars included a few massive Phase 1 Population I stars. Ionized debris expelled by Population I stars that exploded as supernovas enlarged the reach of existing magnetic fields, enabling magnetism to launch Phase 2.

The lines of force in the equatorial region of a magnetic field lie nearly horizontal at a distance from the axis. Closer to the axis, magnetic lines of force 'north' of the equator of the field slope almost vertically up only to bend over and down where the field is depressed, pumpkin-like, at the actual 'north' pole. Lines of force 'south' of the equator slope *down* almost vertically only to bend *up* to find the 'south' pole in its 'dimple.'

Envision strong lines of force extending out scores of light years initially from the axis of an interstellar magnetic field. Envision also more and more Population II stars beginning to follow lines of force *up and away* or *down and away* from the equatorial plane of the field, depending on which pole of the field is negative at the time. Leading stars crest around the 'dimple' and converge closer to the pole. This motion alone would shape proto-galaxies and proto-globular clusters as *half-domes*. What makes the half-domes fully elliptical?

Alternating magnetic field reversals—*again!*

The closer magnetically herded Population II stars converge to an attracting pole, the more they contribute imbalance to the proto-galaxy's magnetic field as a whole. In time, imbalance triggers an MFR. Stars already deep inside the polar indentation—stars 'heavy' with positive charge—are ejected away from what has suddenly become a positive pole.

At this early stage, relatively few stars eject straight out and away from the reversed pole. Large scale expulsions come later. Instead, opposing magnetic lines of force gradually slow and then reverse the entire ovoid stellar migration toward the new negative pole, however many light years distant it may be from the expelling pole.

While stars in the proto-galaxy's 'northern hemisphere' are still in the process of reversing, stars in its equatorial zone are already arcing *southward*. Following magnetism's definitely *non-radial*, long-way-around lines of convergence toward the proto-galaxy's new negative pole, they begin changing the initial 'half-dome' of stars into a fully elliptical globular cluster or galaxy. As more and more Population II stars flock in from the surrounding plane, the above process, repeating over hundreds of millions of years, keeps globular clusters and elliptical galaxies growing larger. Their growth ends when there are no more plane stars to be added. This process of course opens widening gaps between each elliptical stellar community and its neighbors.

Can we know if the prime star-attracting forces hidden in the cores of elliptical galaxies and globular clusters are magnetic fields rather than black holes? Yes! Three evidences can be sought.

First, magnetically ellipted galaxies and globular clusters will be indented, pumpkin-like, at their poles. Light reaching us from Population II stars on opposite sides of these polar indentations effectively disguises them. Population I Stars that explode as supernovas leave trails of opaque dust, but Population II stars cast no shadows. Still, careful spectographic analysis may confirm polar indentations, if they exist.

Second, as surely as globular clusters, elliptical galaxies, *et al.*, *rotate*, studying the way individual stars participate in their rotation will reveal whether gravity or magnetism is the primary controlling force. If gravity—strictly a *radial* force—determines stellar motion in rotating elliptical communities, stellar orbits in the elliptical mass will tend to be *centered on the center* of each galaxy. This means that every star currently orbiting *above* the equator of an elliptical galaxy will eventually dip *below* its equator for half an orbit. Likewise stars currently orbiting *below* its equator will eventually rise *above* for half an orbit. Exceptions would be stars orbiting on the equator itself or transiting the equator due solely to the gravity of neighboring concentrations of stars.

Conversely, if magnetism is dominant, stellar orbits will be affected *by lines of force linked to magnetic poles* more than by gravity's centerward draw. Subject to how recently the last magnetic reversal occurred, a majority of stars in any elliptical mass will favor motion toward just one pole, but not to an extent that disrupts the overall ellipticity of the star mass. Gravity's ability to move stars on orbits linked to the galactic center will be relatively negated.

Although we do not see "half-domed" elliptical galaxies for reasons explained above, some elliptical stellar communities do show slight variations in their overall ellipticity. M104, an enormous galaxy known as "The Sombrero," has a visibly greater mass of stars *below* its 'hat-brim.' That is quite strange, because "Sombrero's" 'hat-brim' dips 6 degrees *below* our line of sight! (W) Though Diagram 7 on page 158 shows dwarf galaxies, ellipticals and globular clusters forming as half-domes, it follows that repeated magnetic field reversals render them full-domed.

Gravity's radius-to-center draw is temporarily more prevalent when magnetism-generated momenta are slowing and reversing due to a recent galactic MFR. Despite the confusion of interrupted stellar orbits, careful tracking will reveal magnetic pole-related motion prevailing statistically over gravity, except perhaps following MFRs.

Third, as surely as the nuclei of elliptical galaxies and globular clusters rotate, their magnetic fields—rotating with them—transfer some angular momentum from the rotating core out to stars at the perimeter. Magnetic fields rotate like semi-solids! Whereas gravity-controlled 'rotation curves' would allow perimeter stars to orbit *slower* at greater distances from the nucleus, the relative rigidity of rotating magnetic fields imparts a "Lorentz force"[2] that *accelerates* perimeter stars to faster orbital speeds than gravity could cause!

Astronomers now know that stars in the arms of spiral galaxies do indeed orbit faster than expected in terms of the mass of galactic nuclei.

This unexpected discovery is one of the conundrums "dark matter" was invented to solve. HOC favors the relative rigidity of galactic and/or interstellar magnetic fields as a better if only partial explanation.

Also note: the semi-solid 'rigidity' of rotating galactic-strength magnetic fields—far from requiring spiral arm stars to spend half of each orbit above a galaxy's equatorial plane and half below, as does gravity—will tend to keep above-plane spiral arm stars above plane and below-plane spiral arm stars below plane all the way around!

That then is how stars born on the *planar* surface of the IHB began congregating in *elliptical* masses. Stellar swarms numbering in the billions became *elliptical* galaxies. Smaller congregations became *dwarf elliptical* galaxies. Still smaller groupings became *globular* clusters. But on which level of the IHB did each category form?

How galaxies, dwarf galaxies, globular clusters and halo stars formed on different IHB 'tiers'

By analogy, *slow* compression may change dust to *clay* but rapid compression may change dust to *rock* or even to the hardness of a gem. So the IHB's four *different* radial convergence rates explained in Diagram 6 below crowded stars enough to form globular clusters on one IHB tier, elliptical galaxies on a second and dwarf ellipticals on a third, but left the remainder as "halo stars" on a fourth. These four tiers are named A, B, C and D. Tiers A and B are located *inside* the Great Magnetic Rift, as shown in the lower half of diagram 6, next page.

Tier A stars were a relative tithe of inside-the-rift Population II stars that formed as MFRs vectored globes of ionized hydrogen straight toward or almost straight toward the cosmic center. Tier A stars thus outpaced stars on tiers B, C and D in their 'race' toward the cosmic center. The more their vectors converged, the more Tier A stars were shepherded magnetically to form the smaller-sized elliptical stellar communities called globular clusters.

Tier B stars, an estimated 90 percent majority of inside-the-rift Population II stars, formed from the much larger number of hydrogen globes that MFRs had vectored *obliquely*, i.e., at angles ranging from 10 to 80 degrees *away* from a direct approach to the cosmic center. The closer Tier B stars converged, the more arcing lines of magnetic force shepherded them to form the much larger elliptical stellar communities we

Diagram 6

How Population II stars formed on 4 *convergence tiers*—Tiers A and B *inside* the Great Magnetic Rift, Tiers C and D *above it*

Tier D: **Population II stars ☼ that formed as MFRs ejected ionized hydrogen radially *above and away* ↑ from the 'Great Rift' had minimal rates of convergence toward the cosmic center. With no stellar collisions forming stars large enough to nova, Tier D magnetic cores were too weak to assemble elliptical stellar communities. Tier D yielded <u>halo stars only</u>.**

➔*Minimal…* **… lateral convergence 🡐**

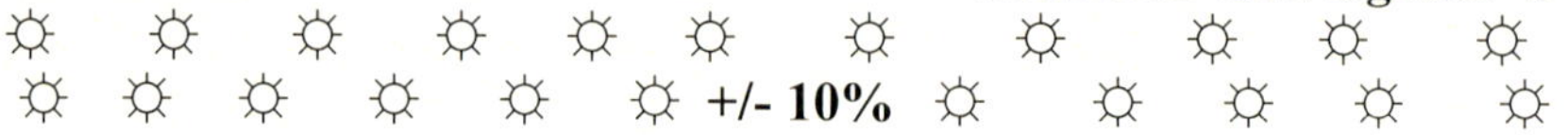

Tier C: **<u>Dwarf elliptical galaxies</u> arose as magnetic poles● amassed Pop. II stars *above* Rift, where lateral convergence was stronger than on Tier D.**

➔ *Moderate…* **…lateral convergence 🡐**

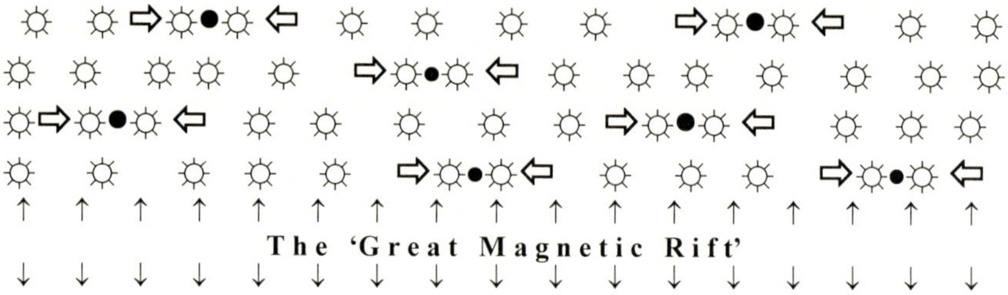

Tier B: **<u>Elliptical Galaxies</u> arose as *strong* magnetic poles● *amassed* Pop. II stars *below* Rift, where lateral convergence was stronger than on Tier C.**

➔ *Greater…* **…lateral convergence 🡐**

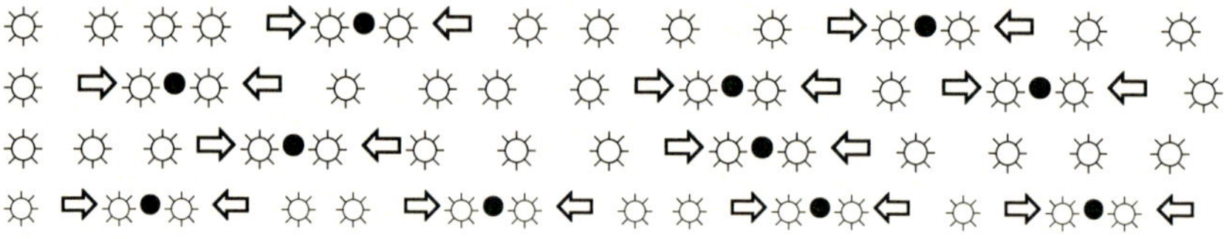

➔ *Maximum…* **…lateral convergence 🡐**

Tier A: **<u>Globular clusters</u> formed amid Pop. II stars vectored more directly toward the cosmic center, where maximum lateral convergence, combined with the highest Velocity X++ rates, assured magnetic fields strong enough to 'elliptize' the last 10% or so of Population II stars.**

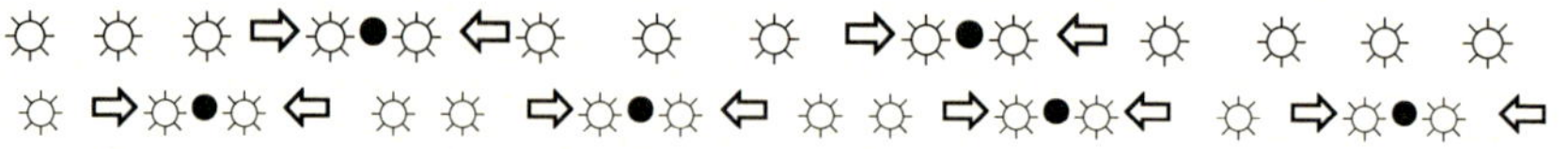

know as elliptical galaxies. Any globular cluster could have become an elliptical galaxy except that the number of Population II stars that MFRs vectored directly toward the cosmic center was so much smaller.

Tier C stars, numerically equal to their Tier B counterparts, formed as MFRs vectored hydrogen globes *away* from the cosmic center at *oblique* angles ranging from zero to 80 degrees *outside and above* the Great Magnetic Rift. These MFRs thus effectively slowed Tier C stars' rate of convergence toward the cosmic center. With this resulting slower rate of crowding, medium-strength magnetic fields shepherded swarms of outside-the-rift Population II stars to form the smaller but initially more numerous elliptical stellar communities known as *dwarf galaxies*.

The further out in **Tier C** that dwarf galaxies formed, the *more dwarfed* those galaxies would be. In fact, dwarf galaxies forming near the boundary between Tiers C and D would even resemble globular clusters in size. HOC says that is exactly why astronomers are now discovering formerly-too-faint-to-be-seen 'compact dwarf galaxies,' or CDGs.

The most dispersed Population II stars formed where MFRs vectored globes of ionized hydrogen vertically or almost vertically *away* from the cosmic center into **Tier D**, the *outermost* realm of the contracting matter sphere. In Tier D, centerward velocities and lateral convergences were minimal, leaving Population II stars in that domain too dispersed and with too little momentum to collide and merge as stars capable of exploding as supernovas. Ergo, Tier D lacked magnetic cores strong enough to gather its stars into elliptical stellar communities. Tier D stars were left to drift in relative isolation until, eons later, subsequent developments added them to galaxies as "halo stars." See Diagram 6 on the previous page and Diagrams 7 and 8 on the following pages.

Chapter 16, "The Great Cosmic Spin-off," describes next what occurred when the contents of Tiers A, B, C and D, converging consecutively around the Cosmic Center, found that contracting space had changed to *expanding* space, hurling globular clusters back to be captured by galaxies and hurling galaxies back to capture halo stars. Read on.

Diagram 7

Magnetism ↗⋎↖ prevails over gravity ⇨✹⇦ by 'globuling' Population II stars *elliptically* in magnetic fields on tiers A, B and C but not D. 'Globuling' resulted in half-domes initially, full domes subsequently. ⋎ and ⋏ indicate that magnetic fields are indented, pumpkin-like, at their upper and lower poles. Light emitted from stars all around the indents renders them indiscernible to the eye.

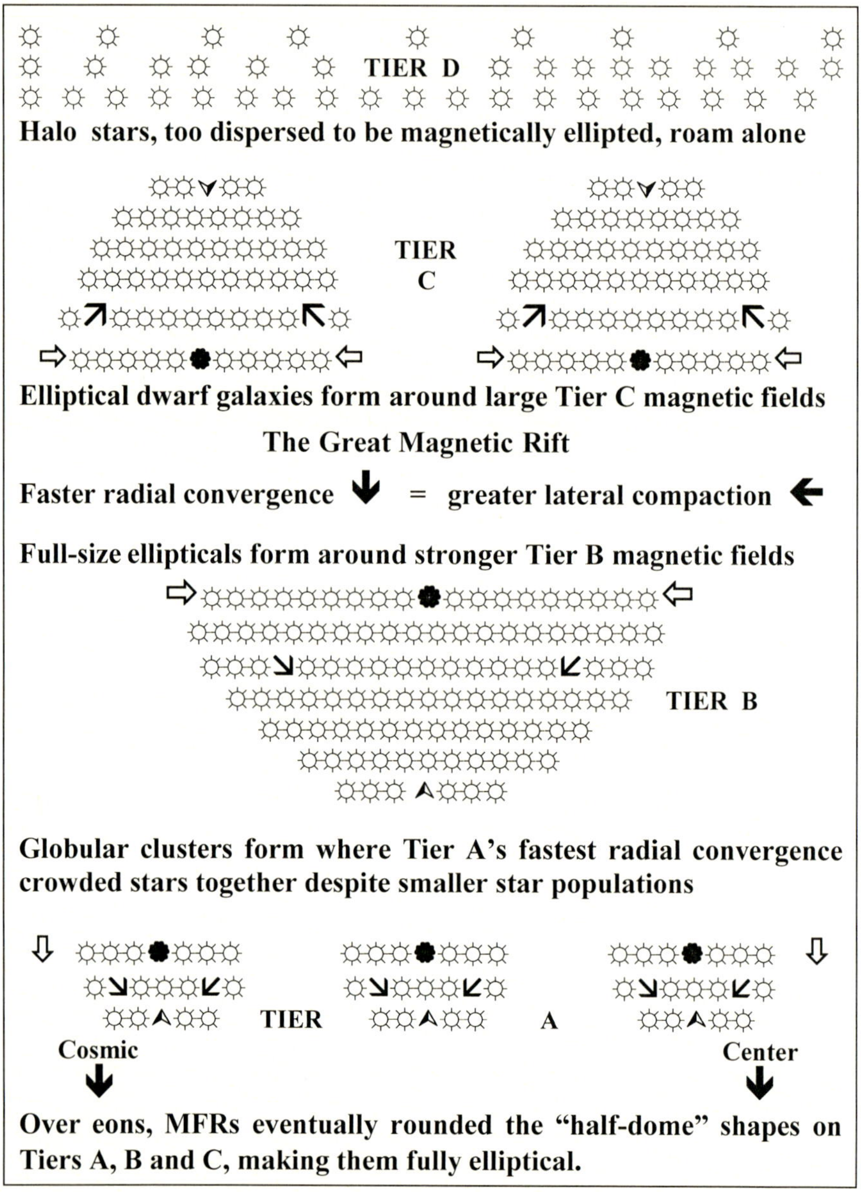

TIER D
Halo stars, too dispersed to be magnetically ellipted, roam alone
TIER C
Elliptical dwarf galaxies form around large Tier C magnetic fields
The Great Magnetic Rift
Faster radial convergence = greater lateral compaction
Full-size ellipticals form around stronger Tier B magnetic fields
TIER B
Globular clusters form where Tier A's fastest radial convergence crowded stars together despite smaller star populations
TIER
A
Cosmic
Center
Over eons, MFRs eventually rounded the "half-dome" shapes on Tiers A, B and C, making them fully elliptical.

Diagram 8

<u>Another view of 4 convergence tiers inside the plane of origin</u>

The entire mass depicted below is shown *contracting* toward the cosmic center, but it is also *rotating* around a cosmic axis, not shown.

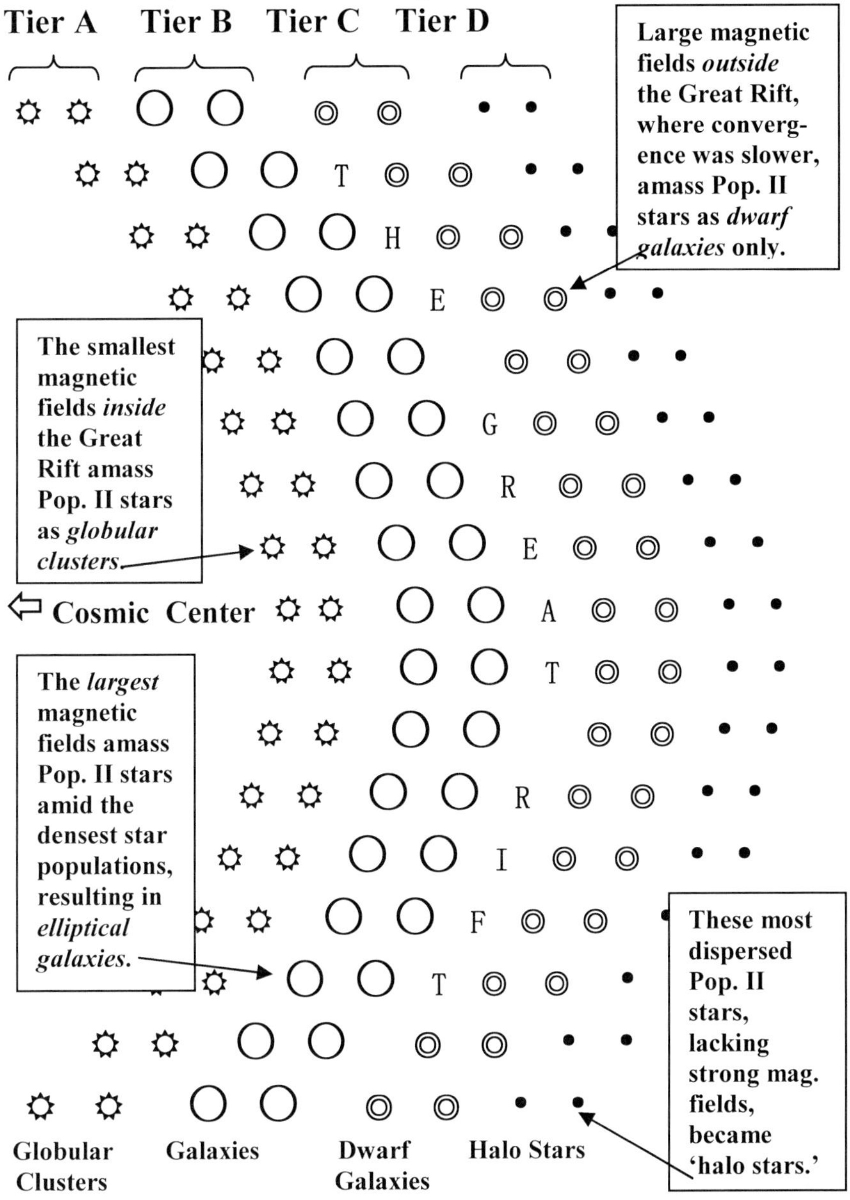
Tier A
Tier B
Tier C
Tier D
Large magnetic fields *outside* the Great Rift, where converg-ence was slower, amass Pop. II stars as *dwarf galaxies* only.
T
H
E
G
R
E
A
T
R
I
F
T
The smallest magnetic fields *inside* the Great Rift amass Pop. II stars as *globular clusters.*
Cosmic Center
The *largest* magnetic fields amass Pop. II stars amid the densest star populations, resulting in *elliptical galaxies.*
These most dispersed Pop. II stars, lacking strong mag. fields, became 'halo stars.'
Globular Clusters
Galaxies
Dwarf Galaxies
Halo Stars

To learn how the 'Great Cosmic Spin-away" would enable galaxies to capture originally separate globular clusters and halo stars, read on!

Chapter Sixteen
The Great Cosmic "Spin-off"

Forces that govern how matter *moves* in HOC

Thus far, Harmonic Origin Cosmology has named *eleven* forces that rule how matter *moves.* Below, one more factor is added in this review:

1. **Velocity X,** the force that separated neutrons and antineutrons at the orisphere, dividing neutrons from antineutrons at Velocity 2X.

2. **The contraction versus the expansion of matter-containing-space toward or away from the cosmic center**. Thus even while matter was moving through space toward the cosmic center at Velocity X, it was also *speeded* toward the cosmic center by the centerward motion of inner space itself. We call that combined velocity "Velocity X+." It, too, was a sub-light speed. Over time, this steady *contraction* of the ionized hydrogen bubble acted as a "matter compacting agent." Enormous quantities of hydrogen and helium were steadily crowded into an ever-diminishing circumference of space-time only later to be borne back outward in matter space's current expansion phase.

3. **The *axial spin* of the entire matter sphere.** The matter and antimatter spheres rotate oppositely with angular momenta conserved. This motion, however, was a motion of matter alone. It was not a motion abetted by a motion in space itself.

4. **The short-range mutual repulsion between particles with like charge, neutrons included.**

5. **"Burst velocities,"** i.e., the velocity that bursting neutrons imparted to protons, electrons and neutrinos. Burst velocities accelerated Velocity X for some protons but retarded Velocity X for others.

6. **The *short*-range mutual attraction** between protons and neutrons.

7. **The *longer*-range mutual attraction** between protons & electrons.

8. **The *bipolar* motion magnetism gives to *ionized matter only*.**

9. **The *radial* motion gravity imparts to *all* matter.**

10. **The ejection velocities** MFRs impart to ionized matter they eject.

11. **The *roiling* motion of the two cosmic circons among galaxies.**

The role of each of the above eleven forces has been explained. Now I add **Force #12—"Spin-off momentum,"** which is simply a derivative of force # 3 above concurrent with a reversal of force #2 above.

As the matter sphere contracted toward the cosmic center during the first few billion years after creation, conservation of angular momentum steadily increased its rotational velocity. At a critical distance from the cosmic center, Tier A's converging swarm of many trillions of globular clusters began reaching what Harmonic Origin Cosmology calls "the Circumference of Deflection," i.e., the point at which conserved angular momentum replaced convergence toward the cosmic center with *divergence* away from it.

In our solar system, gravity draws everything toward the Sun. Conservation of angular momentum counteracts the Sun's gravity enough to maintain planets in orbit. If the Sun and its gravity suddenly vanished, the conserved angular momentum of the planets—changed to linear momentum—would cause planets in the solar system to "spin away," each one moving on its own trajectory away from where the Sun had been.

The cosmic center was a vacuum. It contained no stars, no mass at all to exert a gravitational or magnetic pull on any approaching matter. The contraction of space in the matter realm, supplemented initially by Velocity X and later by Velocity X++, was the only reason the matter sphere was converging toward the cosmic center at all. Conservation of angular momentum was *free* to deflect the esoareon's converging swarm of globular clusters out and away, hurling them back toward a still in-rushing swarm of elliptical galaxies with dwarf galaxies following.

Harmonic Origin Cosmology posits that force #3's conserved angular momentum consecutively hurled everything that each of the matter sphere's four converging tiers brought in back out toward the orisphere. However, force #3 was aided in accomplishing this great deflection by:

Force #2's reversal—the matter sphere began expanding!

Maxing near the cosmic center at 1.618034 times its pre-creation extent continuum 'density,' Valcon's cosmic *eso*volon first *slowed* its rate of contraction in the extent continuum and then *reversed* it, becoming instead a cosmic *exo*volon accelerating its rate of *expansion* back out toward 'mean space density' at the orisphere. This is another factor that frees Harmonic Origin Cosmology from needing to posit anything like "dark energy" to explain why the matter cosmos is not only currently expanding, but also expanding *faster now* than before.

Rather than make this book pricier by including a gallery of color photos depicting the variety of cosmic structures that formed on each of HOC's four tiers, I ask that readers find—via 'search engines' on their personal computers—photos of anything named below that is underlined or followed by (W). Suggestions offered on page 227 under "Notes" for Chapter 15, footnote 1, include www.nasaimages.org, a comprehensive compilation of NASA photos. See also http.//chandra.harvard.edu/photo and www.google.com/sky/.

Tier A lost its myriad globular clusters:

By the time the inmost tier of the matter sphere—Tier A with its myriad globular clusters—was still three billion or so light years from the cosmic center, conserved angular momentum—aided by the onset of spin-off momentum's expansion factor—began batting globular clusters like golf balls in all directions *away* from the cosmic center.

Even as Tier A's trillions of occupants were rebounding *away* from the cosmic center, Tier B's billions of elliptical galaxies *were still rushing in*! When Tier A's globular clusters and Tier B's elliptical galaxies began colliding, the gravity of the latter captured virtually all of what had been Tier A's lode of globular clusters, pulling them one by one into unique and mostly eccentric galactic orbits. It follows that large galaxies captured more globular clusters than small galaxies. It also follows that galaxies close to the leading edge of Tier B captured more globular clusters than galaxies to the rear. Relatively few globular clusters would have slipped between up-front elliptical galaxies to be captured by dwarf galaxies coming in behind ellipticals back on Tier C.

Thus does HOC explain how globular clusters, though formed apart from galaxies, were not only added to galaxies later, but more than that—were added with individually eccentric orbits.

Tiers B and C forfeited their billions of galaxies

Capturing trillions of globular clusters reduced the forward momentum of billions of massive elliptical galaxies minimally. Globular clusters orbiting the nuclei of galaxies now found themselves traveling back toward the cosmos' 'circumference of deflection' *a second time,* borne along this time in the embrace of their captors' gravity. Note that gravity, on this large scale, dominates.

Like the globular clusters before them, large elliptical galaxies too, loaded with angular momentum and feeling the onset of spatial expansion 'underfoot,' began rebounding away from the cosmic center. Some ellipticals underwent glancing collisions with their neighbors or with their dwarf cousins still coming in from further out. Though some collided and merged, the mutual repulsion of exogravity shells prevented many others from merging. Ultimately, though, *all* were deflected away from the cosmic center.

There is a reason, however, why most Tier C dwarf galaxies did not come close enough to the 'circumference of deflection' to collide with newly-outbound large galaxies. During the extra ages of time it took for slower-converging dwarf galaxies to approach that circumference, the accelerating expansion of space—surging like a wave-front ahead of outbound elliptical galaxies—caused further-out dwarf galaxies to begin their deflection at greater distances from the cosmic center. That accelerating wave-front, adding new momentum to both kinds of galaxies, re-vectored them back out into the domain of still-incoming Tier D stars.

Outbound galaxies captured Tier D's halo stars

The stage was now set for a *final* massive entrapment. This time it would be myriad outbound galaxies from Tiers B and C capturing myriad still incoming Tier D Population II stars—the kind now known as "halo" stars. As with globular clusters, each newly captured halo star entered the domain of its galactic captor with its own unique angular momentum. It follows also that Tier D lost its attenuated stellar population without ever reaching the cosmic center's 'circumference of deflection.' Outbound galaxies intercepted them before they got close.

In HOC's creation model, angular momentum conserved at the 'equator' of the rotating matter sphere during its contraction phase had to be much greater than angular momentum conserved close to the *axis* of rotation itself. Hence HOC predicts that anomalies in the distribution of galaxies, globular clusters and halo stars will be found in what could be named the 'Arctic' and 'Antarctic' domains of the cosmos. Reflect also that whichever pole of the cosmos has a negative charge will be attracting galaxies, all of which have a net positive charge, provided they are proximate enough.

That is one explanation HOC offers for a newly discovered very distant phenomenon cosmologists call "The Great Attractor" (W). An alternate explanation for The Great Attractor follows later.

And *that* is how HOC follows an initially *contracting* matter cosmos from its beginning as an extremely thin but solid sphere of neutrons to a multi-planed ionized hydrogen bubble and from that to an *expanding* cosmos of incredibly dispersed galaxies encompassed by globular clusters and halo stars.

By the time HOC's Great Spin-off ended, the original 'planar state' of the matter cosmos had vanished. Galaxies roam everywhere except close to the cosmic center itself. Most galaxies are diverging as they hurtle *away* from the cosmic center. A few move parallel to each other and fewer yet follow *converging* outbound vectors.

Following HOC's Great Spin-off, all galaxies—except those that collided with each other—remained generally elliptical in shape. In my next chapter, Harmonic Origin Cosmology explains why some originally elliptical galaxies began growing 'lenticular disks' or 'spiral arms.'

Chapter Seventeen
Galactic Disks and Arms Appear!

How MFRs add lenticular disks or spiral arms to many elliptical galaxies

Earlier I described magnetic fields elevating some initially plane-bound Population II stars above plane and lowering others below plane to satisfy magnetism's preference for *elliptical* stellar structures. The main byproducts of those early magnetic fields, as we saw, were elliptical galaxies and globular clusters.

I also indicated that magnetic field reversals (MFRs) helped to complete this process, which I suggest should be called "elliptization." I wrote that most stars expelled by the earliest galactic MFRs still remained 'close enough to the action' to be part of the next magnetic 'upsweep.' "Large scale ejections," I also wrote, "would come later." Astronomy indeed affirms that some elliptical galaxies are expelling jets of glowing matter. HOC identifies these jets as caused by galactic-strength MFRs.

Usually the expression "escape velocity" means a velocity that overcomes gravity enough to achieve a stable orbit or even escape entirely. In this chapter the term refers to velocities that enable magnetically expelled stars to recede beyond the closest-in hence strongest magnetic lines of force. I will now explain what resulted from three different categories of "escape velocity" MFRs.

1) *Moderate* 'escape velocity' MFRs expel stars past the control of a galaxy's innermost hence *magnetic-pole-linking* lines of force but leave them subject to the next nearest lines of force—those sloping out just above or just below an expelling galaxy's *equator*. Stars ejected from a galaxy's "north" magnetic pole by moderate escape velocity MFRs, arcing out and "down," initiate the formation of a lenticular disk by spreading out *just north* of an expelling galaxy's equator. Stars ejected by subsequent moderate escape velocity MFRs at the same galaxy's "south" magnetic pole, by arcing out and "*up*," fill in the *southern* face of the galaxy's lenticular disk, making it complete at the galactic equator.

2) *Medium* 'escape velocity' MFRs are those that expel stars further out where the bending effected by magnetic lines of force fails to keep expelled stars close enough to each other to form a single disk around the equator of a galaxy. Instead, these expelled stars become spiral arms by coalescing along divergent magnetic lines of force, each of which, to some degree, is mimicking the rotation of the galactic nucleus! Thus widening *gaps* open between stars adhering to disparate lines of force and the nucleus of the galaxy. The weakest medium-escape-velocity MFRs produce tightly wound spiral arms. Their stronger equivalents yield loosely wound spiral arms. Some of the latter have two or even three interspersed pairs of spiral arms attached to correspondingly smaller nuclei. Invisible magnetic lines of force in orbit control where spiral arm stars align.

Successive MFRs, puffing out stars first from one pole of a galaxy and then from the other, enable spiral arms to completely encircle galactic nuclei. That also explains why stars are not evenly spread in spiral arms but resemble puffs of smoke trailing a steam engine. It follows that galaxies sprouting extensive lenticular disks or spiral arms leave themselves with small nuclei. In other words, HOC credits MFRs as cosmology's hardest-working, most unfairly overlooked Cinderella.

Magnetic fields in globular clusters have been too weak to duplicate the above process on their own smaller scale. That is why we do not have globular clusters sporting lenticular disks or spiral arms.

3) Strong 'escape velocity' MFRs. To explain why some elliptical galaxies sprout *barred* spiral arms, I must comment further about:

Exogravity!

HOC employs new terms (axion, circon, volon, etc.) but avoids—in line with Ockham's Razor—positing utterly strange concepts like 'dark matter,' 'dark energy' or 'an inflationary epoch.' *One* cosmos forming on a spherical plane in pre-existing space is hardly as odd as almost *two billion* universes bursting from a mere point only to undergo immediate destruction, especially when no space-time existed for a burst to occur in.

Also, positing space as contracting initially and then expanding is not a *new* concept so much as a known concept working *bi-directionally*.

Ockham's Razor does allow, though, for new laws to be posited when existing laws simply do not suffice to explain a phenomenon. That is why Harmonic Origin Cosmology by necessity endorses *exogravity,* called *negative gravity* by recent authors—a concept tentatively proposed by Albert Einstein and reinvestigated recently by Mordehai Milgrom with help from Jacob Bekenstein and others. One 2006 article, for example, carries this subtitle: "*Mordehai Milgrom's new physics could overthrow Newton and Einstein—and tear up our whole picture of how the universe is put together.*"[1] In the article itself, Milgrom rejects Big Bang Cosmology's "dark matter":

> The orbital speed of stars circling a galaxy can be teased from an analysis of their combined light. … stars close to the galactic center should orbit faster than stars at the edge because all the mass concentrated at the center of the galaxy pulls most powerfully on the closest stars. The same thing happens in the solar system. Mars moves faster than Jupiter because the sun's gravity pulls harder on it….Orbital speeds…decrease with distance.[2]

Author Adam Frank subsequently describes a problem that has vexed astronomers since the 1970s:

> At a certain distance from the galactic center, the [orbital velocities of] stars in most every spiral galaxy simply do not fall; instead, at some point, they flatten. All the stars in the middle and outer parts of these galaxies orbit *with* the same speed, in seeming defiance of Newton's laws. Why don't the outer stars move more slowly than the inner ones?[3]

As Frank then explains, Big Bang cosmologists seek to resolve the above mystery by resorting again to "dark matter":

> Faced with flat rotation [speeds] that…flout Newton's laws, astronomers assumed the existence of a halo of dark matter around every spiral galaxy. Whatever the stuff was, it did not emit light, but it did exert a gravitational pull. The dark matter tugged on the stars [in outer parts of spiral arms], cranking up their speeds…[4]

The theorists Frank cites do not seem to realize what an incongruous notion they offer. If *spiral* galaxies wear "dark matter haloes," what keeps globular clusters from donning them? Plus—how did galaxies initially squeeze their way *in* through gravitationally powerful haloes of dark matter to occupy space inside them? And, if dark matter exists, what happened to its balancing *anti*-dark matter, or does dark matter also have to violate conservation of charge?

Frank then presents Milgrom's proposition that gravity—at great distances from a major center of mass—actually becomes a *repelling* force. It accelerates matter radially *away!* HOC agrees with Milgrom on this particular issue, but not for the same reasons.

As mentioned earlier, ionized matter is always encompassed in magnetic fields, which rotate like 'semi-solids' if the ionized matter that spawns them is rotating. Unlike gravity, magnetism's "Lorentz force" tends to flatten angular momentum evenly throughout a given rotating system. Thus galactic-strength magnetic fields surely boost the velocity of stars rotating at a distance from galactic centers. But that is not all.

HOC's solution to gravity problems

Probably every astronomy course worldwide credits gravity with infinite reach. "Every particle of matter in the universe attracts every other particle, however minimally," is the mantra. Even thinkers investigating 'negative gravity'—apparently including Milgrom—seem to credit their negative gravity with infinite reach. In Harmonic Origin Cosmology, both modes of gravity exist but are *finite*. Just as magnetism is a force operating on a macro scale with a finite reach, so also gravity functions on a macro scale with a finite reach. If gravity has an infinite reach, why not posit magnetism with the same? With that point settled, the way is open to recognize *exogravity* as an accessory finite force in the cosmos.

In HOC elliptical galaxies *et al.* are enclosed inside 'esograv fields' which in turn are enclosed by concentric 'exograv shields' (not dark matter) of equal volume, hence shorter radii. Exograv shields tend to protect individual stars and galaxies like cosmic 'bumpers,' but—like bumpers on vehicles—exograv shields are not invincible. They keep most stars and galaxies apart; but if approach angles and velocities are acute, two or more stars may connect and orbit within the same esograv space. Even entities as large as galaxies may puncture each other's exograv shields enough to collide and disrupt each other's primal structures.

During the Great Convergence near the cosmic center, angles of approach were oblique enough for exogravity to keep most globular clusters and galaxies from merging. Later, however, when outbound globular clusters met incoming galaxies head on, exogravity was helpless to prevent the captures described earlier. The same was true again later when still-inbound Tier D halo stars met out-rushing galaxies head on!

So, the reason the 'dark matter haloes' posited in astronomical papers emit no radiation is because they do not consist of matter at all. They are only that other kind of gravity. And exogravity shields, like esogravity fields, do not emit radiation.

Next, another cosmic mystery must be considered: why *some* elliptical galaxies sprouted oppositely-directed *barred* spiral 'arms.'

Why galaxy arms may spiral from ends of a bar

Strong **'escape velocity' MFRs**, HOC's third category, expel stars with such force that they do not bend around toward a galaxy's equator at all. Launched straight out bilaterally from both magnetic poles, stars expelled by third-category MFRs elude not only orbiting magnetic lines of force but even the inward radial draw of a galaxy's esograv space! Strong MFRs expel stars all the way out into a galaxy's exograv space, whereupon exogravity *accelerates* their departure even more than a galactic magnetic field's 'Lorentz force' can do.

Exogravity's added acceleration thus keeps expelled stars filling two *bar-like straight lines* all the way out from a galaxy's opposite poles to the perimeter of its exograv shield. Virtually no magnetic bending or rotational lag occurs. Once expelled stars have exited a galaxy's exograv space, acceleration ceases and some expelled stars lag from the ends of the bar.

Apparently third category MFRs occur once per galaxy. Ejections that powerful remove so much ionized mass that a galaxy's magnetic field loses all ability to expel anything more at "escape velocity." Apparently that is why we do not see '*double*-barred' or '*triple*-barred' spiral galaxies in space. Study Diagram 9 on page 171 and then search online for a photo of NGC 1300, a typical barred spiral galaxy.

What, then, determines whether elliptical galaxies remain elliptical or sprout lenticular disks, *tightly*-wound spiral arms, *loosely*-wound spiral arms or *barred* spiral arms? HOC posits the determining factor as a ratio between a given galaxy's *mass* vis-à-vis the degree of *ionization* pervading its mass. Four possibilities emerge:

1) Greater mass vis-à-vis relatively moderate ionization, by strengthening gravity and weakening magnetism, slows the rate at which stars migrate to a galaxy's magnetic poles. MFRs thus fail to expel stars at 'escape velocities.' A galaxy thus remains elliptical, at least much longer.

2) Moderate mass vis-à-vis relatively moderate ionization facilitates relatively weak 'escape velocity' MFRs. Magnetic bending keeps expelled stars hugging a diameter of the expelling galaxy, forming a lenticular disk.

3) Moderate mass vis-à-vis relatively greater ionization facilitates middle-strength magnetic field reversals. These leave a galaxy encircled by spiral arms ranging from tightly-wound to loosely wound.

4) Minimum mass vis-à-vis relatively greater ionization, by weakening gravity, reduces the distance from an elliptical galaxy's center of mass to the inner boundary of its exograv field. But greater ionization intensifies magnetism, thereby speeding the pole-ward flow of strongly ionized stars across vast distances and intensifying the power of the MFRs that eject them across a relatively short distance into exograv space. Dumping millions of stars into exogravity's outbound 'star train' changed less massive but highly ionized elliptical galaxies into *barred* spirals.

What determined which of the above "mass vis-à-vis ionization" ratios a particular galaxy gained? A given elliptical galaxy's initial position in Diagram 8's "Zone B" (page 159) was the deciding factor. Galaxies formed close to the inner surface of "Zone B" tend to be 'lean' on mass but 'fat' with ionization. These galaxies tend to become barred spirals. Galaxies formed in the densest central area of "Zone B" gain greater mass with less ionization, hence tend to remain elliptical, at least for longer periods. Galaxies formed in external areas of "Zone B"—even close to Diagram 8's "Zone C"—make up the remainder.

Diagram 9

How Mid-Velocity MFRs Add Spiral Arms to Some Galaxies

(Weak escape velocity MFRs add lenticular disks, not shown here).

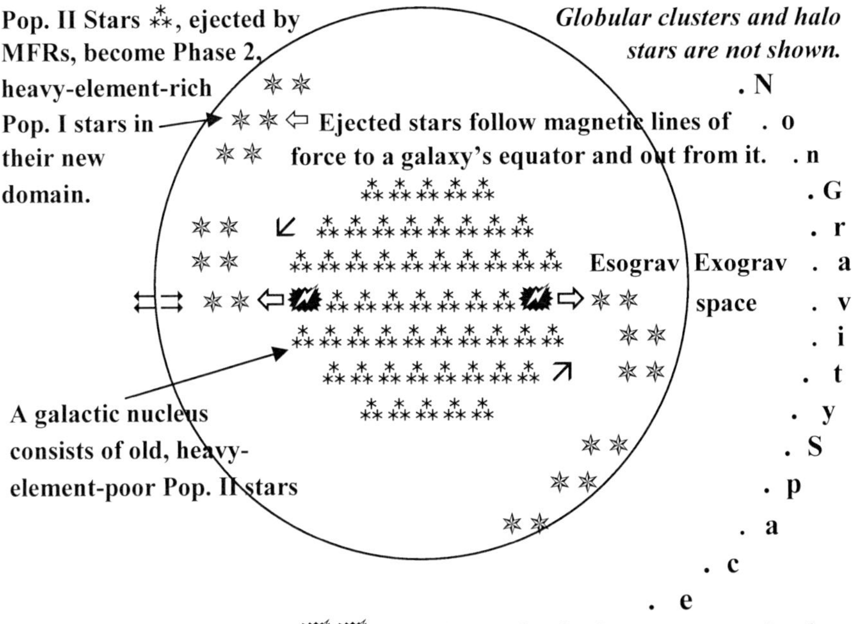
Pop. II Stars, ejected by MFRs, become Phase 2, heavy-element-rich Pop. I stars in their new domain.
Globular clusters and halo stars are not shown.
Ejected stars follow magnetic lines of force to a galaxy's equator and out from it.
Esograv
Exograv space
. N . o . n . G . r . a . v . i . t . y . S . p . a . c . e
A galactic nucleus consists of old, heavy-element-poor Pop. II stars

...but *powerful* MFRs add *barred* spirals to some galaxies

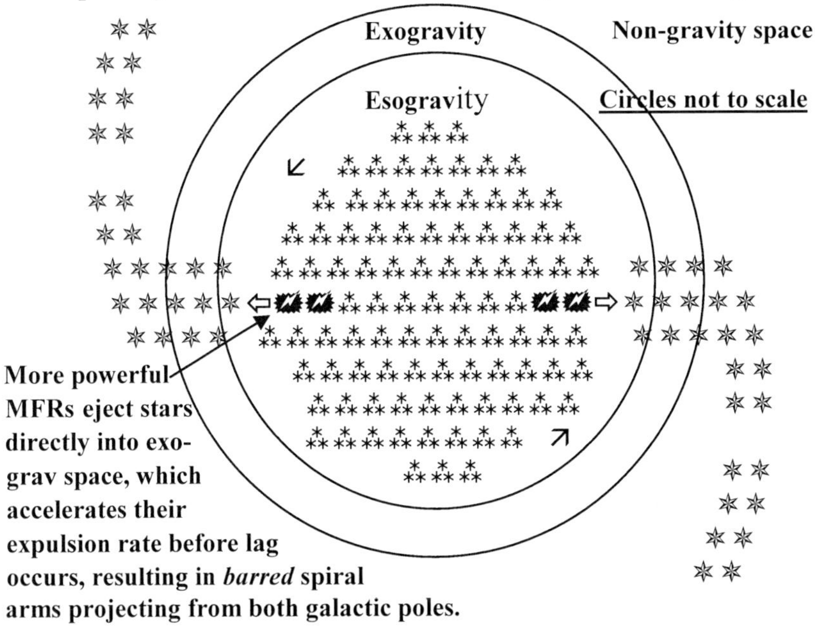
Exogravity
Non-gravity space
Esogravity
Circles not to scale
More powerful MFRs eject stars directly into exograv space, which accelerates their expulsion rate before lag occurs, resulting in *barred* spiral arms projecting from both galactic poles.

Why Population I stars predominate in galactic spiral arms

Clearly, the only stars available to add lenticular disks or spiral arms to galaxies were Population II stars; yet galactic disks and arms feature Population I stars. What changed expelled Population II stars into their Population I counterparts? HOC posits two change agents:

1. MFRs formed Population I stars by ramming two or more Population II stars together, thus doubling, tripling or quadrupling their masses.

In the chaos following MFR expulsions, stars closest to an expelling pole were suddenly thrust away from the pole while other stars were still accelerating toward it. Stars that fused together as a result of catastrophic collisions increased their mass enough or even more than enough to qualify as the first *Phase 2* Population I stars mentioned earlier. Stars with that much extra mass burn hotter and blaze bluer than before.

Before long (astronomically speaking), this new class of stellar giants—exploding as supernovas and novas—spewed their contents, including the first light-blocking heavy elements, throughout the lenticular disks and spiral arms surrounding galaxies that could no longer be called heavy-element-free ellipticals. Astronomers sometimes call the dark lines created by light-blocking heavy elements "dust lanes."

2) MFRs changed other Population II stars into the Population I kind merely by isolating them from the 'esograv links' that increase the longevity of Population II stars.

Even Population II stars that avoided catastrophic merging during expulsions were changed merely by virtue of their new environment. Virtually from the time of their gathering into elliptical communities in Tiers A, B and C of the ionized hydrogen bubble, Population II stars had enjoyed the benefit of 'esograv linkage.' Simply put, the surface layer of every Population II star was *relatively levitated* as the esogravity of proximate neighboring Population II stars tugged from all sides. That relative mutual levitation had reduced the esograv pressure bearing down on the core of individual Population II stars, thereby enabling them to burn their core hydrogen at a slower rate and thus survive much longer.

Violent magnetic field reversals, by disrupting that former closeness, left larger-than-average Population II stars with the full weight of their own masses bearing down on their cores. These stars, too, began to blaze as Population I stars. As subsequent generations of Population I stars coalesced amid the debris left by exploded predecessors, still greater quantities of heavy elements floated as "planetary nebulae" between spiral arm stars. The cosmos was ready at last, not only to continue producing generation after generation of Population I stars but also to birth those solid entities we know as planets, moons, comets and asteroids.

Chapter Eighteen
Gravity Field Reversals

How the cosmos solves its 'electron deprivation' problem

We saw that 90 percent of all electrons released by bursting neutrons on the plane of the matter bubble avoided capture by co-released but much slower moving protons. Bachelor electrons, escaping in all directions inside and outside the matter bubble, left almost all the hydrogen and helium that formed behind them in a state of extreme ionization, otherwise known as 'electron deprivation.'

Widespread electron deprivation was of course essential in the early cosmos. Without it, ionized hydrogen and helium and reversing magnetic fields would not have been there to shape stars, globular clusters and elliptical galaxies, let alone add spiral arms loaded with Population I stars to some of the latter. Stars would have had only *opaque* atomic hydrogen to try to shine through. Yes, electron deprivation was necessary and Valcon ordained a mode of creation that proffered it. However...

Planets designed to serve as settings where Valcon and his citizens minister to each other via all six Locedmedan laws must be free from the flux, snap and crackle of ionized matter. Edens require solid ground made of *atoms*, settings where flora may grow in beauty and abundance and appropriate fauna may teem. For such worlds to exist, sufficient quantities of electrons must unite at last with at least some of the protons that by Valcon's design failed to find them at the beginning.

Only as enough ions become atoms can gravity surpass magnetism as the primary force on the surface of any world. And gravity, to be sure, enables the first two Locedmedan laws—efficiency and predictability—to meet the needs of flora, fauna and citizens much more efficiently and predictably than does magnetism!

Recall again that—by the law of averages—for every 1000 neutrons that decayed on the IHB's original neutron bubble, 2.7 electrons took flight one way or another on each and every protractor degree. Recall also that 50 percent of the electrons departed from the neutron bubble's *inner* surface. Most of these were vectored to pass through or near the cosmic center with continuing motion toward stars and nebulae on the matter sphere's far side. Other electrons traversed the inner vastness of matter space on diagonal short-cuts. All began their journey on straight vectors at the same velocity, but the initial contraction of matter space followed by its later expansion soon altered their straight trajectories and relatively constant velocities.

HOC posits that a majority of matter-space-traversing electrons began meeting/overtaking galaxies *after* the latter had already rebounded away from the cosmic center and completed their capture of hosts of globular clusters and halo stars. That being so, it follows that halo stars, and globular clusters orbiting in the exteriors of galaxies, had 'first grabs' when the incoming electron 'wind' began arriving.

HOC thus predicts that halo stars and globular cluster stars have higher percentages of neutral hydrogen, at least in their surface gases, than do Population I stars in lenticular disks and the inner parts of galactic spiral arms. With halo stars and globular clusters intercepting so many incoming electrons, Population I stars closer to the nuclei of disked and spiral arm galaxies had to resort to their own way of netting electrons.

By exploding as novas and supernovas, Population I stars filled vast spaces with clouds of electron-hungry protons. These clouds of course became huge electron-bagging 'sails' in the lenticular disks and spiral arms of galaxies. It follows that the heavier elements common to such 'sails' snagged far more electrons from the incoming anion 'wind' than hydrogen and helium ions did! Heavy elements in the mix, becoming less and less ionized, began responding more to gravity than to magnetism. As the long era of electron deprivation gave way at last to increased atomization, it became possible finally for 'dry ground' to appear among 'the waters.' Another 'day' was dawning! But first let us ask what does cause Population I stars to explode as novas or supernovas.

Gravity field reversals (GFRs)

Gravity field reversals (GFRs), thankfully, are much rarer than magnetic field reversals; yet gravity field reversals fulfill key roles, one of which is preventing the phenomenon known as 'black holes' from becoming too prevalent in the cosmos!

Once formed, black holes are said to be totally 'self-absorbed,' so to speak, i.e., they become *utterly incommunicado with the rest of creation.* If that were so, black holes would be anti-unified field hence could not exist. In fact, just as magnetism outmuscles gravity elsewhere in the cosmos, magnetism even outmuscles gravity inside black holes. Gravity inside black holes may rein in photons of light, but rapidly recurring MFRs inside black holes keep expelling glowing streams of ionized matter straight out into space via a black hole's magnetic poles. Black holes thus remain 'communicative.'

Gravity always begins with its esograv version pulling in on the inside with its exograv corollary pushing out on the outside. This arrangement allows most stars to keep shining for eons. Massive stars, however, are able to endure only as long as the outflow of energy released at their cores keeps a star's exterior mass from clamping down on the core. When a star lacks enough core hydrogen to sustain its counter-balancing energy outflow, esogravity and exogravity simply switch places! Just as MFRs respond to severe magnetic pole imbalances, gravitational fields respond to critical core-versus-exterior imbalances in stars.

MFRs are instantaneous. Gravity, a weaker force, takes a bit longer to reverse an entire field. This allows intense pressures just enough time to transform the core of some massive stars into pulsars, neutron stars or, less often, into black holes. That is also when hydrogen, helium and other light elements fuse as middle-weight if not also as heavy elements. In time the exterior mass of a star, feather-light in the grip of a newly internalized exograv field, is borne far out into space as a nova if not as a supernova.

Most exploding stars simply expand like a balloon, but Harmonic Origin Cosmology posits exceptions to a balloon shape. If an exploding star's primary magnetic field reverses concurrent with a gravity-triggered explosion, ionized gas hurled away from the field's negative pole follows magnetic lines of force around toward the new negative pole, which also reverses, driving already en route ionized matter back again toward its starting pole. As a result, 'confused' ionized matter becomes concentrated in a band of gas midway between fickle magnetic poles. The result is a "ring nebula." To see "ring nebulae" surviving what began as ballooning clouds, look on the Internet for photos of the Helix Nebula (NGC 7293), the Eight-Burst Nebula (NGC 3132) and Ring Nebula (M57).

Conversely, if an exploding star's primary magnetic field happens *not* to reverse concurrent with the GFR, or if its reversal is delayed, the entire mass of ionized matter joins atomic matter in its outbound rush, resulting in a balloon rather than a ring. Online, search for the Spirograph Nebula (IC418) and Supernova Remnant 1006 as examples.

If a star's primary magnetic field reverses *apart from* a gravity field reversal, ionized matter is expelled first from one pole and then from another with a 180-degree spread. For examples, search the Internet for the Rotten Egg Nebula (OH231.8 + 4.2), the Boomerang Nebula (ESO 172-07) and the Twin Jet Nebula (M2-9) as examples.

The shapes attained by still other nebulae reveal overlapping sequences of GFRs and MFRs, some of which even repeat over time. Search online for the Cat's Eye Nebula (NGC 6543) and the Blinking Eye Nebula (NGC 6826) as examples. Planetary nebulae assume an astonishing variety of shapes when GFRs and MFRs play cosmic 'tag.'

Keep in mind that magnetic field reversals diminish and finally cease as more and more protons in planetary nebulae grab electrons from the steadily inflowing anion wind.

The main point is that GFRs, by eviscerating stars, spread ionized matter from stellar innards across vast regions of space like enormous sails, often reaching more than a light year across! Those 'sails' serve one main purpose: they reap electrons from the anion wind that has been coming across via the cosmic center since creation, searching for protons. That includes protons already incorporated into the nuclei of heavy elements—the substances needed to form planets!

How new stars, planets, moons and comets form in the debris expelled by supernovas and novas

Astronomers generally posit our solar system's planets, moons, asteroids and comets as coalescing from the same cloud of gas and star-dust that birthed our Sun. Harmonic Origin Cosmology posits a different source. Just as globular clusters and halo stars formed apart from galaxies and were added later, so planets, moons and comets coalesce from heavy elements in nova and supernova detritus far from the suns they eventually orbit. Like orphans seeking adoption by 'planetless stars,' proto-planets roam the galaxy. But what is it that launches them on their search?

Electron scarcity in stars assures that the heavy-element-rich clouds GFRs blast out into space must each include several thousand minor magnetic fields. Iron ions in the magnetically-charged detritus quickly congeal as iron spheres *at myriad negative poles* in the debris. As myriad magnetic poles hyper-saturate and reverse, they scatter iron spheres amid the surrounding debris. Barging through element-rich detritus, iron spheres utilize their own esogravity to accrete still other elements that—newly bombarded by free electrons—are being changed from ions to atoms. These other elements include copper, nickel, zinc, tin, silicon, carbon, oxygen, nitrogen, etc.

Do MFRs really eject star and planet-forming masses out of the detritus scattered by GFRs? Log on to any Internet 'gallery' of photos of nebulae and you will notice strikingly finger-like projections of gas and dust being ejected from a generally amorphous background of supernova debris. Subsequent to the omni-directional explosion that generated each cloud *amorphously*, something else is re-concentrating initially-dispersed matter and then ejecting it out of the debris at speeds exceeding the expansion of the debris cloud itself.

When very large MFR-spawned ejections of matter congeal as new stars, of course we see the new stars because they shine! HOC posits that for every large ejection that yields a new star, thousands of smaller ejections too small to be seen congeal as proto-planets, proto-moons and proto comets, all of which—though invisible to us—are being jettisoned into space to find eventual capture by other unexploded stars.

How Valcon assembles solar systems

MFR-expelled iron and rock spheres, layered with other accreted elements, exit the debris clouds that birthed them and hurtle deep into interstellar space. Eons later, captured by esograv fields surrounding other stars, they fall into orbit around their new hosts as rock planets and moons. Following on their heels, another kind of planet—gas giants—accreted at other negative magnetic poles and expelled by powerful MFRs, follow the iron spheres toward eventual capture by other stars. Still other magnetic fields gradually accrete and eventually eject planetoids made mainly of silica and water. These tend to be captured later as asteroids and comets.

Why planets, once captured, tend to orbit *equatorially* and in the same direction

One would expect planets arriving at different angles of approach from different directions to orbit the stars that capture them on diverse planes and in different directions. Yet a majority of planets and planetoids in our solar system orbit the Sun all in the same direction. They also orbit close to our solar system's ecliptic—a plane approximately even with the Sun's equator. Their orbital direction also happens to correspond to the direction in which the Sun itself rotates on its axis. Why?

Obviously the Lorentz force that nudges planets along as the Sun's magnetic field rotates with the Sun is part of the answer. Indeed, a planet orbiting the Sun *against* the Sun's Lorentz force soon loses the momentum it needs to maintain itself in orbit. Any such planet then falls into the Sun! This alone may explain why the solar system has no planets orbiting opposite to the direction of the Sun's rotation.

Possibly the earlier described circonic principle that makes points of maximum and minimum density change orbit *equatorially* in subatomic particles and around very large-scale eso- and exovolons in the cosmos may also be influencing planets to orbit stars ecliptically.

Consider: planets fated to orbit a star high above the ecliptic, i.e., too close to a star's magnetic poles, will be much more influenced by the star's magnetic field than by its gravity. The higher the amount of ionized matter in the planet's mass, the more its orbit will be skewed by the draw of a star's magnetic field. Inevitably, all such planets spiral down into a star's magnetic pole and vaporize. The fact that no planets orbit high above the Sun's ecliptic *now* does not mean that none ever did.

Proto-planetary ionized elements dispersed in nova/supernova debris *must* find enough electrons to change a majority of their ions to atoms before gravity coalesces them as planets and magnetic field reversals eject the resulting planets across interstellar space toward receptive stars. Highly ionized planets, if any exist, fall prey to a capturing star's magnetic field and perish. Even if they could survive, they would not be habitable.

Globular clusters and halo stars easily avoid falling into equatorial orbits around galaxies simply because for them magnetism prevails.

Why rocky planets orbit close, gas giants far out

The exograv shield around a capturing star *slows* the approach of all categories of planets; but denser, faster-moving heavy metal spheres barge in anyway and find orbits as 'terrestrial' planets *closer* to a capturing star. Terrestrial planets are the main worlds prepared as habitats for citizens of the unified field. Did not Valcon, speaking as the Son, declare, "In my Father's 'house' are many 'rooms'" (John 14:2)? [inside quotes added].

Gas giants, slowed on arrival by greater mutual exograv resistance, settle for distant orbits. Each captured planet, according to its mass, adds its own 'push' to the exograv shield of a capturing star. Large solar systems are thus less likely to keep adding new members. Late arrivals to a solar system may bounce away due to ejection by a solar system's exograv shields which HOC posits lie just outside a solar system's Oort Cloud. Entities that make it through an Oort Cloud eventually join a solar system's closer-in "Kuiper Belt," an outer plane from which comets set out on round trips to the inner sanctum of terrestrial planets and back.[1]

Astronomical estimates that the Sun's Oort Cloud extends 1.5 light years out from the Sun link with the assumption that gravity everywhere has an infinite reach.[2] HOC posits the Sun's esograv field as extending approximately one light year from the Sun.

Comets, pulled gradually Sunward from the "K-belt," tend to bring in long watery tails among the generally dry terrestrial planets. Some terrestrial orbs, stealing liquid 'shirts' from the 'backs' of passing comets, gradually become, shall we say, 'moistened.' Earth has already been 'moistened' by a passing comet, as I posit later. Our neighbor Mars has yet to steal a cometary 'shirt' of significant size.

At last, myriad planets suitable for citizens and denizens are prepared across the cosmos. Valcon has provided for the implementation of all six laws of his seventh harmony in the lives of citizens!

What happened to all that antimatter?

Harmonic Origin Cosmology posits that the early attenuation of the rapidly expanding antimatter sphere prevented coalescences of large bodies of antimatter. Indeed, magnetism would have formed globules of ionized anti-hydrogen and unleashed MFRs to hurl them about, but in vain. Gravity was too weak to form anti-stars and arrange them into globular clusters and galaxies when antimatter was so thinly attenuated.

It is possible, however, that antimatter did assemble near the poles of the cosmic axions and may even be co-annihilating with matter there. If so, the result would be extremely bright radiation coming from extremely tiny and very distant sources. Could such be the cause of high-energy gamma rays?

Apart from such encounters, Harmonic Origin Cosmology posits that a majority of the antimatter continues dispersing as a dark, attenuated, starless sphere of anti-plasma compassing the matter cosmos on all sides.

What causes galactic *walls* and *voids*?

This final part of Harmonic Origin Cosmology, introduced on page 138 and mentioned again as #11 in a summary on page 161, offers the most logical explanation for structures as vast as galactic clusters arranged as 'walls' separated by vast, empty, intervening 'voids.' Astronomers, knowing that gravity alone could not yield so great a result, resort again to 'dark matter.' Still, the question remains—why would dark matter construct 'walls' in some areas of space and leave 'voids' in others?

Harmonic Origin Cosmology finds a cause equal to the effect in the dynamics of space itself. To fulfill the unified field's requirement for the *circumference* aspect of a sphere to be manifest in the macro cosmos, Valcon contracted a region of space to serve as an esocircon—a cosmic 'dimple,' if you will—on one side of the ionized hydrogen bubble at its equator. One hundred eighty degrees and billions of light years away, Valcon expanded an inversely equal 'bulge' to serve as an exocircon on the opposite side of matter space.

Strange as it may seem, the 'dimple' and the 'bulge'—each one tens of billions of cubic light years—fulfilled the circonic principle by chasing each other at the speed of light around a circumference of matter space. As matter space's esovolon contracted and its exovolon expanded, the cosmic circons adjusted with it. The more matter space contracted, the quicker the two circons completed each 360-degree circuit. The more matter space expanded, the longer each circuit took.

By the time the ionized hydrogen bubble's four distinct tiers—A, B, C and D—had formed, Valcon channeled his two circonic roilers along a circumference on the boundary between Tiers B and C. That is why many standard galaxies and their dwarf cousins were affected by the passage of the roilers whereas globular clusters and halo stars were unaffected.

Wherever the contracted circon traversed, galaxies were drawn together as clusters. In some cases, galaxies that would not have collided ended up colliding. Galactic clusters brushed aside in the wake of the expanded circon became 'walls.' Space *emptied* by its passage became what astronomers today call 'hallways' extending across the cosmos.

Besides pulling some galaxies closer and pushing others apart, the two cosmic roilers had a third effect as well: they *flipped* some galaxies on edge and *tilted* others to a greater range of plane angles than existed previously. A few galaxies, tilted while undergoing a second or third MFR, ended up with spiral arms on two separate planes!

Recapping the disadvantages of BBC vs. HOC

BBC's disadvantage: Big Bang Cosmology creates two billion universes of *intermixed* matter and antimatter at one point, only to lose 99.9999999 percent of all that mass to immediate matter/antimatter annihilation. Our "matter universe" survived only by a violation of conservation of charge, delicately termed 'charge parity violation.'

HOC's Advantage: Harmonic Origin Cosmology births this one universe with effective separation of equal mass matter and antimatter from the inside and outside of a vast spherical plane in preexisting extent—all with no 'charge parity violation.'

BBC's Disadvantage: Big Bang Cosmology violates the linear nature of space by positing microwave background radiation—despite its omni-directional nature—as emitted from one point billions of years ago. Linear space does not allow radiation emitted from one distant point to be approaching us from every possible direction billions of years later.

HOC's Advantage: In Harmonic Origin Cosmology, microwave background radiation comes primarily from neutrinos annihilating with antineutrinos close to the spherical plane where the cosmos began. Because that source encompasses everything in our part of the cosmos, the omni-directional nature of cosmic microwave background is a given and is consistent with the linear nature of space.

BBC's Disadvantage: Big Bang Cosmology spawns clouds of *atomic* hydrogen which, because it is opaque, required the first stars to be capable of banishing electrons not only from themselves but from the remainder of the opaque hydrogen. Those first stars, it is claimed, enabled subsequent generations of stars to consist mainly of transparent hydrogen, like stars today. BBC thus overlooks a major problem: *stars made of opaque hydrogen, especially huge ones, cannot shine! They can only explode!* BBC also fails to explain where all those banished electrons went! And what kept them away from all that ionized hydrogen?

HOC's Advantage: In Harmonic Origin Cosmology some 90 percent of the hydrogen that formed on a plane called the orisphere is clear, *ionized* hydrogen. There is no need to posit a prior generation of huge UV-emitting stars made of a kind of hydrogen that severely *resists* the flow of energy from a star's interior to its surface.

BBC's Disadvantage: Initially, Big Bang Cosmology conjures Alan Guth's hyper-inflationary epoch—with space expanding at 10^{45} times the speed of light—to *neutralize* too-strong gravity, lest too-strong gravity collapse everything produced by the Big Bang into one enormous black hole. Later, though, BBC invents an opposite contrivance—'dark matter'—as a steroid that strengthens gravity enough to coalesce stars. Major questions are, "What about *anti*-dark matter?" and "If dark matter's gravity is that strong, why is the cosmos still expanding?"

HOC's Advantage: In Harmonic Origin Cosmology, space expands or contracts at sub-light speeds only. Gravity, furthermore, is never too strong; and when it is weak, magnetic fields, MFRs and the initial contraction of the entire matter domain give it all the help its needs to congeal stars out of clouds of ionized hydrogen. Speculative contrivances such as hyper-inflation and dark matter are not needed.

BBC's Disadvantage: Big Bang Cosmologists press Alan Guth's hyper-inflationary epoch into service to resolve a second discomfiting question: what kept that Big Bang, with its enormous heat and pressure, from producing heavy elements billions of years before supernovas began to produce them? Their answer: that incredibly rapid hyper-inflation permitted "instant cooling," ergo the laws of nucleo-synthesis were suspended until the Big Bang was attenuated.

HOC's Advantage: Harmonic Origin Cosmology needs no such artifice but waits for novas and supernovas to do what novas and supernovas do.

BBC's Disadvantage: Big Bang Cosmology fails to explain why each globular cluster and halo star orbits around a galactic nucleus with its own unique angular momentum, whereas everything else in a galaxy shares angular momentum in common.

HOC's Advantage: In Harmonic Origin Cosmology globular clusters and halo stars—formed apart from galaxies—were caught in their embrace when space stopped contracting and began expanding, causing the contents of different 'tiers' in the matter domain to collide

So much for the way the Seven Harmonies call us to understand theology, physics and cosmology. We have yet to explore a more reasoned approach to one aspect of geology and another aspect of history.

Chapter Nineteen
Where Did All the Water Go?

Big Bang Cosmology is one aspect of science that needed correcting, but I have a bone to pick with geologists also. Geologists reject accounts in Genesis, not to mention hundreds if not thousands of traditions worldwide that a cataclysmic deluge occurred during mankind's tenure on Earth. "If at one time a flood covered everything," geologists object, "where did all the water go? That much water would still be covering the entire planet."

Evidence refuting that objection beckons from any globe depicting the Earth, yet remains strangely hidden from trained minds.

Years ago, talking with a professor holding a Ph.D. in geology, I said, "I claim that the earth has only *two* truly major mountain ranges. Agree or disagree?" The geologist disagreed, saying, "The 'ring of fire' surrounding the Pacific Ocean can be considered as one major mountain range for sure, but where do you find a second range on a par with it?"

The 'ring of fire' encompassing the Pacific

He was right about the 'ring of fire' being the first range I had in mind. It is so named because it encompasses the Pacific and features a majority of the world's volcanoes. It includes the Aleutians, the ranges of Alaska, the Rockies, Cascades and the Sierra Nevada, the ranges and volcanoes of Mexico and Central America, the Andes, the Ellsworth and Trans-Antarctic Ranges, the mountains of New Zealand, Vanuatu, New Guinea, the Philippines, Taiwan, Japan, the Kurile Islands and Kamchatka.

To my friend's surprise, I promptly proved my claim that a second major mountain range ranks with the 'ring of fire.' He watched as I traced it on a globe. His next comment was, "Why haven't I heard anyone make this obvious claim before now?" The range I had traced consisted of:

The Pyrenees, Alps, Carpathians, Caucasus, Pamirs, Elburz, Hindu Kush, Karakoram, Himalayas and the Tibetan Plateau

Our conversation had to end. We went our separate ways. Consider now these further insights I would gladly have discussed with my acquaintance had time permitted.

The 'ring of fire' is approximately circular. Note that the second major mountain range traces a remarkably *straight* 6,000-mile-long line from the Pyrenees to the Himalayas. Why does this straight line range, with few exceptions, keep rising to ever higher elevations from an ever widening base the closer it comes to the rim of the *circular* mountain range? Why does it not maintain an average of elevations and a more or less constant base width from west to east?

Something even *stranger* about these two truly major mountain ranges *begs* to be noticed: something geologists ignore to the detriment of their profession. I refer to the potent fact that Earth's straight line mountain range *points toward the approximate center* of its circular mountain range—an orientation one can hardly dismiss as coincidental.

Spin the globe and you will see that the earth's other oceans—the Atlantic, the Indian and the Arctic—are *not* each encompassed by 'a ring of fire.' *Why is the Pacific the only ocean encircled by a 'ring of fire'?* Observe further that the Pacific Ocean *is far larger than the combined surface area of all the other oceans.* Why is the only ocean surrounded by a 'ring of fire' so much larger than the others?

Given that the Pacific is so much larger than Earth's other oceans combined (it covers approximately 50 percent of our planet's surface), should it not perhaps be *shallower* on average than the other oceans? Not at all! The Pacific Ocean, in spite of its enormously greater area, averages approximately *one mile deeper* than Earth's other oceans. Now we come to a more complex question: *Why is the one ocean that is so much larger and deeper the only ocean surrounded by a ring of fire and also the only ocean that has a straight-line mountain range pointing like a 6,000-mile-long arrow toward its center?*

'Catching the drift' of continental drift

Studies of 'continental drift' reveal that North and South America broke away from Europe and Africa and drifted *west* toward the center of the Pacific, Earth's deepest, biggest ocean. Antarctica—separating from

South Africa—drifted *south,* also heading toward the center of Earth's deepest, biggest ocean by a southerly 'great circle route.'

Australia and India, separating from east Africa and southern Arabia respectively, drifted *east* toward the center of the deepest, biggest ocean. New Zealand broke off ahead of Australia; but islands of the Indonesian archipelago trailed behind, like bubbles in a wake on one side of a ship at sea. En route, India separated from Australia and drifted northeastward instead, as if somehow suctioned off its easterly course by the uplifting of the earth's loftiest plateau, Tibet. Africa, Europe and Asia, conversely, show no sign of drifting—with one exception:

The entire eastern fringe of Africa was about to join India and Australia in their 'great eastward breakaway.' But somehow, whatever 'engine' powered that extremely strong *suction* away from the center of Africa toward the center of the Pacific Ocean 'ran out of fuel,' leaving a 4,600-mile-long fissure—'The Great Rift Valley'—stretching from the Sea of Galilee almost to Cape Town, South Africa. A *secondary* eastward breakaway from Africa was averted.

Is it a mere coincidence that the longest fissure on Earth's land surface—the Great Rift Valley—*lies squarely on the opposite side of the earth from the center of its deepest and largest ocean, the Pacific?*

Even more complex and still more intriguing is this question: *Why is continental drift oriented toward the center of the only ocean that is deepest, biggest, surrounded by a ring of fire and uniquely pointed at by a 6,000-mile-long straight-line mountain range?*

What geologists currently theorize

Geologists explain continental drift as caused by 'convection currents' (W). Hotter-than-average molten rock in Earth's mantle, they aver, convects upward to the surface amid cooler-than-average lava and then spreads bilaterally outward, only to be sucked down again as it approaches a 'plate' on which a continent rides. As it is being sucked down, however, it keeps giving the adjacent continental plate a nudge; hence continental drift. These mid-ocean bilateral out-spreadings of upwelled lava, geologists claim, are all it takes to force continents further and further apart over millions of years.

Convection currents of molten material do indeed well up under several of Earth's oceans, *but do they cause so major a phenomenon as continental drift? Could convection currents be mere after-effects of something else that is the real cause of continental drift?* Surely convection currents—were they really *causing* continental drift—would tend to balance each other globally, keeping all oceans approximately the same size. Alas, convection current theory fails to explain why the Pacific is so much larger and deeper than other oceans. Nor does it explain why only the Pacific is encompassed by a 'ring of fire,' let alone why only the center of the Pacific is 'targeted,' so to speak, by a 6,000-mile-long, arrow-like, straight-line mountain range that rises higher and spreads wider as it nears the Pacific.

Nor does convection theory explain why continental drift is oriented—except for India's northeasterly movement—*away from Africa* toward the center of the Pacific.

To illustrate: the fact that hurricanes are often accompanied by tornadoes does not warrant crediting tornadoes as causing hurricanes. Rather, hurricanes and their attending tornadoes are both *by-products* of a much greater 'engine.' What, then, might be 'the grander engine' causing *both* continental drift *and* mid-ocean convection currents?

Positing a different cause of continental drift

Envision an unusually massive comet—Comet X—nearing Earth on its trajectory toward the sun. At the time of Comet X's approach, Earth had hills but no high ranges. There were no oceans, but water could be seen almost everywhere in algae-rich lakes, ponds and marshes. Many lakes were so rich with algae—incipient oil—that creatures somewhat larger than water spiders could walk on them. Deeper lakes owed their depth to meteorite impacts in earlier ages.

Imagine Earth's axis, prior to Comet X's close encounter, as barely tilted relative to the Sun, rendering our planet virtually season-less in that era long ago. Its verdant forests grew even in polar latitudes.

Most of Earth's moisture, moreover, remained absorbed in its porous soil. Water reservoired between the surface and an underlying impervious layer provided a reliable year-round 'water table' for enormous varieties and quantities of flora and fauna, hence there were no deserts. Vegetation, including massive forests, needed only to put down roots a short distance to find adequate water, rain or no rain. Precipitation—falling mainly on or near Earth's polar caps—soaked continuously *under-soil* from both poles toward the equator, where evaporation contributed to recycling water pole-ward.

Recall the description from Genesis 2:5-6: "...the LORD God had not sent rain on the earth...but streams came up from the earth and watered the whole surface of the ground."

Without cycles of seasons, people did not reckon "years" according to Gregorian time. Whatever basis they chose for their calendars, one thing is evident from Genesis chapter 5: either the ancients reached puberty very early or else they were indeed extremely long-lived. Even after the Earth was tilted by Comet X—bringing on seasons, a new phenomenon—the ancient way of counting years must have continued for a time; hence Genesis 9:28 records, "After the flood, Noah lived 350 years...."

Comet X's gravity, deft and sharp as a surgeon's scalpel, was about to do major surgery on an Edenic world. Closing to critical range, Comet X's gravity uplifted—in a matter of minutes—that 6,000-mile-long straight-line mountain range. After the Pyrenees, the Alps, Carpathians, Caucasus, Hindu Kush, Karakoram, Himalayas and the Tibetan plateau stood up to attention! The closer Comet X arced, hurtling eastward, the higher and broader were the ranges its gravity raised.

Like the Earth, Comet X also rotated on its axis. Like many lesser comets and asteroids, Comet X was not uniformly spherical; hence its gravitational effect on the nearest side of the Earth varied from relatively weak when its smaller aspect presented to extremely strong when its massive side was nearest. This factor determined how severely it disrupted the nearest side of the earth at intervals during its fly-by.

At its nearest, over what is now the Pacific side of Earth, Comet X's gravity was strong enough to do more than merely *uplift* part of Earth's mantle. The 'surgeon's scalpel' became more like a cosmic bulldozer, shearing ever deeper. After a few moments of glancing impact, Comet X and its gravity dislodged and siphoned away not only half the earth's crust but even a virtual tithe of the earth's underlying mantle—some of which fell back on Earth's opposite side as Earth rotated! The remaining detritus merged with Comet X or scattered, cooling and hardening as asteroids.

By then, Comet X had tilted Earth's axis to its present angle.

With perhaps a twentieth of Earth's mass suctioned away into space, an entire side of a once Edenic planet became a 13,000-mile-wide 'Great Red Face' (GRF) of molten lava. At its deepest, the GRF may have dipped as much as 1,000 miles below the normal plane of Earth's surface.

All around the 24,000-mile-long perimeter of that vast expanse of exposed lava, a single towering wall of rock marked the zone where Comet X's gravity was strong enough to uplift but not quite strong enough to tear mass away into space. It formed a virtually continuous serrated *upraised edge.* That Great Upraised Wall (GUW)—elevated probably from three to four miles above the average elevation of the still-intact side of Earth—formed a 24,000-mile-long rim for an enormous *lava tub.*

In fact, it was about to serve as a tub-rim separating lava on one side from water on the other. Comet X was dragging an enormous tail. That tail, several million miles long, contained perhaps as much as 160 million cubic miles of water plus enormous quantities of dust and rock. Also, deep in the tail's densest part—shielded from rays of the sun—quantities of liquid nitrogen and dry ice remained still as frozen as when Comet X's orbit took it far beyond even Pluto.

Comet X hurtled onward, its trajectory skewed, of course, by its close encounter with Earth's gravity. Like a marauder in the night, Comet X had stolen half the earth's crust plus a significant part of Earth's underlying mantle of liquid rock. But Earth would not be without reparation. Earth retaliated by severing the gravitational connection between Comet X and its tail. Standing squarely between comet and tail, Earth's gravity began siphoning *down* thousands, then millions and eventually tens of millions of incoming *cubic miles* of water mixed with quantities of dust, rock, liquid nitrogen and dry ice.

For several days, water deluging Earth's undisrupted side began collecting to greater and greater depths behind the Great Upraised Wall, which now began to resemble a four-miles-high 'bathtub wall' behind which water could collect on the earth's still intact side. As for the earth's other side, water falling there—hitting several million square miles of molten lava—boiled away again as clouds of steam. Billowing around to Earth's intact side, the steam cooled and condensed, lengthening the duration of rainfall on that side of Earth out to the "forty days and forty nights" specified in Genesis 7:11.

In a matter of days, water contained by that miles-high upraised wall covered everything on the still-intact side of the earth—everything, that is, except the highest peaks of the straight-line mountain range and the Great Upraised Wall. Meanwhile, three other phenomena occurred:

1. Massive slurries of wet soil flowed down from steep slopes of the Great Upraised Wall and the straight line range.

The same depth of rich, peaty soil that had sustained pre-catastrophe forests was also water-saturated, as explained earlier. Accordingly, that soil, wherever it was uplifted like a wet rug coating the cool side of the Great Upraised Wall and both sides of the straight line range, slumped down in massive slurries that later solidified as foothills below the Great Upraised Wall and the straight-line range. This happened even as intense rainfall was eroding everything erodable.

The porous soil that covered pre-catastrophe Earth had served as one enormous, level, planet-sized reservoir of absorbed subsurface water. That same soil, left uplifted and mounded in the shape of slurried foothills, could no longer contain its enormous reservoir. Sub-soil water draining from high areas gushed out in low areas just as Genesis 7:11 declares: "...all the springs of the great deep burst forth and the floodgates of the heavens were opened."

Layers of vegetation, seared to charcoal by intense heat roiling over from the Great Red Face's vast lava beds and compressed under flows of slurry, over time formed beds of coal. Equally hot seas, lakes and ponds, thick with algae, could not flow fast enough to stay atop spreading slurries. Deeply buried, compressed and hot, they became oil.

2. Mammoths in Siberia froze to the core in liquid nitrogen before decomposition could begin.

In what is now northern Siberia, something happened ages ago that froze thousands of mammoths to the very core of their huge beings so quickly that natural decomposition did not even begin. Reportedly their flesh can still be thawed, cooked and eaten! Only something much colder than ice could freeze animals that large fast enough to prevent the onset of decay. Scientists are at a loss to explain this mystery.

My Comet X scenario offers the following explanation. Indeed, ice alone could not freeze animals as large as mammoths fast enough to prevent the onset of decomposition. Only dry ice or something equivalent to liquid nitrogen could have been cold enough for the task. Rocky emissaries like meteors do not convey liquid nitrogen, *et al.*; but the shaded interior of a large comet's tail could easily bring to Earth elements as cold as one might find out beyond Pluto in the Kuiper Belt.

As sun-warmed outer layers of Comet X's tail were precipitating the Flood, liquid nitrogen, still insulated deep in the core of the tail, cascaded down mainly on northern Siberia. Mammoths breathed in and swallowed material so cold that ice felt hot by comparison. They froze so quickly that their flesh, despite their size, has been preserved.

Later the super-cooled gases that froze them initially evaporated away, leaving ice alone as long-term preserver.

Apart from the super-cooling effect of in-falling liquid nitrogen and dry ice, the vast expanse of molten lava on Earth's disrupted side would have super-heated Earth's atmosphere, making air unbreathable even on the intact side.

3. A misshapen *planet flexed* to become a sphere again.

Like water seeking its lowest level, liquid lava contiguous to that 13,000-mile-wide 1,000-mile-deep-at-the-center 'wound' on earth's 'dis-mantled' side began flowing center-ward from all sides of 'the great planetary wound.' With Comet X's gravitational interference ended, Earth's own gravitational field resolved to restore Earth to be, as close as possible, a spherical orb once again.

Quantities of lava flowing from under Earth's undisrupted side were speeded on their way by a second factor. As tens of millions of cubic miles of water raining in from Comet X's tail added mass over Earth's still intact crust, the weight of so much water pressing down on Earth's undisrupted side helped speed the flow of lava gushing out in all directions from under the Great Upraised Wall.

Inevitably, the pressure of water bearing down from above and the fierce tug of lava flowing beneath began fracturing the earth's undisrupted side into continent-size chunks. The result was continental drift, a new phenomenon! Just as inevitably, widening gaps between what were now drifting 'continental plates' ripped open gaps in the Great Upraised Wall. Massive amounts of water initially contained behind the Great Upraised Wall began torrenting out across the Great Red Face, speeding the cooling and firming of its molten surface.

Within hours, continents—unmooring from what would remain as Africa, Europe and Asia—floated away like ships sailing a red hot sea. Accelerating gradually to several kilometers per hour, the continents rocked and tilted on swirls and waves in the underlying mantle. Water still contained by the Great Upraised Wall swashed back and forth across thousands of miles of crust, stacking layers of silt to greater depths and burying enormous forests and seas gelled with algae at depths that would in time transform them into even more beds of coal and oil respectively.

Water gelled with algae could not float up through layers of soil and sand burying it to ever greater depths. When water finally escaped, algae remained to form oil. Even as he destroyed the earth that was, Valcon was making provision for a technologically advanced civilization to arise.

As continents separated from continents and large islands from continents, each huge 'plate' followed its own 'great circle route' toward the deepest part of the Great Red Face. With the continuity of that 25,000-mile-long Great Upraised Wall fracturing and shearing in thousands of places, miles-high falls of comet-tail water cascaded with fracture-widening force unto the Great Red Face's vast expanse of molten lava.

This steady release of Earth's initially well-contained flood *radically speeded the cooling* of the still red-hot depression Comet X had left in Earth's mantle. Portions of the upraised edge eroded away under the force of powerful cascades. Sections that stayed intact remain today as pieces of Earth's 'great ring of fire' around the Pacific Ocean.

As flowing lava 'fleshed out' Earth's great 'wound,' continental drift slowed eventually to inches per year. Even so, due to the still remaining indent of the Pacific Ocean's floor, our earth is still not the fully spherical orb it once was and still wants to be. Ergo earthquakes and tsunamis still endanger and volcanoes still erupt.

Water in excess of what was needed to fill the Pacific Ocean, flowing back behind continents drifting Pacific-ward, filled Earth's smaller oceans. With more than half of Earth's surface covered by ocean, increased evaporation led to rain as we know it, the new primary source of water on land. Tornadoes and hurricanes became another previously unknown effect.

With the original planet-wide under-soil water table disrupted and rain favoring some latitudes more than others, deserts formed.

Convection currents still welling up mid-ocean form lengthy undersea ranges resembling—as geologists are fond of noting—the seams of a baseball. Mid-ocean convection is all that remains of what was once a planet-reshaping, Pacific-ward flow affecting Earth's entire mantle.

Continental drift was once much more rapid

When lava stops flowing and begins to cool, exposure to wind and rain causes its upper surface to cool and harden first. Lower sections of a lava flow, insulated from wind and rain, may take weeks to harden all the way down as solid rock. Why is this important? It is important because iron atoms in a lava flow constantly orient themselves in relation to the earth's magnetic poles. When a lava flow becomes stationary, absence of turbulence allows every iron atom in the lava to agree as to the direction of the earth's magnetic poles. Once lava hardens, iron atoms within it can no longer revise their orientation. If Earth's magnetic poles were to shift *after* a lava flow solidified, iron atoms in already hardened lava would continue pointing only to where the poles *were*, not to where they would then be.

Curiously, cores extracted from solid lava in eastern Oregon show the orientation of iron atoms that cooled in the upper part of a stationary flow offset from the lower part of the flow by as much as 3 to 6 degrees per day during the cooling period. (W)

Since Earth's magnetic poles do not shift so radically in that brief a time, and since the lava itself had stopped moving, inferably North America—the continent *on which the lava was located*—must have been moving at several kilometers per hour relative to the earth's magnetic poles. Only thus could the orientation of iron atoms at upper and lower levels of a single lava flow be offset so drastically. Geologists simply refuse to believe that something as massive as an entire continent could ever have drifted at several kilometers an hour, so they simply dispute or ignore the findings from Eastern Oregon.

I posit that similar tests in same-period South American lava flows will show approximately the same results in that North and South America were both flowing from east to west. Similar tests in same-period Australian and New Zealand lava flows will show similar results favoring the opposite direction, in that Australia and New Zealand were moving from west to east Similar tests in same-period lava flows in India will fail to show significant results because India was moving northeast, i.e., more or less straight toward Earth's magnetic pole, as my next point explains.

Evidence that India was *suctioned,* not 'convected,' toward Tibet

Lava and ash that volcanoes spew from under Earth's crust, geologists find, cover only a small percent of the earth's land surface. There is one major exception: Tibet, a plateau several times larger than Texas yet averaging more than 10,000 feet above sea level. Geologists find that a large percentage of the surface of the Tibetan plateau is sub-crustal material disgorged from under the earth's crust! Conceivably, it could take a thousand active volcanoes a thousand years to produce such an anomaly, but Tibet has no active volcanoes.

Still, geologists rely again on convection theory to explain the phenomenal uplift of the vast Tibetan plateau. (W) Geologists generally believe that the Indian sub-continent, convected forcefully against southern Asia by underlying currents in Earth's mantle, is the 'engine' forcing both the Himalayas and the Tibetan plateau up to such phenomenal heights. How this mechanism could cause a large majority of the Tibetan plateau to be covered with material from the underlying mantle of the earth is not explained.

The Comet X hypothesis offered here posits instead that the passing comet's gravitational draw uplifted the Tibetan plateau *almost* enough to snatch it away into space but then lost its grip and 'dropped' it back to Earth. The resulting impact caused sub-crustal material to gush up onto the surface through thousands of resulting fissures. Because the uplifted mass, once dropped, did not return to its original density—let alone subside to its original low elevation—a strong suction in the underlying mantle drew mass in *laterally* to fill the resulting subterranean reduction in density.

That strong *suction*—not convection in the mantle—is what pulled India toward the already uplifted Tibetan plateau. Apart from this factor, India would have continued eastward beside Australia. However, India's ongoing collision with Tibet still adds elevation to the Himalayas.

As for Comet X, did Earth's gravity alter the comet's course enough to cause it to plunge into the Sun, as some comets do, or does it still orbit? Perhaps we will never know.

Like cosmology earlier, geology is now revised

I submit that the evidence marshaled here logically points to a flood that *did* indeed cover almost the entire land area represented now by Earth's continents and major islands. Atolls and volcanic islands—recent phenomena—are exceptions. The question "Where did all that water go?" is amply answered. All of it is still here with us. Great Flood traditions in hundreds of aboriginal cultures worldwide are also vindicated, at least in principle. The first time I told the Genesis flood account to my aboriginal friends, New Guinea's Sawi people, they could hardly wait for me to finish so they could give me their version, which even included details about releasing birds to see if they returned. Clearly, for mankind to survive so great a catastrophe, special provision must have been arranged.

Now you also perceive the power of Locedmeda's sixth principle, Recompense. Via the flood and its accessory phenomena, Recompense destroyed mankind's earliest civilization and much of Earth's flora and fauna. Recompense's reaction to evil can be *delayed* with the provisos explained earlier, but *it cannot be stalled forever*!

I trust many will now read Genesis with heightened appreciation.

Chapter Twenty
Valcon's Clandestine Mission on Earth

Incarnated among us two millennia ago, the second Persension of the Value Continuum, joined to humanity as Jesus of Nazareth, devoted the last three years of his 33-year earthly sojourn to concerted ministry. Superimposing Locedmeda's third law, Adaptability, over its second law, Predictability, Jesus put Valcon's conspiracy of mercy (explained in chapter 9) on hold long enough to expose throngs of people in and near Israel to a cascade of responsibility-elevating *public* miracles.

Valcon normally grants physically manifest miracles only to people he foreknows will honor him because of the evidence miracles proffer. He also tends to withhold miracles from foreknown truth haters. *Public* miracles are those Valcon displays to *both* categories of people—dire consequences for the latter group notwithstanding! Did Titus Vespasian's 70 A.D. assault on Jerusalem recompense people who, having witnessed Jesus' miracles, withheld the response such evidence demanded?

Miraculous healing for incurably sick, blind, deaf, mute or lame people increases the culpability of proud, arrogant, scornful, self-excusing onlookers if they remain impenitent despite evidence bestowed.

Even allowing Jesus' relatively brief 'Adaptability-call' to be confirmed later via extra-biblical records unearthed in tels would similarly endanger unpersuadables in later generations. That would be, at best, *counter-conspiratorial*. Apparently Jesus left no such evidences. What remains to detail his remarkable sojourn among us are the four Gospels, a record conspiratorially designed to appear to unpersuadables primarily as fiction accruing like moss to a few pebbles of fact.

Predictability's ubiquitous 'veneering' of almost everything in our earthbound existence with un-miraculous 'naturalism' works, may we say, *miraculously?* Naturalistic veneering serves Valcon by enabling foreknown Valcon-rejecters, for the duration of their earthly existence, to rationalize away the whole notion of redemption as 'illogical.'

Conversely, responders to Valcon—guided by echoes of his Unified Field in creation as well as in their own consciences—find the New Testament to be both convincing and appealing. As Paul said, "The message of the cross is [to reduce their guilt, designed to appear as] *foolishness* to those who are perishing, but to us who are being saved, it is *the power of God*" (I Corinthians 1:18).

This 'message of the cross'—crafted by Valcon to shepherd his friends while befuddling his enemies—is designed to lead responders from every people and tribe to redemption. For that, Valcon must somehow arrange to smuggle this cosmically significant message to myriad villages, cities and palaces where Paul's "full number of the Gentiles" (Romans 11:25), known to John as "some from every tribe, language, people and nation" (Revelation 5:9), have yet to hear it and be redeemed.

Those who supplicate Valcon for mercy in response to his voice in creation (i.e., Melchizedek and Job-types à la Hebrews 11:6) are already redeemed yet remain bereft, knowing nothing of the profound self-sacrifice whereby mercy avails for mankind. They, too, need the message of the cross in order to access the whole counsel of God (Acts 20:27, KJV).

For Valcon himself to preach directly to mankind via redemption-explaining visions, dreams and spectacular signs would have two undesirable effects. First, doing so would elevate those who still persist in rebellion to higher tiers of culpability. Using shining angels as messengers would have the same counter-conspiratorial effect.

Second, Valcon would be keeping his future across-the-cosmos story-tellers from *practicing* how to bear witness for him. Valcon's solution: utilize humble earthborn people, especially those willing to range far afield, as Jesus said, "...for my sake and the Gospel's."

How Jesus expounded 'mission' to his apostles

First, Valcon Incarnate—Jesus—must enable his initial task force, the apostles, to *understand the redemptive message and why it must be launched from Israel to the entire Gentile world.* How did he explain this? In his three years of public ministry Jesus 'micro-taught' a wide selection of *brief* Old Testament texts. Not until the 40-day interval between his resurrection and his ascension did Jesus divulge at length two grander Old Testament themes. The risen Lord taught his disciples again, but with a difference! Rather than briefly exposit a few more disconnected texts, "beginning with Moses and all the prophets, he explained…what was said in all the Scriptures concerning himself" (Luke 24:27). Unveiling two Old Testament *mega themes* Jewish rabbis then ignored and even now still repress, Jesus "opened [his disciples'] minds so they could understand the Scriptures. He told them, 'This is what is written—'"

Recall that Jesus' crucifixion and death had left his disciples dispirited. Peter, for one, thought his only option was to go back to fishing for *fish*, not *men*. No disciple had any inkling that Jesus 'tragic' demise meant salvation for mankind. The way Jewish rabbis interpreted Scripture gave them no warning that Israel's Messiah must come initially to *suffer*!

A contrary factor among Jewish rabbis

Jewish rabbis preferred to define the Messiah's future mission as securing *political emancipation* for Israel. Thus the Jewish people (including Jesus' disciples) expected Israel's Deliverer to lead a Jewish army to victory over Rome, Israel's oppressor. The Son of David replaces Caesar! Jerusalem supplants Rome as capital city of the world.

Raised under rabbinic influence, Jesus' disciples saw their Master's crucifixion and death as incompatible with the role of a political emancipator. Could a crucified *victim* be a regal *victor*? Though Jesus often spoke of freeing people from *sin*, surely freeing Israel from Rome was primary. Jesus corrected these grave misperceptions by teaching:

Mega Theme "A"!

As Luke 24:47, 48 records, Jesus—appearing among his disciples after his resurrection—opened their minds to comprehend two epic Old Testament themes. I call them Mega Themes "A" and "B." To teach Mega Theme "A," Jesus showed his disciples a mosaic of prophetic passages—Genesis 3:15, Isaiah 53, Psalm 16:10 and Psalm 22, for example—portraying Messiah as one who must suffer, die and rise from the dead. With their minds opened to grasp Mega Theme A, Jesus' disciples at last saw their Lord as the one who, from before creation, was destined to offer himself as a *sacrifice* before ascending on high as Savior and Sovereign.

For example, picture Jesus explaining why—two millennia earlier (see Genesis 22:1-12)—Valcon ordained Abraham's near sacrifice of Isaac to happen, not just anywhere, but "in the region of Moriah." Even more specifically, Valcon specified "*on one of the mountains*" near Moriah. Why link Abraham's incredible test to so precise a site? The text reveals that Abraham, nearing the specified site with Isaac, two servants and a donkey, paused to cut wood for the offering. Curiously, neither Abraham's servants nor the donkey carried the wood up the final slope. Telling his servants to "*Stay...with the donkey,*" Abraham required *Isaac* to carry the wood the remaining distance—wood on which *Isaac* was to be offered.

As for the "region of Moriah," Jewish historians identify it as the site where Solomon's temple would stand centuries later. Inferably, that God-chosen hill near Moriah was Golgotha, where Jesus, a 'Greater Isaac,' would later bear the *wooden* cross on which he was to be offered, completing the needful sacrifice of a beloved Son, a sacrifice Abraham and Isaac were privileged to *foreshadow*, but not complete, 2000 years before.

No ram took Greater Isaac's place.

How fittingly Abraham named that hill "The *Lord* will provide."

With Mega Theme A unveiled via such foreshadowings, Jesus' crucifixion became something to fill his disciples with awe, not despair. But to instill a full measure of apostolic spirit, he needed also to open their minds *again*—this time to what I call Mega Theme "B." Only thus could his disciples grasp the Great Commission's significance.

Whereas Mega Theme A already would enable Jesus' disciples to expound the *Tenach* in ways that were beyond the ken of Jewish rabbis, only Mega Theme B could convince them that Mega Theme A's message must be offered to Gentiles as well as to their fellow Jews. Again, Jesus had to counter a bias disseminated by rabbis.

A second contrary factor in rabbinic teaching

Centuries earlier, Valcon had imparted *two categories of law* to guide Hebrew people *morally* but also to set them apart *culturally* from Gentile neighbors. Valcon's *primary* laws defined *ethical purity*. Jesus summarized these laws with, "Love the Lord your God with all your heart and with all your soul and with all your mind....and love your neighbor as yourself" (Matthew 22:37-39 cf. Deuteronomy 6:5 and Leviticus 19:18).

The second category of law consisted of *ritual rules*—directives for cleanliness, offering sacrifice, circumcision, what to eat or spurn, etc. Clearly, Jesus regarded ritual law as given merely to *symbolize* issues implicit in moral law. "Do not boil the flesh of a young goat in its mother's milk,"[1] for example, translates as, "When injuring someone [a criminal, for example] is unavoidable, at least do not add insult to the injury." Over time, however, the Jews inflated ritual law into a maze of redundant rules, some of which overshadowed ethical issues. Ritual observance became an end in itself, fulfilling Isaiah's prophesy (28:13) that, "…the word of the Lord to them will become: Do and do, do and do, rule on rule, rule on rule"—i.e., something less than Valcon desires.

Accordingly a prophet lamented, "For you, this whole vision is nothing but words sealed in a scroll…," adding elsewhere, "These people …honor me with their lips, but their hearts are far from me. Their worship of me is made up only of rules taught by men" (Isaiah 29:11-13). Note Isaiah's phrase *"this whole vision."* Surely it signifies that Israel was ignoring a higher priority while engaging in a shadow-play of ritual.

Linking personal righteousness in large part with ritual observance left Israel shunning un-ritualed Gentiles as unclean. Urging Gentiles to obey Valcon's moral law was valid. Spurning them for non-conformity to Jewish ritual law was not. How then could Jesus inspire his Jewish disciples to mingle compassionately with Samaritans, Romans and Greeks—to say nothing of utter *barbarians*—when his disciples saw contact with such as defiling?

Mega Theme "B"!

Israel's own *Tenach* does indeed reverberate with a grander vision, one that relates blessedly to the entire Gentile world. It was precisely that grander vision that provided Jesus with his Mega Theme B.

To 'unseal' Mega Theme B, Jesus had only to highlight an intensely *missional* message in the *Tenach*—one that rabbis woefully disregarded. Shattering a stereotype that views God as coddling Israel and ignoring Gentiles, Jesus marshaled quote after quote showing the *Tenach* as filled with promises and examples of blessing for Gentiles.

Where, though, does one find a 'missional theme' in Israel's *Tenach*? The answer takes us back 4,000 years to a covenant God ratified with a Chaldean named Abraham (father of nations). As a "**top line**" of that covenant, Valcon promised, "I will bless you…," pledging also to found "a great nation" through Abraham, coupled with a promise to bless whoever blessed that nation-to-be and curse whoever cursed it. Yet any action Valcon may take *against* Gentiles is an occasional exception to the "**bottom line**" purpose he announced as his final promise to Abraham, namely, "All peoples on earth will be *blessed* through you."

How Genesis *emphasizes* a 'blessor franchise'

Valcon iterated both parts of that same covenant with Abraham *a second time* on the eve of the destruction of Sodom and Gomorrah, saying, "Abraham will surely become a great and powerful nation, *and all nations on earth will be blessed through him*" (Genesis 18:18).

Valcon's reminder had the desired effect. Abraham responded by stepping into a role that was new for him. Negotiating with Valcon as an appointed *blessor*, he established a basis whereby mercy could preempt judgment—not just for Lot *et al.* but for all the people of two decadent cities, Sodom and Gomorrah. Indeed, both cities would have been spared had they met the minimal basis Abraham negotiated on their behalf.

Later, responding to Abraham for placing Isaac on that altar in the region of Moriah, Valcon affirmed his covenant a third time, adding a personal oath for powerful emphasis: "*I swear by myself...*that because you have done this and have not withheld your son, your only son, I will surely bless you and make your descendants as numerous as the stars in the sky and as the sand on the seashore.... Your descendants will take possession of the cities of their enemies...." (Genesis 22:15-17). Valcon then also affirmed the last part of his covenant, adding, "...and through your offspring all peoples on earth will be blessed, because you have obeyed me" (Genesis 22:18).

By his own choice, Valcon *bound himself under oath* to fulfill the above promises *on pain of perjury*.

Isaac, Abraham's son conceived in response to a test of faith, was the next patriarch to hear Valcon assure blessing followed by "*through your offspring all nations on earth will be blessed*" (Genesis 26:4).

A third patriarch, Abraham's grandson, Jacob, heard Valcon promise for a *fifth* time: "Your descendants will be *like the dust of the earth,* and you will spread out to the west and to the east, to the north and to the south. All peoples on earth will be blessed through you and your offspring" (Genesis 28:14; emphasis is added in this and also in the above four crucial quotes from Genesis).

The final clause in all five passages proffers a divinely-appointed franchise for Abraham and his progeny by saying, "All peoples on earth will be blessed *through you*" or "through you and your descendants." Valcon chose not angels but Abraham and his progeny to serve as *blessors* for Gentile *blessees*. Abraham *et al.* thus possess what can best be termed a '*blessor franchise.*' But what have they done with it?

Note Valcon's reason for dispersing large numbers of Abraham, Isaac and Jacob's descendants to the four coordinates. It would not be for military conquest, financial gain or resettlement but to "bless all peoples on earth"! Valcon's plan to spread Abraham's descendants like dust to bless all peoples on earth signifies the New Testament's *Great Commission* in Old Testament prototype! Thus did Valcon announce that much of Abraham, Isaac and Jacob's progeny would in time be uprooted from their homeland and sent as blessing-bearers to Gentile realms.

One would think—since Valcon gave that promise *five* times to *three* patriarchs and even confirmed it with an *oath!*—that rabbis would teach such a strongly emphasized promise to Jewish boys preparing for their *bar mitzvahs.* Not so. Rabbis leave God's mission in the shadows.

What of Christian theologians? As Gentiles, surely *they* must honor a five-times-given sealed-by-divine-oath promise of blessing for Gentiles. Surely they would see that "All peoples on earth will be blessed through you" is quoted twice and paraphrased a dozen times in the New Testament. Wouldn't they at least assign that blessed concept an honorific title from Greek or Latin, as they do for other aspects of scripture (*Pentateuch, Decalogue*, *diaspora, imago Dei,* etc.)?

Alas, Christian theologians are almost as remiss as Jewish rabbis. How contentedly they have left a promise given five times to three patriarchs—a promise sealed under divine oath—bereft of even an honorific title from a classical language, let alone extensive commentary.

No matter! Better late than never! If the Ten Commandments can be called "the *Deca*logue," let us here and now affirm God's five-times-given promise of blessing for all peoples on Earth as his "***Penta*logue**"!

That 'Great Commission' would later be echoed by Isaiah's "Go, swift messengers" (Isaiah 18:2) and "Whom shall I send? And who will go for us?" (Isaiah 6:8). Old Testament scripture shows the blessor franchise fulfilled by relatively few—Joseph, Naomi, Elijah, Elisha, Jeremiah, Ezekiel, Daniel and others like them who reached out to Gentiles and blessed them profoundly. Are not they the ones most favored to have their biographies featured in the canon of Scripture?

Does not Genesis, Moses' first book, culminate with Joseph blessing Egyptians as well as his fellow Hebrews? Joseph is the model! Failure to emulate *the Joseph standard* would ever be to live below the ideal of Valcon's *missional covenant.* How, then, did subsequent generations fare or falter in relation to that remarkable 'Joseph standard'? Let's look at the list a little closer.

More biographies with a 'common denominator'

Note the multi-ethnic nature of prominent biographies throughout the *Tenach*. Moses led his **Midianite** father-in-law, Jethro, to trust in Elohim, the true God. Moses also urged Hebrews to show compassion for foreign minorities dwelling amid them. Moses admonished repeatedly: "*Do not mistreat an alien or oppress him, for you were aliens in Egypt*" (Exodus 22:21).[3] In other words, Hebrews must treat aliens the way Hebrews wished Egyptians had treated them when they were aliens in Egypt. When Jesus, centuries later, spoke his famous "Golden Rule," he was simply rephrasing a missional element of Moses' teaching.

Joshua blessed Rahab, a **Canaanite**. Naomi blessed Ruth, a woman of **Moab**. David made restitution for Saul's campaign of genocide against **Gibeonites**, yet brought disrepute upon the blessor nation by violating Bathsheba and arranging for her **Hittite** husband, Uriah, to be killed in battle. For that, Valcon punished David.

Solomon taught Gentiles visiting Jerusalem about Hebrew proverbs and Mosaic Law. He dedicated the temple in Jerusalem as "a house of prayer for all nations." Yet Solomon also marred his legacy with utter decadence. His later devotion to pagan gods and his recourse to slave labor for self-aggrandizing projects became an embarrassment.

Elijah blessed a **Canaanite**—the widow of Zarephath—and Elisha (with help from a Hebrew child-slave in Damascus) blessed Naaman, a **Syrian** leper. Jonah (however reluctantly) blessed **Assyrians** in Nineveh. Daniel blessed **Babylonians**. Esther, Mordecai, Ezra and Nehemiah blessed **Persians**.

Paraphrases of the Pentalogue in the *Tenach*

Biographies displaying multi-ethnic blessor-blessee encounters are supplemented by several hundred clear paraphrases of Valcon's Pentalogic promise. Among the more than two hundred passages Jesus could have cited for his disciples, and perhaps did cite, we find:

> "God be gracious to us… *that your ways may be known on earth, your salvation among all nations*" (Psalm 67:1, 2).

> "*All nations will be blessed by him* [bottom line], and they will call him blessed" [top line](Psalm 72:17).

"It is too small a thing for you...to restore the tribes of Jacob; *I will also make you a light for the Gentiles that you may bring my salvation to the ends of the earth*" (Isaiah 49:6).

"I set you apart. I appointed you as *a prophet to the nations*" (Jeremiah 1:5).

"If you will return, O Israel...*then the nations will be blessed by him and in him will they glory"* (Jeremiah 4:1, 2).

Consider Isaiah's rueful confession (26:18, part b) of Israel's age-long disinterest in fulfilling Elohim's blessor franchise: "We have not brought salvation to the earth; *we have not given birth to people of the world."* Clearly Jews were obliged to help Gentiles experience "new birth"! Three times Psalm 87:4-6 credits Gentiles being spiritually "born" into an obviously spiritual Zion as pleasing to Israel's God. When Jesus chided Nicodemus (John 3:10) for missing what Israel's Tenach had to say about new birth, surely he had Isaiah 26:18 and Psalm 87:4-6 in mind.

How sad that modern rabbis too, like Nicodemus of old, overlook their own *Tenach's* teaching about mankind's need to be born again. They dismiss new birth as a Christian nuance antithetic to Judaism. By unveiling Mega Theme B, Jesus was urging 12 Jewish men not to dismiss these and numerous similar *Tenach* passages as passé "words sealed in a scroll" but as germane evidence of Valcon's yearning to complete a great ingathering of beloved people from among all peoples.

Mega Theme B must have startled Jesus' disciples as had Mega Theme A. Neither Theme A nor Theme B fit the religiously correct thought of the time; yet both pervade the *Tenach,* and both are to be taught as Jesus taught them—in tandem! Both themes, once understood, become far too compelling to be ignored. Now at last Jesus' disciples could grasp the logic of ministry choices they had seen Jesus make in the prior three years—choices that baffled them at the time.

How Jesus himself honored Mega Theme B

Why, for example, did Jesus favor Capernaum—a small town in northeastern Galilee—as his center of ministry operations, rather than Jerusalem in Judea? Almost everyone expected him, if he was truly the Messiah, to 'open an office in headquarters city,' so to speak, and seek to build a political base supported by key leaders in Jerusalem. Jesus showed no interest. Why instead did he favor 'backwater' Capernaum?

The advantage Capernaum afforded

Capernaum yielded Jesus much more than access to Galilee's large Aramaic and Hebrew-speaking Jewish population. Capernaum placed him close to Aramaic-speaking **Syria** and to **Phoenicia**. Capernaum also positioned him just across the Jordan River from Greek and Aramaic-speaking **Decapolis**. Capernaum was proximate also to **Tiberius**, a city catering primarily to Roman military personnel—a force representing still more distant peoples.

What an excellent 'operations center' Capernaum afforded for a *pentalogic* Messiah! Jerusalem could not compete. Once Jesus began working miracles *à la Adaptability* in Galilee, "news about him spread all over *Syria*, and people brought to him all who were ill with various diseases, those suffering severe pain, the demon-possessed, those having seizures, and the paralyzed, and he healed them" (Matthew 4:24). More than that, large crowds, not only from Galilee and Syria, but also from "*...the Decapolis,* Jerusalem, Judea and the region across the Jordan followed him" (verse 25).

It was a foregone conclusion. Dutifully religious Jews from Jerusalem and Judea—guardians of '*correct*' Judaism—were sure to trek to Galilee to evaluate and possibly *forbid* the *strange* interactions Jews in Galilee were experiencing with Gentiles thronging in from surrounding areas. Conversely, had Jesus begun working miracles en masse in Judea, precious few Syrians and Decapolitan Greeks would have ventured that great a distance to hear Jesus teach.

Thus did Jesus fulfill an eight-centuries-old prophecy given to Isaiah [9:2]: "The people living in darkness [e.g., Syrians and Greeks living in close proximity to northeastern Galilee, where even Jews spoke Aramaic more readily than Hebrew] have seen a great light; on those living in the land of the shadow of death a light has dawned."

Jesus' encounter with a Roman centurion

Pleading for Jesus to heal his paralyzed servant, a Roman centurion expressed faith that Jesus could accomplish so remarkable a deed *even at a distance*. Despite the anti-Gentile bias of his disciples and other Jewish spectators, Jesus boldly commended the Roman centurion, declaring, "I have not found anyone in Israel with such great faith." Refreshed to encounter true faith in a Gentile, Jesus predicted: "Many [i.e., Gentiles with similar faith] will come from the east and the west and north and south" [Matthew 8:5-11, with the last four words added from Luke 13:29].

Only later would Jesus' disciples realize that the words he spoke that day linked back to Valcon's promise to Jacob that his descendants—"like the dust of the earth"—would "spread out to the *west* and to the *east*, to the *north* and to the *south* [so that] all peoples on earth will be blessed." Thinking back, they must have recognized the very next statement Jesus made that day as a *de facto* **sequel** to Genesis 28:14, a statement assuring that Gentiles with faith similar to the centurion's "will take *their places* at the feast with Abraham, Isaac and Jacob in the kingdom of heaven."

Jesus and the Samaritan woman

The Samaritan woman Jesus met by the well at Sychar asked if Jerusalem was indeed the primary place where mankind should worship. Jesus replied, ". . . a time is coming when you will worship the Father neither on this mountain nor in Jerusalem. ... a time is coming and has now come when the true worshippers will worship the Father in spirit and in truth…." (John 4:21-23). Then Jesus defined for the woman the Value Continuum's creation-justifying desire for true worshippers, adding, "…they are the kind of worshipers the Father seeks" (verse 23).

Jesus and the Canaanite mother

Later Jesus led his disciples from Galilee via Syria into Phoenicia (Matthew 15:21-28). A Canaanite mother in Phoenicia asked him to heal her daughter. To test his disciples, Jesus at first feigned indifference to her plea. Instead of urging him to show mercy, his disciples—still in the grip of ethnic bias—failed the test miserably by urging him to "send her away."

Affording them a second chance to pass the test, he feigned further indifference with a statement that contradicted his entire public ministry policy up to that time. With utmost incongruity, Jesus said (probably with a twinkle in his eye), "I was sent *only* to the lost sheep of Israel." This time, however, the twinkle must have caught the mother's eye.

Sensing encouragement disguised in satire, the mother knelt before Jesus and repeated her request. This time he responded by paraphrasing the Abrahamic Covenant with a twist of irony that emphasized the Covenant's final promise by way of crudely denying it! He said: "It is not right to take the children's bread [Valcon's covenant blessing for Abraham's descendants] and toss it to their dogs [Gentiles]."

As if God could commit perjury by renouncing his five-times-given, *oath-sealed* promise to "bless all peoples on earth" via the Patriarchs and their descendants! Jesus was emphasizing to his disciples how Valcon's ancient pact with Abraham, Isaac and Jacob would have to be worded for him to be the discriminating Messiah they would have preferred.

Responding to Jesus' satire with a humor of her own, the mother replied, "Yes, Lord, but even [we] 'dogs' eat the crumbs that fall from their masters' table." How beautifully she played her part! "Woman, you have great faith," Jesus replied. "Your request is granted." And he healed her daughter at that moment, from a distance.

Two miraculous feedings and a cleansed temple court

Surely his disciples also recalled the *two* times Jesus fed large crowds by multiplying a few loaves and fish. The first miraculous feeding, proffered for *Jews* in Galilee (Matthew 14:13-21), was balanced by a second miraculous feeding for *Greeks* in Decapolis (Mark 7:31-8:10).

The disciples also must have remembered how Jesus denounced the temple authorities' decision to rezone the temple's *Court of the Gentiles* for commercial use by money-changers. (See Mark 11:15-17.) Stitching two Old Testament quotations (Isaiah 56:7 and Jeremiah 7:11) together as one, Jesus protested, "Is it not written: 'My house will be called a house of prayer *for all nations*'? But you have made it 'a den of robbers.'"

Valcon's Great Commission renewed at last!

With his disciples' minds thus opened to both mega themes, Jesus gave them at last the 'Great Commission.' For 'The Great Commission Part One,' Jesus appointed his disciples to keep Mega Themes A and B as their primary teaching agenda, saying, "**You are witnesses of *these things***" (Luke 24:48). That is what they, his Jewish Apostles, must faithfully impart to the soon-to-emerge Christian Church!

With that aspect of the Great Commission narrated, Luke ends his Gospel, only to open his sequel—the book of Acts—with the 'Great Commission Part Two': *the geographical directive!* "…**you will be my**

witnesses in Jerusalem and in all Judea and Samaria, and to the ends of the earth" (Acts 1:8).

Thus did Jesus initiate the clandestine advance of God's *true* kingdom on Earth and ultimately—via his 'precious-treasure-securing' long-range plan—*in the cosmos!* As it is written, "Of the *increase* of his government and peace there will be *no end*" (Isaiah 9:7).

Earlier, Jesus—recognizing his disciples as still unfit for cross-cultural service—said, "Do *not* go among the Gentiles or enter any town of the Samaritans. Go rather to the lost sheep of Israel" (Matthew 10:5, 6). Yet he also announced in that same discourse that wider ministry awaited them, adding, "On my account you will be brought before governors and kings as witnesses to them *and to the Gentiles*" (verse 18). The time for that wider ministry was now at hand.

Having opened their minds to Mega Theme B—the *pentalogue* in their own *Tenach*—Jesus stood among his disciples on the Mount of Olives and commissioned them at last to proclaim Mega Theme A where Mega Theme B required it to be proclaimed: to all nations. With that, Jesus ascended to heaven, leaving them to ponder the significance of all they had heard and seen since he, three years earlier, had promised to make them "fishers of men."

Shortly thereafter, on the Day of Pentecost, Valcon filled his disciples with the Holy Spirit. Lest they forget that the Spirit was given to aid their proclamation to *Gentiles as well as to Jews*, Valcon even enabled them to proclaim Mega Theme A immediately *in the Gentile languages* known to the throng of Diaspora Jews who had arrived in Jerusalem for the Feast (Acts 2).

How Peter taught both mega themes *initially*

Later, explaining the healing of a lame man to a throng of amazed onlookers, Peter focused everyone's attention on the significance of Jesus' crucifixion and resurrection (Acts 3:13-24). Echoing the two mega themes the Lord had opened his mind to understand, Peter said, "This is how God fulfilled what he had foretold through all the prophets, saying that his Christ would suffer....Indeed, all the prophets...have foretold these days." This was Peter's concise summary of Mega Theme A.

Peter then acknowledged Mega Theme B with this: "And you are heirs of the prophets and of the covenant God made with your fathers. He said to Abraham, '*Through your offspring all peoples on earth will be blessed*.' When God raised up his servant, he sent him *first to you to bless you* by turning each of you from your wicked ways" (verses 25-26).

Peter's "*first*...to bless you" tacitly implied that a *second* goal must be to bless all peoples on earth. Even so, Luke reveals in Acts that Jesus' disciples, despite Jesus' clear teaching and example, failed the call at first.

How they began to put Theme B back in a scroll

Over time, none of Jesus' disciples—though appointed as his 'sent ones' (*apostles*)—showed the slightest interest in proclaiming anything to Gentiles. Did they think foreign-born Jews repeating their Pentecost proclamation for Gentiles was sufficient?

Even when Valcon permitted persecution to drive other believers out of Jerusalem to areas where their message was needed, the apostles stayed put. The 'cloister mentality' that would later inhibit the spread of the message in subsequent eras of church history was already manifesting.

Only Philip—a deacon, not an apostle—was willing to venture outside the Jerusalem 'box.' Entering Samaria, Philip cast aside fear of ritual defilement and reaped a harvest matured from seed perhaps planted in part by that Samaritan woman's earlier witness in Sychar. Finding at last someone willing to work outside the 'monastery' for spiritual recluses that Jerusalem was becoming, Valcon spirited Philip off to a strategic encounter with an Ethiopian proselyte, who promptly took the Jesus message to his homeland (Acts 8:26-39).

At least Peter and John *complemented* Philip's ministry in Samaria—a ministry they would have had no interest in had not Philip ventured out in faith. Later, though, Peter and John returned to Jerusalem, "preaching the Gospel in many Samaritan villages" en route (Acts 8:25). Philip, meanwhile, continued trail-blazing from Azotus northward to Caesarea, lighting still more ministry fires for Peter to keep refueled.

While Peter lingered in Joppa, Valcon arranged an invitation for him to preach to Cornelius, a Roman centurion based in nearby Caesarea. So deeply engrained was Peter's aversion to direct contact with Gentiles that Valcon had to give him a motivational vision *three times* to assure he would not decline Cornelius' invitation (Acts 10:10-16).

Through Peter's obedience, Cornelius and his household received the revelation about Jesus. Peter, at last, had ventured at least to a fringe of the kind of ministry the Lord's Mega Theme B required. Alas, Peter's fellow apostles and other leaders in Jerusalem—learning that Peter had consorted with Gentiles *and even eaten food with them*—came close to impeaching him!

Though Peter defended his actions well, it was clear already that Peter was not to be the primary 'Joseph' who must launch Valcon's Mega Theme message far out into the wider world of Cilicians, Cappadocians, Galatoi, Phrygians, Mysians, Lycaonians, *et al.* That point man would have to be Saul from Tarsus, the hostile Jewish rabbi who became Valcon's special friend—Paul, the "Apostle to the Gentiles."

Paul's clear grasp of Mega Themes A and B

Though Paul was not present at Jesus' mind-opening discourse, the following quotes show how clearly Paul—a few years later—not only grasped the two mega themes Jesus had opened the other apostles' minds to understand, but also the necessity of proclaiming them in tandem.

For example, Paul wrote in Galatians 3:8, "Scripture foresaw that God would justify Gentiles by faith and announced the gospel in advance to Abraham: 'All nations will be blessed through you.'" A few verses later (3:14) Paul explained that "[Christ] redeemed us in order that the blessing given to Abraham might come to the Gentiles through Christ Jesus…."

In Romans 15:8, 9 Paul wrote, "Christ has become a servant of the Jews on behalf of God's truth, to confirm the [five-times-given] promises made to the patriarchs *so that Gentiles may glorify God for his mercy*."

Reasoning with King Agrippa (Acts 26:22-23), Paul said, "I am saying nothing beyond what the prophets and Moses said would happen—that the Christ would suffer and as the first to rise from the dead [recapping Mega Theme A] would proclaim light to his own people *and to the Gentiles"* [acknowledging Mega Theme B].

In Ephesians 3:2-6, Paul wrote, "Surely you have heard about the administration of God's grace that was given to me for you [Gentiles], that is, the mystery that was made known to me by revelation…reading this, then, you will be able to understand my insight into the mystery of Christ [i.e., Jesus' clandestine mission to harvest earth's savable people in a way that does not impart wrath-accelerating insight to those who persist in rebellion. Paul describes that 'mystery' as] "…not made known to men in other generations as it has now been revealed by the Spirit [beginning with Jesus' pre-ascension mind-opening discourse] to God's holy apostles and prophets" [not that all such were giving it priority].

Paul defines the mystery precisely: "This mystery is that through the gospel [the Mega Theme A message] Gentiles [who believe] are heirs together with Israel, members together of one body, and sharers together in the promise [the promise of blessing for all peoples on earth] in Christ Jesus" (Ephesians 3:6).

Paul then explains his role in Valcon's creation-justifying cosmic purpose: "…this grace was given me: to preach to the Gentiles the unsearchable riches of Christ and to make plain…the administration of this mystery, which for ages past was kept hidden in God, who created all things. His intent was that now, through the church, *the manifold wisdom of God* should be made known *to the rulers and authorities in the heavenly realms* [progenitors of new races of worshippers on myriad other worlds] according to his eternal purpose, which he accomplished in Christ Jesus our Lord" (3:8-10, emphasis added).

The word 'administration' denotes measures Paul was taking to assure that the Church would not imitate Israel by burying Valcon's "all peoples on earth" commission under layers of unpentalogic indifference. Recall how Paul—one sad day in Antioch—had to rebuke even Peter and Barnabas for surrendering to unpentalogic bias (Galatians 2:11-14).

The phrase "hidden in God" signifies Paul's recognition that Jesus' Mega Theme A message, though clear enough to save millions of rescuable people, is also by design *not* convincing enough to deprive persistent rebels of the spiritual blindness that insulates them from otherwise immediate wrath.

Christianity's first strategic accomplishment

Inspired mainly by the faithful witness Paul gave to both mega themes in his epistles and his preaching, Barnabas, Silas, Titus, Timothy and Paul's other protégés assured that both mega themes were taught wherever a new category of worshippers—'**Christians**'—were found. But for how many generations would *both* mega themes be taught in tandem?

Substituting Mega Theme A with teaching that ignored or denied the atonement would send the wrong message. Forgetting Mega Theme B would leave the right message 'warehoused' among too few peoples. Deleting both Mega Themes would reduce the church to a social club.

For some two and a half centuries after the Day of Pentecost, Christians promulgated both mega themes faithfully. As long as *both* themes were taught in tandem, Christians remained profoundly motivated to proclaim the true message in more and more languages to *more and more peoples* both inside and, to some degree, even *outside* the Roman Empire. In time, congregations of Christians flourished, despite outbreaks of persecution by Rome, in every sector of the Empire. Christians can be described as draping a 7,000-mile-long, oval-shaped 'lei' of churches around the 'neck' of the Mediterranean Sea!

That was Christianity's first truly major strategic accomplishment.

Christians accomplished this goal despite the relatively low social status of many Christians. An average Christian during those first two and a half remarkable centuries of church history was a slave or a semi-literate working class person. Christians had no bank loans to finance church construction nor presses to publish literature. Anointed by the Holy Spirit for winsome witness marked by compassion for their fellow man, they maintained *three kinds of exponential growth for more than two centuries.* Christians kept advancing exponentially as to (1) their number, (2) the number of churches and schools they established and (3) *the number of cultures they were penetrating with the Gospel.*

What should have been the Church's 2nd goal?

With that 7,000-mile-long lei of churches in place, which *new* goal should Church leaders have urged Christians to strive toward?

Utilizing that 7,000-mile-long 'church belt' as *a staging area—a launching pad*—for outreach to the remaining peoples of the world would surely have been consistent with Jesus' Mega Theme B. Channeling three already-existing categories of exponential growth in pursuit of that *secondary goal* would have swept the Gospel onward into all of northern Europe and even—via Viking contact with Iceland, Greenland, Labrador and Newfoundland—over into eastern sectors of the New World.

Another initiative could have ventured south to pagan Arabs and the peoples of sub-Saharan Africa. A third sweep across Asia to China, Korea and Japan could have led via the Bering Sea into western sectors of the New World—*all in less than one millennium*! Compassionate evangelists would have arrived in many cases well ahead of ruthless political, commercial exploiters, rather than following in their wake centuries later. How many wars and genocides could have been averted! Peaceful trade might have flourished among merchants submissive to biblical ethics.

Vikings in the **north**; Goths, Visigoths, Tartars and Vandals to the **east**; Arabs, Ethiopians, Berbers, Bedouins and others far to the **south**—all could have been brothers and sisters in faith, conveying the Gospel to the four co-ordinates of the world Valcon described in Genesis 28:14. The world stage was set for a momentous spiritual drama.

Alas, a few Christian leaders diverted the Church into pursuing a tragically altered goal.

How a few church fathers *axed* Mega Theme B

Around the time that Constantine, Emperor of Rome, made Christianity the *de facto* official religion of the Roman Empire, the persecution of Christians ended. Bishops, pastors and deacons—preoccupied with consolidating positions of new-found status, influence and personal prestige in the new limelight—began losing interest in evangelizing regions beyond the borders of Empire.

They knew, of course—and everyone in their congregations knew—that Jesus had given the Great Commission. That knowledge nagged their consciences. What to do about a command they no longer wanted to obey or cared to teach?

A few 'church fathers' hit upon a facile solution. *They began to teach that Jesus gave the Great Commission only to the apostles, not to the Church.* They opined that the apostles finished the task. To regard the Great Commission as undone implied that the apostles had failed to do what only apostles could adequately accomplish.

Such leaders could cite Peter's ministry in Babylon, the Apostle Thomas' outreach to India, Matthew's southerly venture to Ethiopia, Andrew's ministry somewhere to the north in Scythia and Paul's coverage of almost everything else. How much bigger could the world be than that? Surely the apostles had finished a task that was for them, not for the church. *Neglecting expansion and consolidating the Church's existing gains* grew, over time, into the watchword for a new era.

Other Christian leaders did not echo this tragic negation of Mega Theme B, but neither did they mount an effective objection! Gradually, a new consensus won the day by their default. Zealous Christians still abounded, of course. Some could have evangelized the Vikings or served Christ among Goths, Visigoths, Tartars, Vandals, Arabs, Berbers or Bedouins. Instead, bishops and elders, in effect, began to advise, "The finest way to serve God is to find a cave and be a hermit. Devote the remainder of your days to perfecting your own holiness. Don't concern yourself to help others find *their* path to holiness. Leave that to God."

Alas, there were too few caves, so isolating oneself in a ridiculous hut atop a pillar called a 'stylos' became an acceptable alternative. Joining a Trappist Order and taking 'an oath of silence' was another way to be a *de facto* hermit without suffering total isolation. Trappist monks not only refrained from preaching aloud; they dared not even say, "Pass the bread"!

How dire the consequences!

Goths, Visigoths, Tartars, Vandals and later Vikings who could have been co-bearers of the gospel to more distant fields instead watched bemusedly as Christianity in southern Europe enriched itself via policies of consolidation. Soon enough, foreign watchers became envious marauders. Pillaging Goths, Visigoths, Tartars and Vandals effectively plunged Christian Europe into its so-called 'Dark Age.' In time, ravaging Vikings from the north added to the suffering that overtook Europe's Christians.

Europe's 'Dark Age' did not have to happen. Europe's Dark Age resulted not only because the Roman Empire's military defenses were crumbling. It was even more a consequence of fourth- and fifth-century church fathers weakening the resolve of Christians to fulfill Mega Theme B by evangelizing Asian and Scandinavian peoples before such people found incentive to become marauders.

Christian growth still continued in some areas—southern England and Ireland, for example. But growth was rarely as exponential as when Mega Theme B remained a key part of the Church's teaching agenda.

Revisionism by Church fathers discouraged Christians from planting churches among the peoples of *Arabia*. Little more than nominal vestiges of Christian teaching were known in Mecca, Mohammed's hometown, only 750 miles south from Jerusalem. Naïve pagans were thus left susceptible to the tragically virused semi-biblical notions Mohammed promulgated. Apart from fourth- and fifth-century church father dereliction from the mission Jesus assigned, western civilization could have been spared 1400 years of on-and-off conflict with Islam.

De-emphasizing evangelism created a void that ritual and ceremony rushed in to fill. Baptism became a substitute for heartfelt faith. Parents, regarding their children as saved by infant baptism (as if any infant is lost at so early an age), grew lax at teaching their children to know God. Faith and moral standards sagged. Missional expansion gave place to continent-wide competition aimed at building not churches but cathedrals that of course had to be ever more enormous and ever more fantastically ornate.

Some who lacked the ability and the patience to persuade by charisma resorted to compulsion. Augustine of Hippo had his fellow Christians called Donatists repressed by force. How shameful of Augustine to misapply Jesus' words in a parable—"Go out into the highways and hedges and *compel* them to come in" (Luke 14:23, KJV), to justify his choice to use force rather than rely on charisma.

Over time, Augustine's example led others to reason that *Jews*—deemed further from the truth than Christian Donatists—could be repressed still more forcibly. By the same logic, *Muslims*—deemed more distant from biblical truth than Jews—could be set upon with *crusades.* Considered equally reprehensible, a few centuries later, were Christian "heretics," many of whom were burned at the stake or tortured with thumb screws and 'iron maidens.'

How ironic that many who were tortured or burned alive as 'heretics' were Christians pleading for a return to New Testament ideals.

A reprehensible omission in our creeds

Church father revisionism still included Mega Theme A in the various creeds it promulgated, but it persistently deleted Mega Theme B from them. Take, for example, the Apostles' Creed. It begins:

> **"I believe in God the Father Almighty, Maker of heaven and earth: And in Jesus Christ, his only Son, our Lord; who was conceived by the Holy Spirit, born of the virgin Mary, suffered under Pontius Pilate, was crucified, dead and buried; he descended into hell; the third day he rose again from the dead; he ascended into heaven…."**

Did Jesus rise from the dead and ascend to heaven on the same day? In the same week? In the same month? No! Forty days intervened. Apparently, for framers of the Apostle's Creed, whatever transpired during that 40-day interval was not significant enough to be included in a creed that millions of Christians would subsequently memorize and share with their children.

How tragic! It was during those 40 days that Jesus "opened [his disciples'] minds" to see Mega Themes A and B as foundational to their message as his Apostles. Our Lord waited until then to make it clear that *both* themes must be taught to the soon-to-emerge Church, thus launching both themes to "the ends of the earth." *Surely that was worthy to be included in anything destined to be called an Apostles Creed.*

The Great Omission!

Revisionist church fathers omitted Mega Theme B, thus inaugurating the beginning, as far as Christian authorship was concerned, of what may be called *The Great Omission.* All the commonly popular creeds list wonderful things for Christians to believe without mentioning a single thing Valcon might want us to do for his kingdom and the redemption of mankind.

Compounding the tragedy, missionless creeds became templates birthing almost equally missionless *systematic theology*. Of course, many Christians still surpassed both their creeds and their theology by their willingness to serve God. A majority, however, accepted revisionism's lower standard as normative.

Amending the Apostles' Creed is long overdue! After **"...he rose again from the dead,"** insert the following sentence: **"He commissioned his church, beginning with the Apostles, to proclaim repentance and forgiveness of sins to all nations. He ascended into heaven...."**

How might church history have unfolded if tens of millions of Christians over the last 1700 years had memorized that one added sentence! Surely thousands more cross-cultural emissaries would have been launched. If the three kinds of exponential growth that the Church sustained for its first two and a half centuries had been extended out to a millennium, people at the ends of the earth could have found redemption.

May I urge anyone who, from this time forward, quotes the Apostle's Creed, to include that added sentence?

Problems would still have arisen, yes; but by and large, what a comparatively blessed millennium would have ensued. Not until western Europe launched its age of exploration in the sixteenth and seventeenth centuries did the body of Christ, his bride—the truly Christian church—begin trying to make up for centuries of time lost because of the Great Omission. Read about the Moravians, William Carey, Robert Morrison, Hudson Taylor and many others in histories by Kenneth Scott LaTourette and Stephen Neil.

I trust I have clarified what scripture reveals as Valcon's major concern since the call of Abraham. Just as the first two centuries of the

Christian era were remarkably 'all peoples' oriented, so also the Church, in these last two centuries, has begun recovering fresh momentum toward completing Valcon's ancient, oath-sealed commitment to "bless all peoples on earth."

One day, somewhere on Earth, the last person from the last *ethnos* will have his or her name entered in heaven's "register of the peoples" (Psalm 87:6). This will complete what Paul called "the full number of the Gentiles" (Romans 11:25), at which point—as Jesus forewarned—"the end will come" (Matthew 24:14).

From firstfruits to harvest, but soon—gleaning!

Jeremiah declared, "Israel was holy to the Lord, the *firstfruits* of his harvest" (Jeremiah 2:3, emphasis added). Any mention of a firstfruit offering, of course, suggests a *harvest* to follow, which in turn gives place to a final phase called *gleaning* (see the book of Ruth). What, then, comprises the harvest? What must conform to the gleaning?

As surely as Old Testament Jewish believers from Abraham to the likes of Simeon and Anna (Luke 2:25-38) comprise the firstfruits (a relatively small offering), the enormously greater number of Gentile believers gathered in over the last two millennia suggests the corollary of a harvest. What, then, correlates to a subsequent gleaning?

In Romans 11:25 Paul wrote, "Israel has experienced a hardening in part"—i.e., a stubborn rejection of Jesus that persists "*until* the full number of the Gentiles has come in." After that, Paul declared, "all Israel will be saved." What sort of catalyst concurrent with the completion of the harvest could persuade hosts of Jews to acknowledge Jesus at last?

When the long ago promised Rapture suddenly lifts God's 'harvest' up from this planet, Hindus, Buddhists, Muslims, atheists and agnostics by the hundreds of millions will find the event not only extremely startling, but utterly baffling. Who among those left on the earth will be best able to fathom what the Rapture proves?

Jews who had not yet believed.

Ruing at last their choice to be the odd party out in God's plan that began with them, surely they will supplicate Adonai for the privilege of manifesting their reconciliation through *some* form of service. I suspect they will discover—though they are far too late to share in the harvest—that Adonai, foreseeing their repentance, has kept something else in reserve for them.

According to the Law, if Jews were harvesters, Gentiles could be *gleaners*. If, however—as a result of Judaism's historical obstinacy—devout Gentiles replaced Jews as harvesters, surely Jews may return as 'gleaners' to complete the paradigm. Inferably, Jews will serve heartily as gleaners who bring still more people to faith during a relatively brief but chaotic phase following the Rapture. After that, ultimately we will all be manifested as one people (Ephesians 2:14-22 and 3:6).

Jesus promised that no aspect of the Law will fail "until everything is accomplished." With gleaners appointed, scripture's firstfruits-harvest-gleaning triad will have found fulfillment.

Chapter Twenty-One
The Problematic Nature of Proof for Infinity

Some of you may be thinking, "Even these chapters do not persuade me to believe in a God I cannot see. Seeing is believing!" Consider again this question: *how* exactly would you require Valcon to make himself visible? If he appears to you in the form of a man, you could still say, "He is only a man." If he took the form of a mile-tall man who talks very loudly and works miracles, that would still not prove to you that he has infinite capacities. You might even dismiss him and his miracles as illusions generated by state-of-the-art holographic projections.

My point: because God by definition is infinite, a scientific proof of God would have to prove his infinity, which in turn requires an infinite proof. My second point: because man is finite, he cannot conceive, nor can he comprehend, an infinite proof; so a scientific proof of God is unattainable. But that fact by no means proves God does not exist!

Imagine yourself as Valcon for just a moment

Imagine for a moment that you are an infinite Being, by nature inherently, intrinsically, unavoidably *invisible* to everything finite. Also imagine that you create finite beings in order to love them and to be loved by them. What would *you* do to win their love, assuming you have granted them freewill which must remain free? Suppose you give them a demonstration of your *power* by creating an incredibly vast, complex universe founded upon a grid of beautifully symmetrical but hidden laws known only to you as Creator. Suppose again that some of the finite beings you have created credit that universe as existing on its own without you!

What else can you do to win love when sheer power fails to awe?

Those finite beings who *do* believe you exist because of the power you have manifested provide you with a second option—let them employ their finite persuasions to help you win love from the others! Granting responders a deeply comforting, uplifting, character-instilling experience of your touch upon their lives motivates them to testify that you are real. Their testimony, added to your own witness to yourself in creation, persuades some of the others to believe in you, leaving a remnant who reject the witness of your helpers as naïve.

Your final recourse for the holdouts—if you are unwilling to ignore them indefinitely as they ignore you—is to resort finally to an *intellectual* appeal by rendering unhidden the entire set of hidden laws which logically explain your existence, their existence and creation itself in a remarkably integrated way. Imagine that you unveil that set of, shall we say, **22 laws** replete with predictions whereby their validity can be tested and proved.

Imagine finally that knowing those 22 laws comes with the ultimate **"catch 22"** because part of that set of laws requires everyone who perceives them as verified to acknowledge your right to rule your universe, or—if due acknowledgement is refused—to be punished as usurpers. As a patient, merciful Being you may delay precipitating the day of reckoning, except that endless delay is also legally prohibited.

When that day dawns, would-be usurpers enter a valley of *decision.*

I have sought God's help to discover the Unified Field. I believe what is presented herein *is* the Unified Field. Of course my belief alone does not confirm that these 22 laws are the Unified Field. All I can say now is that, to my knowledge, what is offered herein is the only symmetry-manifesting set of laws currently candidating for the position.

Moreover, this candidate field, as you have seen, offers explanations about the past unfolding, present function and future destiny of the cosmos, some of which—if not considered axiomatic—can at least be tested via existing technology. To the degree that other minds verify these laws as axioms tested and proven, mankind's responsibility before Valcon rises or remains unchanged. It follows that people who are already at peace with Valcon are not obliged to learn what this candidate Unified Field is all about, even if it is subsequently confirmed as valid. Surely, though, their friendship with Valcon will render them *curious* to discover what is stated about someone they love and who has redeemed them.

Areas of concern

To maintain his aforementioned conspiracy of mercy, Valcon has often refrained from defending his beloved by overtly miraculous means.

Should the laws offered herein be verified as axioms tested and proven, Valcon may not be so hindered from that time forward. Valcon sees executives abusing corporate privilege; educators, entertainers and the media turning the minds of their constituencies against him; parents abusing children, children defying parents, politicians subverting public interest, perverts stalking innocent prey, spouses abandoning their mates, feckless judges undoing sound legal precedent, tribalism undermining the common good, gambling dens and brothels exploiting human weakness.

Valcon also detests the elitist philosophy that abets self-inflicted genocide by promoting abortion, *excessive* birth control and homosexuality. As child-rearing skills wane, parents entrust their children to corrupting educators. Women are chided for wanting to mother children more than to earn workplace bonuses and benefits.

How foolish to foster simultaneously an economy based upon anticipation of population growth alongside policies that undercut population growth! If tens of millions of aborted babies plus the millions who have been denied existence because of excessive birth control and homosexuality were alive, they would right now be buying homes, vehicles, furniture, clothing and groceries, and rearing another 10 million or so babies of their own to stimulate the economy even more.

How ironic! Predatory systems—those threatening to overthrow the more generous freedom-bestowing societies—are those that generally eschew abortion, *excessive* birth control, homosexuality and divorce! They infiltrate the cities of the free with sustained high birth rates while free societies thin their ranks in demographic suicide. Never in history have invaders been so naively welcomed by those they intend to victimize. Yet even within the predatory systems, Valcon awaits the love of those he foreknows will repent.

You cannot know how much Valcon wants *you* to be *with* him. "Yes" is a little word, but say it to him from your heart and it will accomplish more and mean more than everything else you have ever said or done. Say it *now*.

Then take the next step—find a church that honors your Triune Creator, his Scriptures and his redeeming atonement. Make friends with those who truly are Valcon's people. Serve him as he enables you among those who are not his friends. Plead with them as I, by writing this, have pleaded with you. Enjoy his blessings here and now while awaiting the ultimate blessing of full restoration with him in ages to come.

You may contact the author at:

unhidden22laws@gmail.com.

Don’s books and DVDs may be ordered at:

www.donrichardsonbooksales.com

OTHER BOOKS BY DON RICHARDSON:

Peace Child
(available also on audio CD and DVD)

Lords of the Earth
(available also on audio CD)

Eternity in Their Hearts

Secrets of the Koran

Notes

Chapter 8

[1]Joseph Padinjarekara, *Christ in Ancient Vedas*, rev. ed. (Kerala, India: Mukti Publications, 2007), pp. 93-96.

Chapter 11

[1]Ian McCausland, "Anomalies in the History of Relativity," *Journal of Scientific Exploration* 13:2 (1999), p. 274.

[2]M. Froeschlé, F. Mignard, and F. Arenou, "Determination of the PPN Parameter γ with the Data" (no date), p. 50. Research essay on the Internet at *http://www.rssd.esa.int/hipparcos/venice-proc/poster01_03.pdf.*

[3]McCausland, *Ibid.*

[4]Eric J. Lerner, *The Big Bang Never Happened: A Startling Refutation of the Dominant Theory of the Origin of the Universe* (New York: Random House, 1991). Quoted in "Newton, Mach and Einstein's Infinite Mass Paradox" at *http://www.spaceandmotion.com/Physics-Albert-Einstein-Cosmology.htm.*

[5]Roy C. Martin, Jr., *Astronomy on Trial* (Lanham, MD: University Press of America, 1999), p. xv.

Chapter 12

[1]*New Strong's Concise Dictionary of the Words in the Hebrew Bible with their Renderings in the King James Version* (Nashville: Thomas Nelson, 1995), p. 55.

[2]Internet site *www.biblestudytools.net/Lexicons/Hebrew*, online version of Francis Brown, S. R. Driver and Charles A. Briggs, *The Brown Driver Briggs Hebrew and English Lexicon* (Peabody, MA: Hendrickson Publishers, 1996).

[3]Michael D. Lemonick, "Let There Be Light," *Time* 168:10 (September 4, 2006), 42-51.

[4]Neil deGrasse Tyson and Donald Goldsmith, *Origins: Fourteen Billion Years of Cosmic Evolution* (New York: W. W. Norton, 2004), pp. 41-43.

[5]Stephen Hawking, *A Brief History of Time* (New York: Bantam Books, 1988), p. 136.

[6] William E. Carroll, "God and Physics: From Hawking to Avicenna," quoting Stephen Hawking and Roger Penrose, *The Nature of Space and Time* (Princeton: Princeton University Press, 1996), p. 71. Available on the Internet at *www.muslimphilosophy.com/sina/art/gpa.doc.*

[7]Lemonick, *op. cit.*, p. 46.

[8]Tyson and Goldsmith, *op. cit.*, p. 51.

[9]"Astrophysicists Devise New Method for Investigating Dark Matter," a "Headlines at Hopkins" News Release of Johns Hopkins University, February 9, 1995. Available online at *www.jhu.edu/news/home95/feb95/darkmatt.html.*

[10]Lemonick, *op. cit.*, p. 47.

[11]*Ibid.*, p. 48.

[12]William C. Mitchell, "Big Bang Theory Under Fire" (as published in *Physics Essays* 10:2 [June 1997]), at *http://nowscape.com/big-ban2.htm.* Mitchell points out numerous problems in Big Bang Cosmology, including what he terms "logical inconsistencies of BB theory."

[13]*Ibid.*

[14]Lemonick, *op. cit.*, p. 44.

Chapter 13

[1]Commentary at end of online book review for *Cosmos* magazine (August 2005), found at *http://www.cosmosmagazine.com/reviews/136/the-little-book-scientific-principles-theories-and-things.*

[2]Albert Einstein, *Sitzungsber* (Preuss. Akad. Wiss., 1917), p. 142. (English translation in *The Principle of Relativity* [Dover, NY, 1952], p. 177.) This quote appeared in a paper Einstein authored in 1917, as reported by Lucy Calder and Ofer Lahav in "Dark Energy: Back to Newton?" (London: University College, 2008, p. 12). See http://arxiv.org/ftp/arxiv/papers/0712/0712.2196.pdf. The same quote was included in *Ideas and Opinions (1919-1954)* by Crown Paperbacks (1954), noted at *http://www.spaceandmotion.com/Physics-Metaphics-Relativity-QT-Cosmology.htm#11.*

[3]*New Strong's Concise Dictionary of the Words in the Hebrew Bible*, p. 135.

Chapter 14

[1]Nancy Atkinson, September 23, 2008, "Scientists Detect 'Dark Flow': Matter From Beyond the Universe," at *www.universetoday.com.*

[2]So many excellent sources of photographs of such phenomena are available that even a partial list is inadequate. The vast majority of sources are secularly oriented, and I cannot endorse much of the content, conclusions drawn, etc. However, the photographs are well worth viewing; so to facilitate interested readers' search, I include several suggestions here. BOOKS: (1) Eric Chaison and Steve McMillan, *Astronomy Today*, 6th ed. (New Jersey: Prentice Hall, 2007). (2) Giles Sparrow, *Cosmos: A Field Guide* (London: Quercus Publishing Ltd., 2006). (3) Raman Prinja, *Visions of the Universe: The Latest Discoveries in Space Revealed* (New York: Barnes & Noble Books, 2005). (4) Martin Rees, ed., *Universe: The Definitive Visual Guide*, compiled by DK Publishing-New York (Penguin Books Australia, 2005). This book contains hundreds of awe-inspiring photographs and other visuals from around the solar system to the outer reaches of space. PERIODICALS: (1) *Astronomy* (e.g., the December 2005 issue features several pages with photos of nebulae—pp. 14-15 and 76-79). (2) *Sky and Telescope* releases an annual edition of a soft-cover book titled

Beautiful Universe, a magnificent photo gallery of outer space. (3) *Discover* and (4) *Scientific American*, periodicals that do not focus on astronomy but do contain periodic reports that include photographs.

Chapter 15

[1]Thousands are available online. Interested readers may want to start their photographic journey at one of the following (though by no means exclusive) Web sites: (1) *www.nasaimages.org*: the most comprehensive compilation of NASA still photographs, film and video; (2) the "Gallery" link at *http://imgsrc.hubblesite.org* (3) *http://chandra.harvard.edu/photo* (the Chandra x-ray observatory); (4) *www.google.com/sky/*; and (5) *www.sciam.com* for the periodical *Scientific American.*

[2]Lorentz force is the tendency of a rotating magnetic field to drag particles of matter along as it rotates.

Chapter 17

[1]Adam Frank, "Gravity's Gadfly," *Discover* (August 2006), 33-37.

[2]*Ibid.*, p. 34.

[3]*Ibid.*

[4]*Ibid.*

Chapter 18

[1]Sparrow, *op cit.*, pp. 88-89.

[2]*Ibid.*

Chapter 20

[1]This command appears three times in the Old Testament—a rare occurrence: Exodus 23:19b and 34:26b, and in Deuteronomy 14:21d. Even today some Jewish rabbis and scholars regard a thrice-given command of Almighty God as weightier than commands given once or twice.

[2]The full narrative of the life of Joseph is told in Genesis, chapters 37 through 50.

[3]The same command and accompanying reminder ("you were once aliens in Egypt") are reiterated three other times in the Torah: Exodus 23:9; Leviticus 19:33, 34; and Deuteronomy 10:18, 19. It is rare indeed to find a command given four times within such a relatively brief span of Scripture.